AS-Level Psychology

The Revision Guide

Editors:
Rachel Selway, Dominic Hall, Andy Park.
Contributors:
Radha Bellur, Richard Carciofo, Charley Darbishire, Chris Dennett, Christine Johnson, Tracey Jones, Asraf Sattar, Denise Say, Emma Singleton.

Proofreaders:
Sue Hocking, Teresa Jamieson, Christine Johnson.

Published by Coordination Group Publications Ltd.

This book is suitable for:

AQA A, Edexcel, OCR.

There are notes at the tops of double pages to tell you if there's a bit you can ignore for your syllabus.

ISBN-10: 1 84146 978 5
ISBN-13: 978 1 84146 978 2

Groovy website: www.cgpbooks.co.uk
Jolly bits of clipart from CorelDRAW®
Printed by Elanders Hindson Ltd, Newcastle upon Tyne.

Contents

We deliberately haven't put any answers in this book, because they'd just be saying what's in the revision guide. So instead, here's how to write answers, and do well.

What is Psychology?

These two pages give you a very quick intro to psychology: the guys who kicked the whole thing off, the four big different types of psychology and three very impressive beards. Don't spend ages learning this stuff cos it's really just an overview of stuff you'll cover in detail later on.

Psychology's a Science With Lots of Theories and Few Facts

Psychology is "**the scientific study of experience and behaviour**."
This basically means that psychologists look at what people and animals do, why they do it and how they feel.

A lot of psychology sounds like **common sense**, but it's a science, so everything's got to be investigated.
You've got to come up with a **theory** about something and then **scientifically test** it.

It's very difficult to prove things in psychology, so there are loads of disagreements and a lot of theories that sound rubbish. But you can't just say they're rubbish, that'd be too easy, you've got to use theories and experiments to show it.

Many Important Guys Helped Start Psychology

Here are the serious-looking guys that started it all. You don't need to understand or learn all the weird terms yet.

The first person to call himself a psychologist was **Wilhelm Wundt** (1832 - 1920). In the 1870s, he founded the first experimental laboratory and developed a theory called **structuralism**.

Charles Darwin (1809 - 1882) was a 19th century biologist, who found evidence for evolution. **Social Darwinism** was the application of his theory of **natural selection** to human society.

Charles Darwin

Sigmund Freud

Sigmund Freud (1856 - 1939) was a psychiatrist in 19th century Vienna. Using information from his patients, he developed the **psychodynamic** or **psychoanalytic** theory of personality development. He had a major impact on psychology.

J.B.Watson (1878 - 1958) developed a theory called **behaviourism**, using **conditioning** to explain behaviour in a more scientific, objective way.

Carl Rogers (1902 - 1987) was a leading figure in person-centred therapy and **humanist psychology**.

There are Lots of **Branches** of Psychology

The guys above helped kick off psychology, but things have changed since, and now there's no such thing as 'structuralism' or 'social Darwinism'. Instead, the main branches of psychology are the **psychodynamic**, **humanist**, **behaviourist**, **cognitive**, **social**, **physiological**, **developmental** and **individual differences** approaches (phew!). Remember that these approaches are based on **theories**, not facts, so they're not necessarily true.
Here's some info on some of them, but there's lots more detail on the rest throughout this book...

1 — Freud's **Psychodynamic Approach** Focuses on Unconscious, Internal Conflicts

According to the psychodynamic approach:

1) The mind is split into three parts — the id, ego and superego. The **id** contains our innate, aggressive and sexual instincts. The **ego** is our conscious mind and the **superego** our conscience.
2) The id, ego and superego are often in **conflict**, leading to anxiety.
3) The ego protects itself with **defence mechanisms**, such as repression, denial and displacement.
4) There are five stages of **psychosexual development** — the oral, anal, phallic, latency and genital stages. If a child has a serious problem or excessive pleasure in any of these stages, they can become fixated with that stage. The **fixations** can continue into adult life.
5) What we experience in childhood can lead to unconscious conflicts when we are adults, affecting our behaviour.

Freud's theories were based on in-depth case studies of himself and his patients, who were mainly white, middle-class Viennese women. His theories have consequently been criticised as they may not apply to the rest of the population.

2 — The **Humanist Approach** Focuses on the Higher Motivations of Humans

1) Humanists think that humans are very different from animals. Humans play, are creative, have humour and are driven by a desire to grow and develop their **potential**, rather than being blindly driven by stimuli.
2) The humanist approach focuses on **self-development** and **higher motivations**.
3) It depends on the idea that individuals are **unique** and have **free will**.

The humanist approach has been criticised for being **unscientific**, untestable and vague.

What is Psychology?

3 — The **Behaviourist Approach** Made Psychology More Objective and Scientific

1) This approach focuses on **behaviour** — in particular, the **stimuli** that trigger behaviour and the **responses** to the stimuli (the behaviour itself).
2) Behaviourists think that what goes on in the mind ('the black box') doesn't matter.
3) They argue that all behaviour is learned through **conditioning** (see the boxes below).
4) Behaviourists think that human and animal behaviour is basically the same, so the same laws apply to each. This makes sense in terms of the theory of evolution.
5) There are two forms of **conditioning** that can explain learnt behaviour:

Classical Conditioning — **Ivan Pavlov** noticed that dogs he was experimenting on would salivate to the sound of the door opening. They had '**learned**' that the sound of the door meant that food was on its way. So they had developed an **association** between the **stimulus** (the door) and their **reflex response** — salivation.

Ivan Pavlov

Operant Conditioning — developed by **B.F. Skinner** from **Edward Thorndike's** instrumental learning. Skinner concentrated on the **effects** of behaviour rather than the behaviours themselves. Experimenting on rats, Skinner found that if a rat was rewarded with food for a specific behaviour, this **reinforced** that behaviour, making it more likely to occur again.

Behaviourism has been **criticised** for ignoring the role of **thoughts** and **emotions** in behaviour — behaviourism can't be a complete explanation of behaviour as it takes no interest in what happens inside the mind.

4 — The **Cognitive Approach** Focuses on Internal Processes

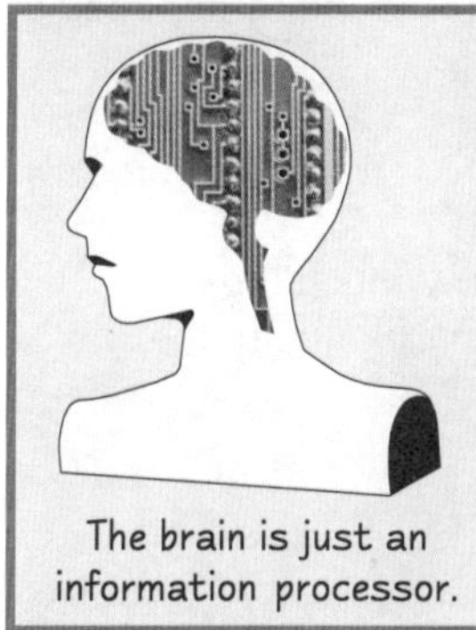

The brain is just an information processor.

1) The cognitive, or **information processing** approach, was developed due to dissatisfaction with the behaviourist approach, which fails to account for internal processes. For example, behaviourism can't explain how we perceive things or acquire language.
2) Cognitive psychologists focus on **internal processes** to understand behaviour, such as how we perceive or remember things.
3) They think that **computer** systems are a simple analogy to the human mind. They use computer models to try and understand human cognition (thinking).
4) Using concepts from information-processing, cognitive psychologists describe the brain as a **processor** with which we input data and produce output.

Cognitive approaches are often laboratory based and **artificial**, so lack **validity** in the real world, known as '**ecological validity**'.

Practice Questions

Q1 What are the four main branches of psychology?

Q2 Who was the first person to call himself a psychologist?

Q3 What is the 'black box'?

Exam Questions

Q1 Outline and evaluate the psychodynamic approach. [8 marks]

Q2 Discuss the main differences between the cognitive approach and the behaviourist approach. [12 marks]

It's Psychology, Jim, but not as we know it...

There are so many different types of theory that call themselves 'psychology'. Some of them are a bit more like biology, some are more like computing, and some... are Freud's theories. The interesting thing about his weird ideas is that it's hard to prove them wrong. So they're still around and that means you've got to learn them.

Assumptions and Applications of the Cognitive Approach

Ignore these pages if you're doing AQA. *Cognitive psychology is all about using how we act to guess what our heads are doing. If you can do that and toss in some fancy diagrams you're well on your way.*

Cognitive Psychology Looks at How We ***Interpret*** the World

1) Cognitive psychology is all about **how** we think.
2) Cognitive psychologists try to **explain behaviour** by looking at our **perception**, **language**, **attention** and **memory**.
3) Humans are viewed as rational, **logical** beings.
4) **Computers** and computer models are used to explain how we think and behave. Humans are treated as **information processors** (computers) and behaviour is explained in terms of **information processing** (how computers deal with information).
5) But cognitive psychology has **limitations**. Research is often carried out in artificial situations (laboratories, using computer models) and the role of emotion and influence from other people is often ignored. For these reasons some argue that the results aren't valid in the real world.

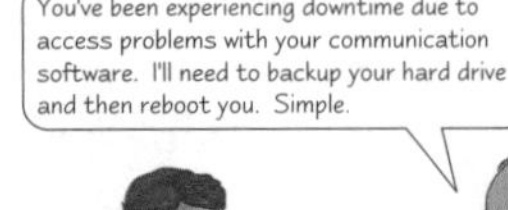

You've been experiencing downtime due to access problems with your communication software. I'll need to backup your hard drive and then reboot you. Simple.

Cognitive Psychology Developed as the ***Computer Age Developed***

1) Cognitive psychology is sometimes called the **information processing** approach. 'Information processing' is just a fancy term that's normally used to describe how computers deal with stuff.
2) As computers developed, people saw similarities with how computers and humans make sense of information.
3) Computer terms are used in cognitive psychology:
   The brain is described as a **processor** (the thing that makes things happen) — it has data **input** into it, and **output** from it. Some parts of the brain form **networks** (connections of bits). Other parts work in **serial** (info travels along one row) or in **parallel** (info travels to and fro along lots of paths at the same time).
4) Cognitive psychologists use computers to create **computational models** of the human mind.

Cognitive Psychologists Use ***Four*** Main Research Methods

Here's a quick phrase to learn before you read on: "ecological validity" — it's the measure of how much the result of an experiment is true for the rest of the world. If a result has low ecological validity, it might work fine in the lab, but as soon as you try and use it to explain real life behaviour, you find it just doesn't work.

1 — Laboratory Experiments

A lot of research in cognitive psychology happens in **laboratories**. This is very **scientific** and reliable as it is possible to have great control over variables in a lab. However, this type of research doesn't tell us much about the real world — it has low ecological validity.

2 — Field Experiments

Field experiments take place in a **natural** situation, so they have more ecological validity, but there's less control of other variables. For example, studies of memory or attention in a school environment.

3 — Case Studies

Cognitive psychologists often make use of **case studies** of one or a few patients to test their theories. For example, **brain damaged** patients are often studied so that the damaged parts of the brain can be compared to the observed differences in behaviour.

There are some **difficulties** with the use of case studies. It is hard to make generalisations from the study of subjects with brain damage to 'normal' individuals. Also, individual differences between people mean that one subject may respond in a way that is totally different from everyone else.

4 — Brain Imaging

Brain imaging can now be carried out during a cognitive task.
For example, MRI scans have been used to show the blood flow in different brain areas for different types of memory tasks.

The main criticism of cognitive psychology is that it's removed from the 'real world' and that it fails to take **individual differences** into account by assuming that all of us process stuff in exactly the same way.

Assumptions and Applications of the Cognitive Approach

Case Studies Provide Support for the Cognitive Approach

The case study of HM showed how short-term and long-term memory must each be based in different structures of the brain. Cognitive psychology splits the different types of memory up into different units, assuming that the brain deals with them separately (see pages 6-9). So, the case study of HM provided support for cognitive psychological thinking.

Milner et al (1978) — case study of HM

Diagnosis: HM was a patient with severe and frequent epilepsy. His seizures were based in a brain structure called the hippocampus. Doctors decided to surgically remove the hippocampus.

Results: The operation reduced his epilepsy, but led to him suffering memory loss.
He could still form short-term memories (STMs), but was not able to form new long-term memories (LTMs). For example, he could memorise a number and recall it 15 minutes later, but if given something else to think about during the 15 minutes, he couldn't recall the number. He could read something over and over without realising that he had read it before. He also moved house and had difficulty recalling the new route to his house. However, he could still talk and show previous skills (**procedural memory**).
From tests, they found HM's **episodic memory** (for past events) and **semantic memory** (for knowledge, e.g. word meanings) was affected more than his **procedural memory**.

Cognitive Psychologists Apply **Animal Research** to Humans

Cognitive psychologists study **non-human** animals mainly so they can **apply** the results to human cognitive abilities. Discovering whether chimpanzees can learn language, for example, helps psychologists develop theories about how humans learn language.

However, there are so many **differences** between humans and animals that results can be explained wrongly. For example, you might conclude that chimpanzees can't learn a **spoken** language because they lack the **cognitive** abilities. In fact, however, it is more likely to be because they lack the **physiological** attributes, like a voice box.

Gardner and Gardner (1969) — teaching ASL to a chimp

OCR Core Study

Method: Washoe, a chimpanzee, was raised like a human child and taught American sign language (ASL).

Results: By the end of the 22nd month of the project, Washoe had learned 34 signs.

Conclusion: The development of language in the chimpanzee appeared to follow the **same patterns** as language development in children (both children speaking and using ASL). Washoe learnt language at similar rates to children of the same age. Additionally, language acquisition seemed to require **interaction** with caregivers and communication in everyday situations. However, she did not learn **grammar**.

Evaluation: There are **ethical** considerations, in that Washoe was taken from the wild and deprived of other chimpanzees for companionship. There are also issues of **external validity** — it is not possible to accurately generalise results from a chimp to human children.

Practice Questions

Q1 List four research methods used by cognitive psychologists.

Q2 Behaviourists focus on behaviour. What do cognitive psychologists focus their studies on?

Q3 Who was HM?

Exam Questions

Q1 Describe how cognitive psychologists make use of brain damaged people to study 'normal' human cognition. [8 marks]

Q2 Describe how cognitive psychologists apply animal research to humans. [8 marks]

Syntax error. Funny line does not compute. Insert file 'humour for books'.

I'm not sure I like being compared to a computer. But then, you've got to admit, it does make people easier to understand. I mean, our thinking is just down to a load of neurones carrying signals — a bit more complex than a computer, but not far removed. Maybe we'll know enough about the brain one day to build new computer-people from scratch. Freaky thought.

Short-Term and Long-Term Memory

These pages are for AQA only, so ignore them if you're doing OCR or Edexcel.

I used to worry that I could remember where I was in, say, May '84, but I couldn't recall why I'd just walked into a room. But it's due to the difference between short-term and long-term memory. Or something... I forget the exact reason.

Memory is a **Process** Where Information is **Retained** About the Past

Memories are thought to have a physical basis or '**trace**'. Most psychologists agree that there are three types of memory, **sensory memory (SM)**, **short-term memory (STM)** and **long-term memory (LTM)**.

SM is visual and auditory information that passes through our senses very briefly. SM disappears quickly through **spontaneous decay** — the trace just fades. SM isn't around for very long, so most studies are on LTM and STM.

STM and LTM differ in terms of:

1) **Duration** — How long a memory lasts.
2) **Capacity** — How much can be held in the memory.
3) **Encoding** — Transferring information into code, creating a 'trace'.

STM has a **limited capacity** and a **limited duration** (i.e. we can remember a little information for a short time).

LTM theoretically has an **unlimited capacity** and is theoretically **permanent** (i.e. lots of information forever).

Research Has Been Carried Out into the Nature of **STM and LTM**

Peterson and Peterson (1959) Investigated STM Using Trigrams

Peterson & Peterson (1959) investigated the duration of STM.

Method: Participants were shown **nonsense trigrams** (3 random consonants e.g. CVM) and asked to recall them after either 3, 6, 9, 12, 15 or 18 seconds. They then had to count backwards in 3s between seeing the trigrams and recalling them. This was an **'interference task'** — it prevented them repeating the letters to themselves.

Results: After **3 seconds**, participants could recall about **90%** of trigrams correctly.
After **18 seconds**, only about **2%** were recalled correctly.

Conclusion: When rehearsal is prevented, **very little** can stay in STM for longer than about **18 seconds**.

Evaluation: Nonsense trigrams are artificial, so this study lacks **ecological validity** — the results might not apply to real life settings. Meaningful or 'real life' memories may last longer in STM.

Bahrick et al. (1975) Investigated LTM in a Natural Setting

Bahrick et al. (1975) studied VLTMs (very long term memories).

Method: 392 people were asked to list the names of their ex-classmates. (This is called a **'free-recall test'**).
They were then shown photos and asked to recall the names of the people shown (**photo-recognition test**) or given names and asked to match them to a photo of the classmate (**name-recognition test**).

Results: Within 15 years of leaving school, participants could **recognise** about **90%** of names and faces.
They were about **60%** accurate on **free recall**. After 48 years, recognition was still good, at about **75%**, but free recall had declined to about **30%** accuracy.

Conclusion: The study shows evidence of **VLTMs** in a **'real life'** setting. Recognition is better than recall, so there may be a huge store of information, but it's not always easy to **access** all of it, i.e. all the information's there, you just need help to get to it.

Evaluation: This study showed better recall than other studies on LTM, but this may be because **meaningful** information is stored better. However in a 'real life' study like this, it's hard to **control** all the variables, making these findings less reliable — there's no way of knowing exactly **why** information was recalled well.

Other studies have also looked at VLTMs. Waganaar and Groeneweg (1990) found that 30 years after being imprisoned in concentration camps, people could still remember extensive details from their experience.

Short-Term and Long-Term Memory

STM and LTM Have Very **Different Capacities**

Jacobs (1887) studied the capacity of STM.

Method: Participants were presented with a string of letters or digits. They had to repeat them back in the same order. Initially, there were 3 digits, then 4, etc, until the participant failed to recall the sequence correctly.

Results: Participants recalled, on average, about **9 digits** and about **7 letters**. This capacity increased with **age** up to a point.

Conclusion: Based on the range of results, Jacobs concluded that STM has a **limited storage capacity** of **5-9 items**. Individual differences were found, such as STM increasing with age, possibly due to increased brain capacity or memory techniques, such as **chunking** (see below). Digits may have been easier to recall as there were only 10 to remember, compared to 26 letters.

Evaluation: This research is **artificial**, so more meaningful information may be recalled better, perhaps showing STM to have an even greater capacity.

7, plus or minus 2, is known as 'Miller's magic number'.

Miller (1956) reviewed research into the capacity of STM. He found that people can remember about seven items. He argued that the capacity of STM is **seven, plus or minus two**. He also suggested that we use '**chunking**' to combine individual letters or numbers into larger more meaningful units. So 2,0,0,3,1,9,8,7 is about all the digits STM can hold. 'Chunked' into the meaningful recent years of 2003 and 1987, it's much easier to remember. In fact, STM could probably hold about seven such pieces of chunked information (2003, 1987, 1999, 2001...), increasing STM's capacity.

Encoding is About the Way Information is Stored in Memory

In **STM**, we try to keep information active by repeating it to ourselves. This means it generally involves **acoustic** coding. In **LTM**, encoding is generally **semantic** — it's more useful to code words in terms of their meaning, rather than what they sound or look like (although encoding in LTM **can** also be visual or acoustic).

Encoding of memories can be visual (pictures), acoustic (sounds, e.g. 'dog' and 'dot' are acoustically similar) or semantic (meanings, e.g. 'dog' and 'canine' are semantically similar).

Baddeley (1966) investigated encoding in STM and LTM.

Method: Participants were given four sets of words, either **acoustically similar** (e.g. man, mad, mat), **acoustically dissimilar** (e.g. pit, cow, bar), **semantically similar** (e.g. big, large, huge) and **semantically dissimilar** (e.g. good, hot, pig). Participants were asked to recall them either immediately or following a 20-minute task.

Results: If recalling the word list immediately (therefore from **STM**), participants had problems recalling acoustically similar words. If recalling after an interval (from **LTM**), they had problems with semantically similar words.

Conclusion: The patterns of confusion between similar words suggest that **LTM** is more likely to rely on **semantic** encoding and **STM** on **acoustic** encoding.

Evaluation: There are other types of LTM (e.g. episodic memory, procedural memory) which this experiment doesn't consider.

Practice Questions

Q1 Describe two differences between STM and LTM.

Q2 Define encoding, capacity and duration.

Q3 Describe the findings of one study of STM.

Exam Questions

Q1 Compare STM and LTM in terms of capacity, duration and encoding. [6 marks]

Q2 Describe and evaluate studies into the duration of STM and LTM. [8 marks]

Remember the days when you didn't have to remember stuff like this...

How long you remember something depends on how much it means to you personally. So trivial things that are going to have no bearing whatsoever on your life are quickly forgotten. But more important stuff tends to stay in your head a whole while longer. Not sure if that makes this stuff easy or hard to learn — but try to remember it for more than twenty minutes.

Models of Memory

Ignore these pages if you're doing OCR.

This page is all about why you can't remember the last page. Maybe you didn't rehearse it enough, or maybe you only looked at the letters instead of trying to understand the facts. Or maybe you spilt tea on it and can't read the words...

Atkinson and Shiffrin (1968) Created the *Multi-Store Model*

The multi-store model is made up of three memory stores — a **sensory store**, a **short-term store** and a **long-term store**. Information from our environment initially goes into **sensory memory**. If you pay attention to it, or think about it, the information will pass into **short-term memory**. Some information may be processed further (you might rehearse it to yourself, for example), and will therefore be transferred to **long-term memory**.

Support for the model

1) The **Primacy Effect** — Research shows that participants are able to recall the first few items of a list better than those from the middle. The model explains this because **earlier** items will have been **rehearsed** better and transferred to **LTM**. If rehearsal is prevented by an interference task, the effect disappears, as the model predicts.
2) The **Recency Effect** — Participants also tend to remember the last few items better than those from the middle of the list. Earlier items are rehearsed, so transfer to LTM, whilst **later** items are recalled because they're still in **STM**.
3) People with **Korsakoff's Syndrome** (amnesia developed due to chronic alcoholism) provide support for the model. They can recall the **last** items in a list (unimpaired recency effect), suggesting an unaffected **STM**. However, their **LTM** is very poor. This supports the model by showing that STM and LTM are **separate stores**.

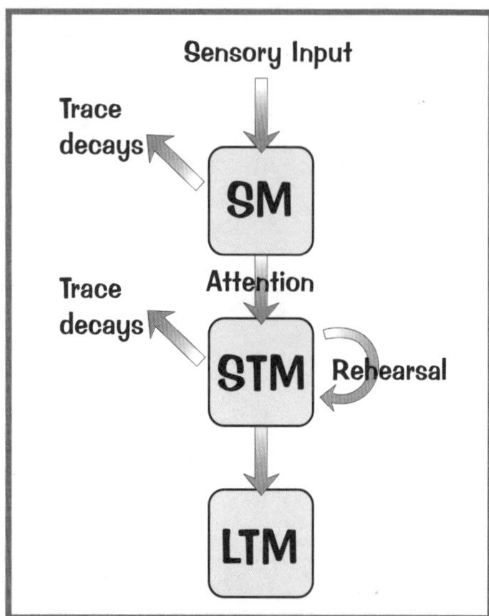

Limitations of the model

1) In the model, information is transferred from the STM to LTM through **rehearsal**. But in **real life**, people don't spend time rehearsing, but they do transfer information into LTM. Rehearsal is not always needed for information to be stored and some items can't be rehearsed e.g. smells.
2) The model is **oversimplified**. It assumes there is only one long-term store and one short-term store. This has been disproved by evidence from **brain damaged** patients, suggesting several **different** short-term stores, and other evidence suggesting different long-term stores.

Baddeley and Hitch (1974) Developed the *Working Memory Model*

Baddely and Hitch developed a multi-store model of STM called the 'working memory model'. It has **3 parts**:

Rehearsal
Articulatory-Phonological Loop
Central Executive
Visuo-Spatial Sketchpad
Rehearsal

1) The **central executive** can be described as attention. It has a limited capacity and controls two 'slave' systems that also have **limited capacity** —
2) The **visuo-spatial sketchpad** (STM for visual and spatial information).
3) The **articulatory-phonological loop** (holds speech-based information). It contains a **phonological store** (the inner ear) and an **articulatory process** (the inner voice).

Studies using '**interference tasks**' support the model — if participants are asked to perform two tasks using the same system at once, their performance will be affected, e.g. saying 'the the the' while silently reading something is very difficult. Both these tasks use the articulatory-phonological loop, which has limited capacity — it can't cope with both tasks, so performance on one, or both, will be affected.

Shallice and Warrington (1974) found **support** for the model through their case study of KF. **KF** was a brain damaged patient who had an impaired STM. His problem was with immediate recall of words presented **verbally**, but not with visual information. This suggested he had an impaired **articulatory loop**, therefore providing evidence for the working memory model's view of STM.

A potential criticism is that the idea of a central executive is **simplistic** and **vague**.

Models of Memory

Craik and Lockhart (1972) Developed the **Levels of Processing Model**

Craik and Lockhart's levels of processing model focuses on the processing of incoming information.
They discussed three levels of processing called **physical processing**, **phonemic processing** and **semantic processing**:

1 **Physical processing** occurs at a 'shallow' level and analyses information in terms of its **physical** qualities, e.g. **a word is typed in black ink.**

2 **Phonemic processing** occurs at a 'deeper' level than physical processing. It focuses on the **sound** of information, e.g. **pea rhymes with bee.**

3 **Semantic processing** occurs at the 'deepest' level and analyses the **meaning** of information, e.g. **a pea is a vegetable.**

The levels of processing theory suggests that information **processed** at a **deeper** level should be **recalled** better.

As the idea of deep and shallow processing was thought to be a bit **simplistic**, Craik and Lockhart included ideas of **elaboration**, **organisation** and **distinctiveness**.

They predicted that information will be recalled better if it has been **elaborated** (e.g. explained more, perhaps with examples), or **organised** (e.g. if participants had to sort information into categories), or made **distinctive** (e.g. said with a funny voice).

They found **support** for their model.

Craik and Tulving (1975) also did a series of experiments to support the model. They found that words processed **semantically** were recalled best, **phonemically** second best and **physically** worst.

The theory has been **criticised**:

1) There is a **circular argument** over what **depth** really is. In this model, the definition of good recall is something that comes from deep processing. The definition of deep processing, though, is something that leads to good recall. However, with elaboration, organisation and distinctiveness added to the model, this criticism doesn't work so well.
2) The model ignores the **distinction** between STM and LTM.
3) The model may also be confusing **effort** with **depth**.

Practice Questions

Q1 What is the recency effect?

Q2 How many components does the working memory model consist of and what are they?

Q3 Give two criticisms of the levels of processing theory.

Q4 Give two criticisms of the working memory model.

Exam Questions

Q1 Compare and contrast the multi-store memory model and the working memory model. [8 marks]

Q2 Evaluate the levels of processing model. [10 marks]

Memory, all alone in the moonlight... something about the moon... la la la...

I don't know about you, but I find these pages pretty boring. Kind of learnable, but still boring enough that you find yourself face-down on your desk in a pool of dribble, with a biscuit stuck to your forehead. Don't fret anyway, it's not long before you can start learning about the gory experiments with electric shocks and nastiness. Much better than this stuff...

Forgetting

Ignore these pages if you're doing OCR. *Forgetting is great — such an easy way to not answer difficult questions. Just screw your eyes up, point your head towards the sky, wibble and say 'Ooh, I know it, it's in there, err, I can't remember'.*

Forgetting is When Learnt Information **Can't Be Retrieved**

Experiments on memory assume that if you can't retrieve a memory, it's forgotten. Forgetting is thought to happen when information is **unavailable** in **STM** and **inaccessible** and/or **unavailable** in **LTM**.
In other words, we can forget because:

1) The information was never **stored** — an **availability** problem, e.g. you didn't pay attention when the information was presented.
2) The information was stored, but is hard to **retrieve** — an **accessibility** problem, e.g. you read something once, a long time ago, and now need a lot of help to recall it.
3) The information is **confused** — there is an **interference** problem, e.g. two pieces of learnt information are too similar, and you can't tell them apart easily.

Decay and Displacement are Theories Explaining Forgetting in **STM**

Theories suggest that information in STM might either just disappear with time, or get pushed out by new information:

Trace Decay Theory

Memories have a physical basis or '**trace**'.
This trace **decays** over time unless it is passed to LTM.
This explains the findings from the **Peterson and Peterson (1959)** experiment — when rehearsal of information was prevented, very little information stayed in STM for longer than about 18 seconds (see page 6).

However, we can't be sure that the trace really decayed instead of being overwritten by new information (**displacement**).

Reitman (1974) gave participants words to learn, then made them listen for a tone as an interference task, preventing rehearsal. There was no new information to push out the old. So if recall was impaired this would suggest the reason was decay, not displacement.
There was a slight, but not huge, reduction in recall so we have some evidence for decay.

Displacement Theory

Displacement theory suggests that new information physically overwrites old information. **Waugh and Norman (1965)** found that with lists of digits, participants were much better at recalling digits from near the **end** of the list than near the beginning. This supports displacement theory.

However, they did a similar experiment with the digits presented at different **speeds**. They found that recall improved when digits were presented faster, which suggests that **decay** rather than displacement was to blame.

Seeing as there is evidence for both the decay and displacement theories of forgetting in STM, a possible explanation could be that **both** are true. There is no reason why **decay and displacement** can't both cause forgetting in STM.

Forgetting in **LTM** Could Be Caused By a **Lack of Availability**

An argument of **decay** or **interference** can be applied to **LTM**. However, in LTM, studies have found more problems in recall if you take in new information rather than just having a relatively information-free break.
Therefore, **interference** is a more likely explanation than decay, as new information affects the recall of old information.

Interference can be retroactive or proactive.

Retroactive interference is where **new** information interferes with the ability to recall **older** information.

Proactive interference is where **older** information interferes with the ability to recall **new** information. This interference can be removed, though, if useful information is given as a prompt (a **cue**). (This explanation has been criticised as it suggests forgetting is better explained as **retrieval failure**, and it doesn't easily explain forgetting in the **real world**.)

Other factors influence forgetting.

We have more chance of retrieving the memory if the **cue** is **appropriate**. Cues can be **internal** (e.g. your **mood**) or **external** (e.g. **context**, like surroundings, situation, etc). We remember more if we are in the same **context / mood** as we were in when we encoded the information originally. This is known as **cue-dependent learning**.

Forgetting

Tulving and Psotka *Investigated Forgetting in LTM*

Tulving and Psotka (1971) — forgetting in LTM

Method: Tulving and Psotka compared the theories of **interference** and **cue-dependent forgetting**.
Each participant was given either 1, 2, 3, 4, 5 or 6 lists of 24 words. Each list was divided into 6 categories of 4 words. Words were presented in category order, e.g. all animals, then all trees etc.
After the lists were presented, in one condition, participants had to simply recall all the words — **total free recall.**
In another condition, participants were given all the category names and had to try to recall words from the list – **free cued recall.**

Results:

1) In the **total free recall** condition, there was strong evidence of **retroactive** interference. Participants with 1 or 2 lists to remember had higher recall than those with more lists to remember, suggesting the later lists were **interfering** with remembering the earlier lists.
2) In the **cued recall** test, the effects of retroactive interference **disappeared**. It didn't matter how many lists a participant had, recall was still the same for each list (about **70%**).

Conclusion: The results suggest that interference had not caused forgetting. Because the memories became accessible if a cue was used, it showed that they were available, but just inaccessible.
Therefore, the forgetting shown in the total free recall condition was **cue-dependent forgetting**.

Evaluation: Cue-dependent forgetting is thought to be the best explanation of forgetting, as it has the **strongest** evidence. Most forgetting is seen to be caused by **retrieval failure**. This means that virtually all memory we have is available in LTM, we just need the right cue to be able to access it.
However, the evidence is **artificial** (e.g. recalling word lists), lacking meaning in the real world.
Also, it would be difficult, if not impossible, to test whether all information in LTM is accessible and available, and just waiting for the right cue.

Jasper couldn't quite recall what his mother had told him about these things.

Practice Questions

Q1 Give two explanations of forgetting in LTM.

Q2 Outline two explanations of forgetting in STM.

Q3 What is meant by cue-dependent forgetting?

Q4 Outline the main features of displacement theory.

Exam Questions

Q1 Outline and evaluate two explanations of forgetting in LTM. [8 marks]

Q2 Outline and evaluate one theory of forgetting in STM. [8 marks]

Remember, remember the 5th of October...

This is a great page for playing psychologist. You can easily make up lists of words and then get your friends to read them. Give them an interference task and then test them. What fun. I love psychology experiments. I'm always doing experiments on my friends, though they've gone off the idea a bit since that incident with the misplaced electrode.

The Role of Emotional Factors in Memory

These pages are just for AQA A. *Emotion affects memories. In fact, interestingly enough, highly emotional material can be either* ***more*** *memorable or* ***less*** *memorable. These pages are all about how nobody really knows why...*

'Flashbulb Memories' Are Really Vivid Memories of Emotional Events

Brown and Kulik (1977) noticed that people were able to **recall vividly** what they were doing when highly important and dramatic events occurred, such as the assassination of President Kennedy.

1) Recent events that probably caused flashbulb memories include September 11th and Princess Diana's death.
2) Flashbulb memories don't have to be **negative** — they can be about dramatic **positive** events too, e.g. Gainsborough Trinity winning the FA cup. OK, it hasn't happened yet, but if it did, I'd remember it vividly...
3) They are almost as if a **photograph** is taken at the time and stuck on the memory.
4) They are **enduring** and **accurate**.
5) They seem to **contradict** the idea that thorough processing in STM is required for a memory to become an LTM.
6) Flashbulb memories support the idea that **emotional factors** and **distinctiveness** are important in memory.
7) Brown and Kulik thought that a special **mechanism** in the **brain** must be responsible for flashbulb memories.

*Other Researchers Suggested **Theories** on Flashbulb Memories*

Many researchers have put forward different theories to explain the **cause** and **reliability** of flashbulb memories.

Cahill and McGaugh (1998) suggested that adrenaline is involved.

1) They argued it wouldn't be useful to remember everything as we'd just be overloaded with information.
2) What would be useful, though, would be a biological mechanism that could **regulate** what we remember by deciding the **importance** of events.
3) They argued that when our emotions are highly **aroused**, we produce the hormone **adrenaline**, which has 2 effects:
   a) In the **short-term**, it makes us **ready** to respond to the situation.
   b) In the **long-term**, it affects our **memory**, helping us remember important situations, and affecting our responses to similar situations in the future.
4) When rats were injected with a stimulant drug with a similar effect to adrenaline, they learnt a new task much faster than normal. This supports the theory.

Since the highly emotional and dramatic event, Emma had more things to worry about than her flashbulb memory.

McCloskey et al (1988) studied the reliability of flashbulb memories.

1) Shortly after the explosion of the space shuttle Challenger, they asked participants for their memories of the event.
2) They retested them nine months later and found that there were some **discrepancies** between the original and later recall.
3) This suggests that flashbulb memories are also subject to **forgetting**.

Conway et al (1994) disagreed with McCloskey et al.

1) They felt the Challenger explosion was **not a significant** enough event in peoples' lives.
2) They interviewed people in various countries a few days after Margaret Thatcher's surprising and important resignation, then again at a later date.
3) They found **86%** of the UK participants to have flashbulb memories after 11 months, compared to **29%** in other countries.
4) They argued that an event with a distinctive **meaning** is more **memorable**. Margaret Thatcher's resignation would be more **meaningful** to people in the UK than to people in other countries, making it also more memorable.

Sheingold and Tenney (1982)

They found adults could recall events that caused significant **emotion**, for example, the birth of a child. This was a **retrospective** study (looking back at events from the past). The problem with it is that we don't know about the original events, so it's hard to check the accuracy of their recall.

The Role of Emotional Factors in Memory

Repression is the Motivated Forgetting of Uncomfortable Memories

Freud (1915) said that '**repression**' was a way of protecting the ego (conscious mind) from uncomfortable memories. Anything that might be traumatic is removed from conscious thought through **motivated forgetting**. So traumatic memories are more likely to be forgotten than happy ones. In fact, anything that has been forgotten could have been repressed, because it is always possible that unconsciously, we were uncomfortable with it.

It is hard to **prove** this theory, but **Herman and Schatzow (1987)** found that **28%** of women who had experienced incest in childhood had memory deficits and evidence of **repression**. Other studies also **support** the theory:

Williams (1994) found evidence of repression.

Method:	129 girls who were admitted to hospital in 1970 due to a sexual assault were interviewed 17 years later.
Results:	**38%** of the women had **no recall** of the original incident. Of those who did remember, **16%** said they had at one time been unable to recall the event, but then recovered their memory. Women who were **younger** at the time of the assault or who knew those who had abused them were more likely to forget.
Conclusion:	The findings **support** the theory of repression, but also suggest that **recovery** occurs.
Evaluation:	This was a very **biased** sample (almost entirely poor urban women), so there could be another reason for the poor recall. Perhaps the original accounts were **fictitious**, or perhaps later in life, the women were just **unwilling** to talk about such personal matters.

Bradley and Baddeley (1990) found that **emotionally arousing** words (e.g. fear) were more **difficult** to retrieve than emotionally neutral words (e.g. cow), but they could still be retrieved in time. They concluded that emotional arousal or anxiety causes **repression** but that this effect **lessens** with time.

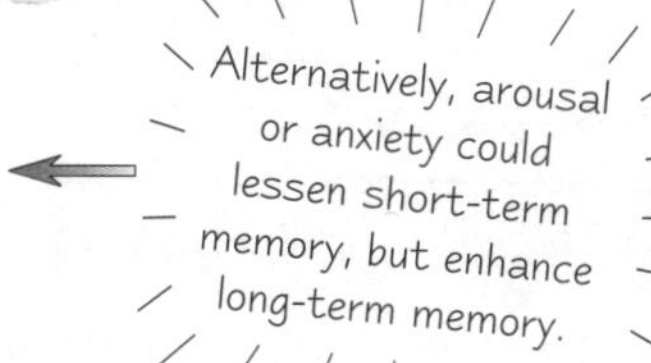

Alternatively, arousal
or anxiety could
lessen short-term
memory, but enhance
long-term memory.

Myers and Brewin (1994)

Method:	The length of time it took participants to recall **negative** childhood memories was measured for '**repressors**' and other personality types. 'Repressors' are people who deal with anxiety by being **defensive** — they have low levels of anxiety, but high levels of defensiveness.
Result:	Repressors took **longer** to recall negative childhood memories than other personality types, but also had more **early** negative memories and reported more **difficult** relationships with their parents.
Conclusion:	The findings suggest that individuals with more **anxiety-inducing** memories are more likely to become repressors in order to **repress** these negative childhood memories.
Evaluation:	Again, this may reflect an **unwillingness** to recall rather than repression.

Practice Questions

Q1 Explain the term 'flashbulb memory'.

Q2 What type of events can lead to 'flashbulb memories'?

Q3 What is repression?

Q4 What did Myers and Brewin discover about repression?

Exam Questions

Q1 Explain how emotion can inhibit memory. [10 marks]

Q2 Discuss how emotion can enhance memory. [10 marks]

I'm so unhappy, but I can't remember why...

There seems to be evidence for repression, but you'd think that if it was entirely true, we'd all have forgotten September 11th and other horrific events. But no, we've got really vivid memories of those. Well, I'm confused. What makes one awful thing more likely to be remembered and another more likely to be forgotten? I have no idea, ask someone else...

The Role of Reinforcement in Learning

This topic is for people doing OCR and nobody else. *Leading on from how we remember things — psychologists are also interested in how we learn behaviours and how we can use special techniques to remember stuff better.*

One Simple Form of Learning is **Classical Conditioning**

Classical conditioning was first shown by **Pavlov**. It's a simple form of learning where a behaviour is **associated** with certain stimuli. Some people believe that **all behaviour** is learnt through simple associations like this.

Pavlov (1927) carried out research on the digestive system of dogs. The dogs were attached to machines collecting their saliva. Pavlov accidentally noticed that the dogs salivated at the sound of the door opening when someone brought them food. Salivating is a **reflex** response to the presence of food, but the dogs had **learned** to salivate at the sound of the door. The dogs had made an **association** between the door opening and food.

In classical conditioning, a certain stimulus (**unconditioned stimulus** or **UCS**) triggers a natural reflex (**unconditioned response** or **UCR**). When some other stimulus (**conditioned stimulus** or **CS**) is repeatedly presented with the UCS, over time it will elicit the UCR by itself. The response is then called the **conditioned response**, or **CR**.

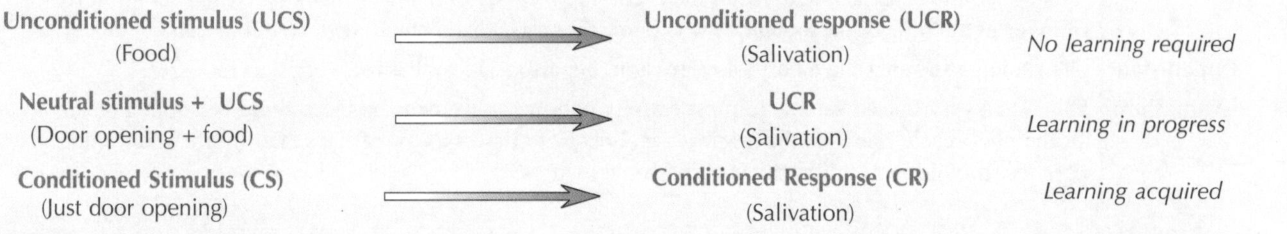

This has since been shown with other weird, abstract stimuli like **bells** ringing and **lights** flashing, not only doors.

Behaviour Can Also Be Modified Through **Reinforcement** and **Punishment**

Operant conditioning and **instrumental learning** are both forms of learning where behaviour is made more likely to happen again following **rewards**, and less likely following **punishment**.

Thorndike (1911) demonstrated instrumental learning

Aim:	Thorndike thought that learning could develop through **trial and error**, rather than just by **association** as with classical conditioning. He called this trial and error learning **'instrumental learning'**.
Method:	A hungry cat was placed in a **puzzle box**. A fish was placed outside the box.
Results:	The cat jumped up and down, scratching and pawing until it accidentally jumped onto the latch that opened the box. The second time this happened, the cat took **less time** to get out of the box. Eventually, the cat learned to release the catch **immediately**.
Conclusion:	These findings show part of the **'Law of Effect'** — behaviours followed by something positive are more likely to reoccur than behaviours followed by something negative or neutral. So **positive** effects (**rewards**) lead to behaviour occurring **more often**, while **negative** effects (**punishments**) lead to behaviour occurring **less often**.

Skinner (1938) developed Thorndike's theory further with his own theory of operant conditioning.

1) Skinner placed rats into cages with a **lever** sticking out.
2) If the rats pressed the lever **accidentally**, the food pellets came down a chute.
3) The rats eventually **learned** that pressing the lever led to food appearing.
4) The food acted as a **reward**, **reinforcing** the chance of the behaviour occurring again.
5) The experiment was repeated with other **consequences** of pressing the lever e.g. electric shocks.
6) He concluded that, apart from nothing happening, there are four possible **consequences** of any behaviour:

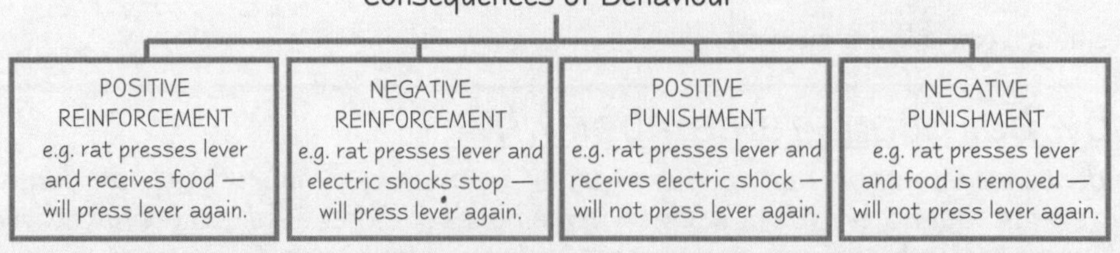

Consequences of Behaviour
POSITIVE REINFORCEMENT
e.g. rat presses lever and receives food — will press lever again.
NEGATIVE REINFORCEMENT
e.g. rat presses lever and electric shocks stop — will press lever again.
POSITIVE PUNISHMENT
e.g. rat presses lever and receives electric shock — will not press lever again.
NEGATIVE PUNISHMENT
e.g. rat presses lever and food is removed — will not press lever again.

The Role of Reinforcement in Learning

Learning and Remembering Are Not The Same Thing

Sometimes, you might say you're learning something, when really you're just trying to memorise it. There's a proper difference between **learning** and **remembering**. Here it is:

> **Remembering** is just about the **retention** of **information**.
>
> **Learning** is about **adapting** to an environment, discovering new **meanings** and **reorganising** cognitive structures.

Memory Techniques Help You Remember Stuff

There are a number of different **memory techniques** you can use to help you remember information better:

1. **Rehearsal** means **repeating** information. This **strengthens** memory traces, making that information easier to retrieve from memory.
2. **Elaboration** involves adding **detail** to the information to be remembered. Associating extra facts with the information gives you more to grasp onto when trying to recall it.
3. '**Method of loci**' is a technique of **imagining** you are walking along a path you know well, e.g. your walk to school. As you mentally walk along, you **associate** facts with locations. Then when you come to recall the information, you can revisit the path, and the locations will act as cues to the facts to be recalled.
4. The **context** in which we **encode** information has an association with the information itself. So, information will be easier to recall if you're in the same context as when you learnt it. This could be the mood you're in, the place, the company, even the weather.
5. **Organisation** involves reordering information into a new **system** that makes more sense. For example, facts could be grouped together into **categories**, or arranged in alphabetical order. This creates more associations, which means there's more links to get you to the facts.

Practice Questions

Q1 Give an example of an unconditional stimulus and an unconditional response.

Q2 Give an example of a neutral stimulus in classical conditioning.

Q3 According to Thorndike, what effect do punishments have on behaviour?

Q4 Explain the 'method of loci' technique.

Exam Questions

Q1 Discuss the methods we can use to memorise material better. [8 marks]

Q2 Explain the difference between classical conditioning and instrumental learning. [12 marks]

Pavlov — that name rings a bell...

I personally like to try these little learning experiments out on the family pets. Just ring a bell a few seconds before you present Rodney the guinea pig with some carroty treats. Keep doing the same every day, and after a little while, you can ring that bell just for fun, and wet yourself laughing as he does a few back flips with sheer excitement.

Eyewitness Testimony

This topic is for everybody. *If you witness a crime or an accident, you have to report what you saw, and your version of events could be crucial in prosecuting someone... But your memory isn't as accurate as you might think...*

Eyewitness Testimony Can Be **Inaccurate** and **Distorted**

Eyewitness testimony (EWT) is the **evidence** provided by people who **witnessed** a particular event or crime. It relies on **recall** from memory. EWT includes, for example, **descriptions** of criminals (e.g. hair colour, height) and crime scenes (e.g. time, date, location).

Loftus and Palmer (1974) investigated how EWT can be **distorted**.
They used **leading questions**, where a certain answer is subtly implied in the question:

OCR Core Study

Loftus and Palmer (1974) studied eyewitness testimony.

Method: Participants were shown films of a multiple car crash. They were then asked questions including 'How fast do you think the cars were going when they **hit**?' In different conditions, the word 'hit' was replaced with **'smashed'**, **'collided'**, **'bumped'** or **'contacted'**. A week later, they were asked if they had seen any broken glass. (There was no broken glass in the films.)

Results: Participants who were asked the speed when the cars **'smashed'** reported **higher** speeds than participants in the other conditions. More participants in the **'smashed'** condition also claimed to have seen **broken glass**.

Conclusion: **Leading questions** can affect the **accuracy** of people's memories of an event.

Evaluation: This has implications for questions in **police interviews**. However, this was an artificial experiment — watching a video is not as **emotionally arousing** as a real life event, which potentially affects recall. In fact, a later study found that participants who thought they'd witnessed a **real** robbery gave a more **accurate** description of the robber.

Loftus and Zanni (1975) also considered **leading questions**. They showed participants a film of a car accident, then asked them either 'Did you see **the** broken headlight?' or 'Did you see **a** broken headlight?' There was no broken headlight, but **7%** of those asked about '**a**' broken headlight claimed they saw one, compared to **17%** in the group asked about '**the**' broken headlight. So, the simple use of the word 'the' is enough to affect the accuracy of people's memories of an event.

Facial Recognition is Also Important in EWT

Witnesses often have to try and recall the **individual facial features** of a criminal so that police can try and make an **identikit** image. There is debate, however, over the **reliability** of these images based on research into how we normally identify faces:

Young et al (1987) studied memory of faces.

They found that people recognise faces better using the face as a **whole** rather than individual features. This has important **implications** as **identikit** pictures used by the police are based on individual features rather than how the face holds together as a whole.

Bruce and Valentine (1988) investigated motion in faces.

They attached lights to faces and filmed them in the dark. They found participants watching the movements of the lights could often identify the **emotion** and sometimes recognise the **person** just by the movements of the face. Police **identikit** pictures, however, are just motionless faces, so do not tap a large volume of facial knowledge.

Bruce and Young (1986) studied mechanisms of facial recognition.

They studied brain damaged patients, and suggested that recognition of **unfamiliar** faces relies on **feature** detection (eyes, nose, etc.), as in identikit pictures, whereas recognition of **familiar** faces relies on recognition of the **configuration** of the whole lot. This therefore lends **support** for the use of police identikit images, because presumably identikit images are of strangers.

Eyewitness Testimony

Reconstructive Memory is About Filling the Gaps in Memory

1) **Bartlett** believed that when we remember something, we only store **some** elements of the experience.
2) We **reconstruct** events using these elements, filling in the **gaps** in the memory with our own **schema**.
3) Schema are **ready-stored opinions** and **expectations** which we use for quick judgements to deal with the world.
4) Our **culture**, **beliefs**, **prejudices** and **previous experiences** all help build our schema.
5) For example, a '**granny schema**' might be that all grannies have white curly hair, like knitting, and say 'haven't you grown'. Of course, not all grannies do, but you might use this granny schema to fill in the gaps in the vague memory you had of someone's granny.

Bartlett (1932) demonstrated reconstructive memory.

Method: Participants were shown a short story from a different culture, which therefore contained **unfamiliar** material. After a number of days, participants were asked to **recall** the story.

Results: The recalled stories were always **shorter** than the original. Many parts were recalled from the participants' own cultural perspectives, with certain facts **changed** to fit. For example, 'canoe' was changed to 'boat'. The recalled version soon became very **fixed** over time with only minor variations.

Conclusion: The **meaning** of a story is remembered, but the gaps are filled in with more familiar material to make the story **easier** to remember. This has an effect of **skewing** information to make it fit our schema.

Comment: It is possible that errors occurred from **conscious guessing** rather than participants actually believing that their recalled stories were the same as the original. Later studies have found that if participants were told from the beginning that **accurate recall** was required, errors dropped significantly.

Sulin and Dooling (1974) found support for Bartlett's findings.

Method: A story was read to participants, who were told it was about either Gerald Martin (a fictional person) or Adolf Hitler. They were then given a few sentences and asked whether they came from the text. Some sentences didn't come from the text, but were concerned with well-known facts about Hitler.

Results: Participants who thought the story was about Hitler were more likely to claim the key sentences were in the text.

Conclusion: Participants' previous knowledge (schema) **distorted** their recall, as in Bartlett's study.

Schemas are Used During Both *Encoding* and *Reconstruction*

1) The way information is **initially perceived** and **stored** is affected by schema and stereotypes.
2) Research shows that people can be mistaken in their initial **encoding** of events, leading to mistaken recall.
3) So schemas and stereotypes are used when **forming** a memory as well as when trying to **reconstruct** a memory.

Practice Questions

Q1 What are schemas?

Q2 What are eyewitness testimonies?

Q3 Describe the study by Loftus and Palmer.

Q4 Describe the main findings of Bartlett's 1932 study.

Exam Questions

Q1 Describe research on face recognition. What do these findings show us about EWTs? [12 marks]

Q2 Outline Bartlett's research on reconstructive memory and explain why this is significant in EWTs. [12 marks]

A tall thin man, quite short, with black, fair hair — great fat bloke she was...

Well, now I haven't a clue what I've really experienced in my life. Did that man I saw shoplifting really have stubble, scars, a pierced chin and a ripped leather jacket, or is that just my shoplifter-stereotype kicking in? In fact, come to think of it, I couldn't actually tell you whether my granny has a hairy chin or not. I think she does, but then I think all grannies do...

Variations in Cognitive Performance

Just for OCR. That's all. *Cognitive performance differs between cultures because of environmental factors, and between people because of disorders (e.g. autism) and individual differences.*

People With **Autism** Normally Have Communicative, Social and Linguistic Problems

1) A person with autism will tend to have the following characteristics:
   - Be **withdrawn** and poor at forming relationships.
   - Be unlikely to **respond** to environmental stimuli, especially people.
   - Have **communication difficulties**, such as abnormal speech.
   - Have **compulsive** and **ritualistic behaviour**, including an obsession with **sameness**.
2) **Very occasionally**, people with autism are **exceptionally gifted**, in areas such as music, mathematics and art.
3) There are thought to be two types of autism —
   a) The **Kanner** type tend to have **learning disabilities** and additional **problems**, such as epilepsy.
   b) The **Asperger** type (**Asperger's syndrome**) tend to have normal or above normal intelligence and few neurological problems.

Someone with Autism may **Lack a "Theory of Mind"**

1) A **theory of mind** is our understanding that other people see the world in **different ways** from our own.
2) **Young children** don't have theory of mind — they don't understand that other people think or see things differently.
3) To have a social or emotional **relationship** with another person, it's important to understand their different emotional state or point of view, and therefore to have a theory of mind.
4) If autistic children don't develop a theory of mind, it may explain why they may find **social contact** difficult.

OCR Core Study

Baron-Cohen et al (1985) studied theory of mind in autistic children.

Method: Three groups of children were studied — children with autism, children with Down Syndrome and 'normal' children. The experimenter had two dolls, Sally and Anne. Sally had a basket, Anne a box. Children were asked to name the dolls (the **naming question**). Then Sally was seen to hide a marble in her basket and leave the room. Anne took the marble and put it in her box. Sally returned and the child was asked 'Where will Sally look for her marble?' (**belief question**). The correct response is to point to the basket, where Sally believes the marble to be. They were also asked 'Where is the marble really?' (**reality question**) and 'Where was the marble in the beginning?' (**memory question**). Each child was tested twice, with the marble in a different place the second time.

Results: **100%** of the children got the **naming** question, **reality** question and **memory** question correct. In the **belief** question, the children with Down Syndrome scored **86%**, the 'normal' children **85%**, but the children with autism scored **20%**.

Conclusion: The results were not due to **learning disabilities**, as both the autistic children and those with Down Syndrome had similar mental ages. The findings therefore seem to suggest that autistic children have **under-developed theories of mind**. They seem unable to predict or understand the beliefs of others.

Evaluation: As **dolls** were used, it may be that children with autism had a more highly developed theory of mind and understood that dolls did not have beliefs. However, when **Leslie and Frith (1988)** did a similar study with real people and not dolls, the same results were gained.

Perception is a Cognitive Process Which Differs Depending on Certain Factors

Perception is a process where the brain receives **raw information** from the environment through our **sense organs** and uses it to help us make **sense** of our environment. Perception can be **affected** by a number of factors.

1) The **environment** affects **what** and **how** we perceive, e.g. a dark room may be perceived very differently from a lit one.
2) Our previous **experience** and **learning** affects how we perceive things, which leads to **cross-cultural** differences.
3) Substances such as **alcohol** and **drugs** affect our perception.

When we see things differently from how they really are, it is called a **visual** (optical) **illusion**. The **Muller-Lyer illusion** is an example of a visual illusion.

The two lines appear to be different in length, but they are actually the **same**. The arrows at the end of the lines give different **cues** to the length of the lines. Visual illusions are created when cues to depth and size '**trick**' our eyes.

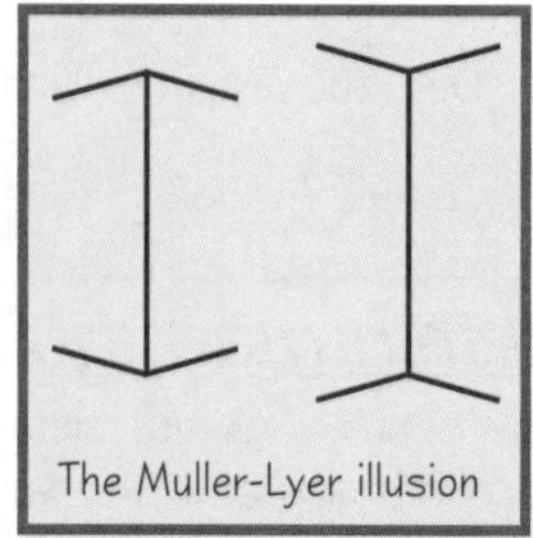
The Muller-Lyer illusion

Variations in Cognitive Performance

Cross-Cultural Differences in Cognition Must Be Due to Environmental Factors

1) Similarities in behaviour between people suggest that some behaviours may be **innate** (inborn).
2) However, there are often large **differences** in behaviour between different cultures.
3) These cross-cultural differences are unlikely to be innate, as it is unlikely that people from one culture would be so genetically different from people from another culture. So the differences must be caused by **environmental factors**.
4) When studying other cultures, a researcher who is an outsider may bring some **bias** to what they observe — they may not understand why people act a certain way, and so interpret it wrongly, e.g. play-fighting as aggression.
5) Additionally, tests used may not be **fair** or **appropriate**, e.g. IQ tests may not cross easily to another culture.
6) Unfortunately, cross-cultural studies are often **ethnocentric**, i.e. from one point of view; typically a white, western, middle-class point of view. This view is often perceived as the 'correct' one, to which other cultures are compared.
7) **Deregowski**'s review of **picture perception** in non-western cultures (below) has been described as ethnocentric, but the results offer an insight which would be useful in designing perception studies for the relevant cultural groups:

OCR Core Study

Deregowski (1972) reviewed picture perception in non-western cultures.

Method: Deregowski **reviewed** research from studies including:
Participants from non-western cultures were shown a **simple picture** consisting of an elephant, a man and an antelope. First the elephant was in the background, then in the foreground.
Participants were asked which was **nearer**, the antelope or the elephant.
Other participants had a similar task with **3D** drawings.

Results: Children and adults from **African** tribes found it **difficult** to answer the question for both the simple picture and 3D picture. Many non-western cultures could not see depth in pictures, preferring traditional **split-style drawings** to **perspective** drawings. (Split-style drawings are where all the parts of an animal or object are shown, such as the elephant shown here.)

Conclusion: Many non-western people have not **learnt** to perceive and integrate the **depth cues** in western-style pictures. This is because pictures are not used as a means of **communication** and so do not need to convey information accurately, being used mainly as symbolic **art**. Therefore, pictures cannot be used as a '**universal language**'.

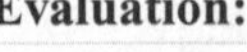

Evaluation: The results can be interpreted as **ethnocentric** as much of the research was conducted around 100 years ago by missionaries with very ethnocentric attitudes. These anecdotes also lack detail and so cannot be analysed thoroughly. Reviews such as this are very useful but potentially can misrepresent information as the reviewer has not conducted the research themselves.

A split-style elephant*

*CGP would like to point out that these tyre tracks were added for your amusement only and we in no way condone the running over of elephants. No animals were harmed in the construction of this graphic.

Practice Questions

Q1 What is ethnocentrism?
Q2 Briefly describe theory of mind.
Q3 What is perception?
Q4 What are visual illusions?

Exam Questions

Q1 Discuss Baron-Cohen's study. [6 marks]

Q2 Discuss cross-cultural experiments and outline one cross-cultural study. [12 marks]

Here's a quick picture perception test — what's this... }^^^^^^:-)

Wow, we all differ a lot in what we see, think and how we interpret the world. I mean, I'm looking at my plant's big pink flowers, but how would I know if you see the same as me? The thing we both call 'pink' could look totally different in both our heads. Your 'pink' could be my 'green'. If I got inside your head I might see green 2D speckles. Or lots of 0s and 1s...

Answer to the picture perception test was... Inspector Gadget

Theories of Child Development

OCR and Edexcel only. *Developmental psychology focuses on how we develop as children and how this affects our future lives. Things are going to get theory-tastic but the three main ones are covered on these two pages — here we go...*

Piaget's Theory is the Most Well Known Theory of Cognitive Development

A child's mental abilities and skills develop with time — things like paying attention, learning, thinking and remembering. But as with so much in psychology, there are many theories as to how this happens.

Piaget suggested four major periods of cognitive development

1. The **sensorimotor stage** (birth to 2 years) — The child **advances** a great deal in this stage. At the beginning, there are only simple **reflex** activities such as sucking. Gradually, through repetition, the child learns more complex routines. After about 8 months, the child has **object permanence** — it realises that objects continue to exist even when it can't see them. Finally, at about 18 months, it shows **representational thought** — it searches for missing objects (therefore it must be able to have thoughts about things when it can't see them), and shows the beginnings of language.

2. The **pre-operational stage** (2 to 7 years) — The child becomes more confident in **constructing** and **using** mental symbols (e.g. language) to think about **situations**, **objects** and **events**. However, it can't **conserve** — it can't understand that the properties of something don't change if its appearance changes (e.g. that there's still the same amount of liquid even if it's poured into a taller glass, also see the study below). Piaget didn't believe that children at this stage have acquired the ability to **think logically**, hence this is the **pre**-operational stage. Piaget divided the pre-operational stage into:
   a) The **pre-conceptual period** (2 to 4 years) — The ideas, thoughts and processes of the child are simple compared to adults. The child shows **animism** (pretending stuff's alive), **transductive reasoning** (concentrating only on one aspect to work something out, e.g. if a car has wheels, and a random thing has wheels, then that thing must be a car) and **egocentrism** (viewing the world from their own perspective and having difficulty seeing anyone else's point of view).
   b) The **intuitive period** (4 to 7 years) — The child becomes **less egocentric** and better at classifying objects due to their perceptual attributes, e.g. size, colour.

3. The **concrete operational stage** (7 to 11 years) — The child learns **new ways of thinking** about **new objects**, **events** and **situations**. It can **conserve** and think **logically**, but only about **real**, not abstract situations.

4. The **formal operational stage** (11 to 12 years) — The child is now able to think about **abstract** ideas that have no basis in reality. It can also think about **hypothetical** events.

Samuel and Bryant tested Piaget's theory of conservation

Conservation is recognising that the **properties** of an object or substance don't change when their appearance changes. For example, if a ball of plasticine is stretched to look longer, children who can conserve will understand that there's still the **same amount** of plasticine.

OCR Core Study

Samuel and Bryant (1984) varied conservation tasks.

Aim: Younger children were thought to fail Piaget's conservation tasks because they think that because a question is asked twice, two different answers are required. This was to be investigated.

Method: 252 children aged between 5 and 8 ½ years were split into four groups according to their age. Each group was then divided into 3 subgroups —
a) The **standard group** — traditional conservation task — two questions: Children were shown two rows with the same number of counters and asked if they had the same number. Then one row of counters was spread out, and the child was asked again.
b) The **one judgement** task — Only one question was asked, after the counters were moved.
c) The **fixed array control** — They saw only the display **after** it had been changed.

Results: They found younger children did better in the **one judgement** condition than the standard condition, but older children always did better overall.

Conclusion: The study supports Samuel and Bryant's argument that two questions may confuse children. But, it still shows that conservation improves with age, so it doesn't disprove Piaget.

Comment: Younger children may have performed worse because they were intimidated by the experimental situation.

Theories of Child Development

Social Learning Theory Suggests Aspects of Our Behaviour are Learned

Social learning theory (or behavioural theory) suggests that behaviour is learnt in three different ways:

1) **Classical conditioning** — A child learns to associate a **neutral stimulus** with another stimulus, and so **responds** to the neutral stimulus as they would to the other, e.g. a child may learn to **associate** the sound of an ice cream van jingle with ice cream and begin to lick their lips.
2) **Operant conditioning** — If a **response** results in a particular **consequence**, the child can learn to use this response again. Consequences include:
   a) **Reinforcers** e.g. if a mother praises her child for sharing a biscuit, the child is more likely to do it again.
   b) **Punishments** e.g. if a child is shouted at for touching a glass beaker, they may be less likely to do it again.
3) **Observational Learning** — A child learns through **observation** and **imitation** of others. For example, if a child hears a person criticising another they may start to criticise them too.

Sometimes it's hard to explain what behaviour is being learnt.

Freud (1909) Talked About 'Psycho-Sexual Development'

Freud explained development in terms of **the id,** (the basic animal part of you which obeys the pleasure principle), **the ego** (the conscious part) and **the superego** (the **moral centre**) (see page 2).

Freud thought children of 3-6 years old take on their parents' **moral standards**. These form the child's superego. Then the child doesn't need an adult to tell them that what they have done is bad or wrong.
Additionally, Freud said that children go through **five** stages of **psycho-sexual development**:

a) **Oral stage** (birth-1 year)
b) **Anal stage** (1-3 years)
c) **Phallic stage** (3-6 years)
d) **Latency period** (6-12 years)
e) **Genital stage** (12 years +)

In each stage the **libido** (sexual energy) is focused on different things — the mouth in the oral stage etc.

Freud suggested children can become **fixated** with things due to experiences during these different stages. For example, a child who experiences very harsh toilet training in their anal phase may develop obsessive or stubborn behaviour.

Freud (1909) — The case study of Little Hans

This study is based on observations of a child named Hans who developed a **fear** of horses. Freud interpreted this fear as being **symbolic** of fear of his father and so believed this provided evidence for the **Oedipus complex**. (This is the theory that the son has incestuous feelings for his mother, and intense jealousy of his father.) He argued that in the phallic stage, the child develops a strong attachment to the parent of the opposite sex. In boys this can result in desire for an exclusive relationship with the mother and jealousy of the father. This could in turn lead to **castration anxiety**, brought on by a father's irritation with his son's attachment to his mother and also his son's fascination with sexual organs. In this case, Freud argued that castration anxiety was symbolised by the boy's fear of the horse biting him.

This whole study ran to a 100 page book in which Freud provided further evidence by interpreting Hans' dreams and conversations. However, the study was based entirely on observation and interpretation, and Freud got some of the information from Hans' father, without interviewing Hans directly. It was also sometimes based on 'leading questions' (see page 16) which made Hans reply in a way to support Freud's interpretations.

OCR Core Study

Practice Questions

Q1 Name the five stages of development suggested by Freud.
Q2 Give examples of reinforcers and punishments in social learning theory.
Q3 Define conservation in Piaget's theory.
Q4 Describe the case study of Little Hans.

Exam Questions

Q1 Compare two theories of child development. [12 marks]
Q2 Evaluate Piaget's theory of conservation with reference to research evidence. [8 marks]

Stages of development — crying, shouting, sulking, drinking...

Personally, I think Freud was a nutter. A funny thing about him is that a lot of his ideas came from studying himself. You'd think he'd be a bit embarrassed to admit to all the mother-fancying and general obsession with genitals. You'd also think that back in 1909, people might have told him to shut up, but no. Wonder how he got away with it...

The Development of Attachments

This bit's for OCR and AQA A. *An 'attachment' is a strong, emotional bond between two people. Psychologists are interested in how and when our first attachments form and what influences them.*

Schaffer Identified the Following Stages in Attachment Formation:

1) The **pre-attachment phase** — During the first **two to three months** of life the baby learns to **separate** people from objects but doesn't have any strong preferences about who cares for it.
2) The **indiscriminate attachment phase** — Between **three and seven months** it starts to clearly **distinguish** and **recognise** different people, smiling more at people it knows than at strangers. However, there are still no strong preferences about who cares for it.
3) The **discriminate attachment phase** — From **seven months onwards** it becomes able to form **true, emotionally strong attachments** with **specific** people. This is shown by being content when that person is around, distressed when they leave and happy when they return. It may be scared of strangers and avoid them.
4) The **multiple attachment phase** — From about **nine months** it can form **attachments to many people**. Some attachments may be stronger than others and have **different functions**, e.g. for play or comfort, but there doesn't seem to be a limit to the number of attachments it can make.

Schaffer and Emerson (1964) — evidence for stages of attachment

Method: 60 babies were observed in their homes in Glasgow every four weeks from birth to about 18 months. Interviews were also conducted with their families.

Results: Schaffer's stages of attachment formation were found to occur. Also, at 8 months of age about 50 of the infants had more than one attachment. About 20 of them either had no attachment with their mother or had a stronger attachment with someone else, even though the mother was always the main carer.

Conclusion: Infants form attachments in **stages** and can attach to **many people**. **Quality of care** is important in forming attachments, so infants may not attach to their mother if other people are more sensitive or loving.

Comment: There is now a lot of evidence to support Schaffer and Emerson's results and the proposed stages of attachment formation, but there are also criticisms of the study. For example, Schaffer and Emerson used a **limited sample** and the evidence from interviews and observations may be **biased** and **unreliable**.

Additionally, there are some cross-cultural differences that should be considered. **Tronick et al (1992)** found that infants in Zaire had a strong attachment with their mother by six months of age but didn't have strong attachments with others, even though they had several carers.

*Different Factors **Influence** the **Development** of **Attachments***

1) The **age** of a child may be important. Some researchers, such as **John Bowlby** (see page 25), have claimed that attachments should develop before a certain age (e.g. 3-5 years), otherwise they will never properly develop.
2) The **quality of care** that a child receives may be crucial for forming attachments. Just being around a child may not be enough — parents need to be caring and sensitive to its needs (this is shown in Schaffer and Emerson's results).
3) A child's **temperament** may make it easier or harder for them to form attachments, regardless of the quality of care that they receive. Some aspects of temperament may be inborn.

There are many ways to form a strong attachment with your child.

The Development of Attachments

*An Infant's **Reaction** in a **Strange Situation** Shows if it's **Securely** Attached*

Ainsworth et al (1978) — The Strange Situation

Method:	12-18 month old infants were left in a room with their mother. Different scenarios occurred — a stranger approached, the infant was left alone, the mother returned. The infant's reactions were constantly observed.
Results:	About 20% of infants were **'anxious-avoidant' (type A)** — they ignored their mother and didn't mind if she left. A stranger could comfort them. About 65% were **'securely attached' (type B)** — content with their mother, upset when she left, happy when she returned and avoided strangers. About 15% were **'anxious-resistant' (type C)** — uneasy around their mother and upset if she left. They resisted strangers and were also hard to comfort when their mother returned.
Conclusion:	Infants showing different reactions to their carers have different types of attachment.

The findings above have been shown many times in the USA, but it was not known whether they could be applied to other cultures. Cross-cultural studies have since occurred:

Van Ijzendoorn and Kroonenberg (1988) — cross-cultural studies

Method:	The findings from 32 studies of 'the strange situation' in different countries (e.g. Japan, Britain, Sweden, etc) were analysed to find any overall patterns.
Results:	The percentages of children classified as Type A, B or C were very **similar** in the countries tested.
Conclusion:	There are cross-cultural similarities in raising children, producing common reactions to 'the strange situation'.

*There are Important **Findings** from Strange Situation Research*

1) **Attachment type may influence later behaviours.** Securely attached children may be more confident in school and form strong, trusting adult relationships. 'Avoidant' children may have behaviour problems in school and find it hard to form close, trusting adult relationships. 'Resistant' children may be insecure and attention seeking in school and, as adults, their strong feelings of dependency may be stressful for partners.
2) **Some cultural differences are found. Grossman et al (1985)** claimed that more 'avoidant' infants may be found in Germany because of the value Germans put on independence — so 'avoidance' is seen as a good thing.
3) **The causes of different attachment types are debatable.** The causes may be the sensitivity of their carers and/or their inborn temperament.
4) **The strange situation experiment doesn't show a characteristic of the child.** The experiment only shows the child's relationship with a specific person, so they might react differently with different carers, or later in life.

Practice Questions

Q1 Outline Schaffer's stages of attachment formation.

Q2 Explain some of the factors that influence attachment formation.

Q3 Explain the differences between type A, B and C attachments.

Q4 What have cross-cultural studies shown about attachments?

Exam Questions

Q1 Describe research on the development of attachments. [6 marks]

Q2 Outline the 'Strange Situation' experiment. [6 marks]

Try and get all these theories of attachment firmly stuck in your head

Next time you're in trouble at college and your parents are called in to 'discuss your behaviour', try sobbing gently under your breath, 'I think it's all my anxious-resistant attachment formation, it's left me insecure and needy of attention'. It's a desperate attempt, but it might just make your parents feel bad enough to let you off.

Explanations of Attachment

This is for OCR and AQA A only. *These pages deal with the five different psychological explanations for how and why attachments develop between infants and their carers. Simple eh — you'd think, but this is psychology...*

Psychodynamic Theory *Offers an Explanation for Attachment Formation...*

Sigmund Freud claimed we are born with a part of personality called the **'id'** (the animal bit, see page 2).

The id is only concerned with our **biological needs** — it demands food when we're hungry, makes us sleep when we are tired, etc.

A baby will cry when it needs something, like when it's hungry. Its mother will then feed it and this will give the baby pleasure because the need is removed. So the baby will make a **link** between having its mother around and having its biological needs for food, warmth, etc fulfilled. This is why babies 'attach' to their mother.

...As Does ***Behaviourist Theory***

Like Freud's theory, the behaviourist theory focuses on the baby wanting its needs fulfilled. However, the behaviourist theory of **conditioning** gives a more precise explanation for how attachments form:

Classical Conditioning. This is about learning **associations** between different things in our environment. Getting food naturally gives the baby **pleasure**. The baby's desire for food is fulfilled whenever its mother is around to feed it. So an **association is formed between mother and food**. So, whenever its mother is around the baby will feel pleasure — i.e. 'attachment'.

Operant Conditioning. **Dollard and Miller (1950)** claimed that babies feel discomfort when they're hungry and so have a desire to get food to **remove the discomfort**. They find that if they cry, their mother will come and feed them — so the discomfort is removed (this is '**negative reinforcement**'). The mother is therefore associated with food and the baby will want to be close to her — because if the mother is close, food will be too. This produces 'attachment behaviour' (distress when separated from the mother etc).

Behaviourists have shown that we can learn by **making associations** — so this could easily apply to forming attachments, and food is a very obvious reinforcement.

However, even though babies do spend most of their time either eating or sleeping, it doesn't mean that they automatically attach to the person who feeds them.

In fact, **Schaffer and Emerson (1964)** found that many babies did not have strong attachments with their mothers, even though she fed them. **Good quality interaction with the baby seemed more important** — the baby will attach to whoever is the most sensitive and loving (see page 22). This is also shown in Harlow's study of monkeys:

Harlow (1959) showed the need for 'contact comfort'.

Method:	Experiments were undertaken where rhesus monkeys were raised in isolation. They had two 'surrogate' mothers. One was made of wire mesh and contained a feeding bottle, and the other was made of cloth but without a feeding bottle.
Results:	The monkeys spent most of their time clinging to the cloth surrogate and only used the wire surrogate to feed. The cloth surrogate seemed to give them **comfort** in new situations.
Conclusion:	The monkeys needed '**contact comfort**' as much as food and would attach to the source of this comfort, not the source of food. This **contradicts** the Freudian and behaviourist focus on feeding as the cause of attachment.
Comment:	The results of this experiment might not apply to humans, seeing as it used monkeys. Additionally, isolating monkeys is not a very **ethical** method of studying attachment development.

Mummy?

Explanations of Attachment

We're Not Done Yet — There's the **Ethological Approach**...

Ethology is the study of animals in their natural environment. **Konrad Lorenz (1935)** found that geese seemed to automatically 'attach' to the first thing they see after hatching. This is called **imprinting**.

Imprinting seems to occur during a **'critical period'** — in this example, in the first few hours after birth. After imprinting on something the geese would follow it and use it as a 'role model'. Normally geese would see their mother soon after hatching but Lorenz showed that they could imprint on other things, including him, if they were seen first.

Imprinting is a **fast**, **automatic** process which may be hard to change later. It is unlikely to occur in humans. Our attachments take a **longer** time to develop and we do not automatically attach to particular things — quality care seems more important in human attachment formation (see Schaffer and Emerson, page 22).

...and **John Bowlby's Evolutionary** Theory...

Bowlby (1951) argued that something like imprinting may occur in humans.
He developed several main claims:

1) We have **evolved** a biological need to attach to our main caregiver — usually our biological mother. This one special attachment is called **monotropy**. Forming this attachment has survival value as staying close to the mother ensures food and protection.
2) This attachment gives us a **'template'** for all future relationships — we learn to trust and care for others. It also acts as a **'safe base'**, giving us confidence to explore our environment.
3) The first 3-5 years of life is the **critical period** for this attachment to develop — otherwise it may never do so.
4) If the attachment doesn't develop or if it is broken, this may seriously damage social and emotional development (see page 26).

Comments on Bowlby's theory:

1) There is some **evidence** for his claims (see page 26).
2) The claims about monotropy are not supported by **Schaffer and Emerson's (1964)** findings that many children form multiple attachments, and may not attach to their mother (see page 22).
3) There is **mixed evidence** for claims of a **critical period** for attachments to develop (see pages 28-29).
4) Attachments are very important in childhood but the effects of a lack of attachment or having an attachment broken may not be as bad as Bowlby claimed (see pages 26-29).

Practice Questions

Q1 How are the psychodynamic and behaviourist theories of attachment similar?
Q2 Explain how classical and operant conditioning could be involved in forming attachments.
Q3 Why does Harlow's study contradict the psychodynamic and behaviourist theories of attachment?
Q4 What is meant by 'imprinting'?
Q5 Outline Bowlby's claims.
Q6 Why do Schaffer and Emerson's findings contradict Bowlby's claims?

Exam Questions

Q1 Outline one theory of attachment. [8 marks]
Q2 Explain two criticisms of the theory outlined in question one. [6 marks]

Monkey lovin'...

As I'm sure you're beginning to realise, psychology is all about theories. You can't get too caught up in them, and you certainly don't need to agree with all of them — but what you have to do is remember the different theories, how they were developed and what the different opinions about them are — only then can you make your own judgements about them.

The Effects of Deprivation and Separation

Just for AQA A. *The attachments we form are very important and there can be serious consequences if they're broken. These pages are all about separation and deprivation, and how they're not the nicest things that can happen to a kid...*

Separation and Deprivation are Different in Psychology

Separation is where a child is away from a **caregiver** they're attached to (like their mother). It's about a **relatively short** time, just hours or days, but not a longer or permanent separation.

Deprivation is about the loss of something that is **wanted or needed**. So, 'maternal deprivation' is the loss of the mother (or other attachment figure). A more **long-term** or even **permanent** loss is implied.

Separation Can Have Major Effects

According to several studies, infants or children who have been separated may react through the following stages. The stages are referred to as the **'PDD model' — Protest, Despair, Detachment**:

1) **Protest** — During the first few hours, the child will **protest** a lot at being **separated** from its mother (or other attachment figure), by crying, panicking, calling for its mother, etc.

2) **Despair** — After a day or two, the child will start to lose interest in its surroundings, becoming more and more **withdrawn**, with occasional crying. They may also eat and sleep less.

3) **Detachment** — After a few days, the child will start to become more **alert** and interested again in its surroundings. It will cry less and may seem to have **'recovered'** from its bad reaction to the separation. However, its previous attachment with its carer may now be permanently **damaged** — the trust and security may be lost.

One study to look at...

Robertson and Robertson (1968) — evidence for the PDD model

Method: Several children who experienced short separations from their carers were observed and filmed. For example, a 17 month old boy called John stayed in a residential nursery for nine days while his mother had another baby.

Results: John showed the signs of passing through **'protest'** for the first day or two. Then he showed **despair** — he tried to get attention from the nurses but they were busy with other children so he 'gave up' trying. Then he showed **detachment** — he was more active and content. However, when his mother came to collect him, he was reluctant to be affectionate.

Conclusion: The short-term separation had very **bad effects** on John, including possible **permanent damage** to his attachment with his mother.

Some comments on the PDD model include:

1) These findings suggest that **separating a child from its carers should be avoided** whenever possible. This has important implications for childcare practice, e.g. children should be allowed to visit, or remain with, their mothers during a stay in hospital.

2) The findings of some studies are **open to question**. For example, the effects on John may not have been simply due to separation from his mother — he was also in a strange place and getting much less care and attention than he was used to.

3) **Many factors** influence how a child reacts to a separation. These include age (older children will cope better), the quality of the care received during the separation, the individual temperament of the child and how often it has experienced separations. So, **separations do not necessarily produce the PDD effects**. They may even be good for the child (see pages 32-33).

The Effects of Deprivation and Separation

*John Bowlby (1953) Studied Longer Term Maternal **Deprivation***

Even if short-term separation may not necessarily be bad for a child, **John Bowlby** argued that long-term **deprivation** from an attachment figure could be harmful. He produced his **maternal deprivation hypothesis**:

1) Deprivation from the main carer during the **critical period** (the first 3-5 years), has harmful effects on a child's emotional, social, intellectual and even physical development.
2) Long-term effects of deprivation may include **separation anxiety** (the fear of another separation from the carer). This may lead to problem behaviour, e.g. being very clingy, and avoiding going to school. Future relationships may be affected by this emotional insecurity. Bowlby's research showed evidence for this.

Bowlby (1944) — The 44 Juvenile Thieves

Method: Case studies were completed on the backgrounds of 44 adolescents who, because of stealing, were referred to the clinic where Bowlby worked.

Results: It was found that 17 of them had been separated from their mothers for at least six months, some time before five years of age. Some of them didn't seem to care about how their actions affected others. They had no guilty feelings and were called '**affectionless psychopaths**'.

Conclusion: Deprivation of the child from its main carer early in life can have very **harmful long-term consequences**.

Some comments on Bowlby's maternal deprivation hypothesis include:

1) Other evidence supports Bowlby's claims. **Spitz and Wolf (1946)** found that babies cried more than normal when they were (briefly) maternally deprived. **Goldfarb (1943)** found that orphanage children who were socially and maternally deprived were later less intellectually and socially developed.
2) The evidence has **criticisms**: Bowlby linked the thieves' behaviour to maternal deprivation, but **other things were not considered**, e.g. whether the poverty they grew-up in led them to steal. Spitz and Wolf didn't study **long-term effects**. The children in Goldfarb's study may have been most harmed by the **social deprivation** in the orphanage rather than the maternal deprivation.

Even when deprivation has harmful effects, these may be reversed with appropriate, **quality care**. For example, **Skeels and Dye (1939)** found that children who had been socially deprived (in an orphanage) during their first two years of life quickly improved their IQ scores if they were transferred to a school where they got one-to-one care.

Practice Questions

Q1 Explain the difference between the definitions of separation and deprivation in psychology.

Q2 What is meant by 'PDD'?

Q3 What factors affect how a child reacts to separation?

Q4 Explain Bowlby's maternal deprivation hypothesis.

Q5 Why does the 44 thieves study support Bowlby's hypothesis?

Q6 Give a criticism of the 44 thieves study.

Exam Questions

Q1 Outline the possible effects of maternal separation and maternal deprivation. [6 marks]

Q2 Describe and evaluate Bowlby's maternal deprivation hypothesis. [12 marks]

The PDD model can also be applied as a reaction to excessive study

So, if your mum leaves you alone for a while when you're little you might well become a bank robber — sounds like a pretty poor excuse to me but there you go. It's certainly interesting stuff. Even if you don't agree, the bottom line is you have to learn the theories, who came up with them, and what their pros and cons are — it's a world of pain.

The Effects of Privation

These pages are for AQA A and OCR. *Maternal privation is a bit different to maternal deprivation.* ***Privation*** *means never having been able to satisfy a certain need. So,* ***maternal privation*** *is when a child has* ***never*** *had an attachment to their mother or another caregiver. (In contrast to deprivation where an attachment has formed but is broken).*

Privation Means Never Having Been Able to Satisfy a Need

Rutter (1981) claimed that the effects of maternal privation are more likely to be **serious** than the effects of maternal deprivation. Evidence for this comes from **case studies** of children who have suffered difficult conditions or cruel treatment.

Some Case Studies of Privation Include:

Curtiss (1977) — The Case of Genie

This reported the case of a girl who suffered **extreme cruelty** from her parents. Her father believed that she was retarded and kept her strapped to a high chair with a potty in the seat for most of her childhood. She was beaten if she made any sounds, and didn't have the chance to play with toys or with other children or to form an attachment.

She was finally discovered when she was 13 years old. She was **physically under-developed** and could only speak with **animal-like sounds**.

After a lot of help she later learned some language but her **social and intellectual skills never seemed to fully develop**.

Koluchova (1976) — The Case of the Czech twin boys

This is the case of **twin boys** whose mother died soon after they were born. Their father remarried and their stepmother treated them very cruelly. They were often kept locked in a cellar, had no toys and were often beaten.

They were found when they were seven with rickets (a bone development disease caused by a lack of vitamin D), and **very little social or intellectual development**.

They were later adopted and made **much progress**. By adulthood they had above average intelligence and had normal social relationships.

There are a Number of Limitations to this Evidence

1) The children were **not just maternally privated** — they were also privated of general social and intellectual stimulation, and generally treated horribly. So we can't tell what caused the problems.
2) The case studies show **mixed results** for how much children can **recover** from privation early in life. Some recovered well (the Czech twins) but others didn't (Genie).
3) **Differences between the cases** may explain why some recovered better than others did. We should consider:
   a) Length of privation (Genie was the longest).
   b) Experiences during the isolation (the twins may have attached to each other).
   c) Quality of care after the isolation (the twins were adopted, but Genie was passed between psychologists and eventually put in an institution).
   d) Individual differences, including ability to recover (Genie may have been retarded at birth).

The evidence suggests that **recovery from privation is possible**. However, because of the lack of control over what had happened to the children, we can't know for sure exactly what they experienced, e.g. whether they had ever had even a brief attachment. We therefore can't ever be sure why the twins recovered more than Genie.

More controlled, scientific evidence is needed, but it would be ethically very wrong to actually put children in situations of privation to see what might happen. Some studies of children raised in institutions have given some evidence of the effects of privation, but we still can't be precisely sure of the reasons behind the effects seen.

The Effects of Privation

Hodges and Tizard (1989) Studied Children in Institutions

Studies of children raised in **institutions** (e.g. orphanages) may provide **more accurate records** of what the children experienced, seeing as they can be properly scientifically observed over a long period of time. **Hodges and Tizard** studied children in institutions:

Hodges and Tizard (1989) studied children raised in institutions.

OCR Core Study

Method: This was a longitudinal (long-term) study of 65 children who had been placed in a residential nursery before they were four months old. By four years of age they had each had about 50 different carers, so had been maternally privated. At this time, some returned to their natural mothers, some were adopted and some stayed in the nursery.

Results: At 16 years old, the **adopted** group had **strong** family relationships, although compared to a control group of children from a 'normal' home environment, they had weaker peer relationships. Those who stayed in the **nursery** or who returned to their **mothers** showed **poorer** relationships with family and peers than those who were adopted.

Conclusion: Children can **recover** from early maternal privation if they are in a good **quality**, **loving** environment, although their social development may not be as good as children who have never been privated.

Comment: The sample was quite **small** and more than 20 of the children couldn't be found at the end of the study, so it's hard to generalise the results. However, **Rutter et al (1998)** studied 111 Romanian orphans adopted by British families before they were two years old. The children were initially below normal development, but by four years of age were normal. However, the **older** a child was when s/he was adopted, the **slower** the development was.

*Psychological Research Suggests Two **Long-Term Effects** of Privation*

Privation of attachments early in life will have a damaging effect on all aspects of development, although how damaging it will be depends on several factors such as the length of privation. Children can recover to some extent, but **permanent** effects are possible. This can happen in two ways:

1) **Reactive attachment disorder — Parker and Forrest (1993)**
This is a rare but serious condition in which children seem to be permanently damaged by early experiences such as privation of attachment. The symptoms include an inability to give or receive affection, poor social relationships, dishonesty and involvement in crime.

2) **The cycle of privation**. Some evidence (**Quinton et al 1985**), suggests that children who experienced privation may later become less caring parents. Therefore their children are privated of a strong maternal attachment and may then be less caring to their children, and so on.

Practice Questions

Q1 Explain the difference between privation and deprivation.

Q2 What happened to Genie and how well did she recover?

Q3 What happened to the Czech twins and how well did they recover?

Q4 Explain a limitation of case study evidence.

Q5 What does Hodges and Tizard's study show about privation?

Q6 Describe reactive attachment disorder.

Exam Questions

Q1 With references to examples, explain what is meant by 'separation', 'deprivation' and 'privation'. [9 marks]

Q2 Outline research findings on the effects of privation. [15 marks]

Developmental problems — enough to make you develop mental problems

There's some pretty grizzly case studies of seriously abused children on these pages . Not the nicest of topics to be studying, though it is interesting to see how these theories of severe privation fit in with the earlier ones about children separated from their parents and so on. My advice would be get the theories and case studies in your head quickly and move on.

The Effects of Early Childhood Experience

This is for OCR only. *Developmental psychology is all about how children learn and develop — behaviourists think it can all be explained by conditioning. Some other guys think kids learn stuff through observation and imitation...*

The **Behaviourist** Approach to Development is Pretty Scientific

Behaviourism developed in early 1900s America and remained influential during most of the century. It was pioneered by **John Watson** who proposed three main assumptions, explained below, which the approach was based on.

1) Virtually all behaviour is **learnt** from the environment. The only exceptions are inborn reflexes and instincts, e.g. the reflex to blink when we get dirt in an eye.
2) **Both humans** and **animals** learn their behaviours using the same principles of learning.
3) For psychology to be **scientific** we should only study **observable behaviour** which can be analysed in quantitative terms e.g. how many times a person does something. The 'mind' can't be seen or measured, so can't be scientifically studied.

Following these assumptions, behaviourists would usually do **experiments on animals** to study how they, and therefore how we, learn.

Behaviourists Proposed **Two Types** of Conditioning:

Classical Conditioning

In early 1900s Russia, **Ivan Pavlov** was studying how dogs' salivation helps them to digest food, when he noticed that they would sometimes salivate before they got food. He realised they had **associated** food with another stimulus, such as the sound of the door opening. He later made dogs associate food with bells, lights and other abstract stimuli. Applied to humans, this process of learning is shown below:

Having needs dealt with and gaining comfort naturally makes a baby happy — it has not learnt to be happy, it is an inborn reflex. So, comfort is an **unconditioned stimulus (UCS)** that produces happiness — an **unconditioned response (UCR).**

Hearing a voice would not normally make the baby happy. It must **learn** to respond to it, so it is a **conditioned stimulus (CS)**. When the baby has its needs taken care of (food, warmth, clean nappy etc.) and so becomes comfortable, it will hear its mother talking. Later, it will become happy at the sound of its mother's voice alone — a **conditioned response (CR)** — the baby has learnt to become happy in response to something that previously did not make it happy.

Operant Conditioning

Classical conditioning only applies to reflexive responses. **B.F. Skinner** studied how animals can learn from the **consequences of their actions**. Consequences can be classified as follows:

1) **Positive reinforcement**. This is when something 'desirable' is obtained in response to doing something e.g. after murmuring, the baby gets attention (the positive reinforcer). The baby is likely to murmur again.
2) **Negative reinforcement**. This is when something 'undesirable' (the negative reinforcer) is removed when something happens, e.g. after crying, a dirty nappy is removed. The baby is likely to cry the next time the nappy is dirtied.
3) **Punishment**. This is when something 'undesirable' (the 'punisher') is received when something happens e.g. after picking up something dangerous, a slap is received. The baby is unlikely to do it again.

There is a lot of evidence to show that animals and humans can learn by conditioning (see pages 68-71) but conditioning can't explain all human behaviour. We also learn by observation, as shown by **social learning theory**.

The Effects of Early Childhood Experience

Social Learning Theory *(SLT) Accepts that Cognitive Processes are Important*

SLT developed in the 1950s. It agrees with behaviourism that people can learn by conditioning but also claims that they learn a lot by **observation** and **imitation** of role models. This involves **cognitive processes** like **perception**, **attention** and **memory**. People must focus their attention on the model, perceive what they do and remember it in order to learn how to do it too.

A study by Bandura shows how children will imitate adult role models.

Bandura et al (1961) — observational learning of aggression

OCR Core Study

Method:	Children were individually taken to a play area where they saw an adult play either aggressively or non-aggressively with a 'Bobo doll' (a blow-up toy). They were later taken to another play area and then rated for how much aggression they showed.
Results:	The children who observed the aggressive role model showed the most acts of aggression, e.g. hitting the Bobo doll with a mallet. Boys were also generally more aggressive.
Conclusion:	Children can **learn aggression by observation** of adult role models.

Also see page 72 for another Bandura study, showing the effects of observing a model receiving reinforcement.

Some ***Comments*** *on SLT, Behaviourism and Bandura's Research:*

1) SLT shows that **reinforcement is not needed for learning**. We can learn just by **observing**. However, the reinforcement the model is seen to receive may have an effect — for example, if you see a model punished for an action, you're unlikely to copy it (see page 72).
2) Bandura's study has **ethical issues** — for encouraging aggression in children. No follow-up was done, so it isn't known if there were any long-term effects. Also, the situation is unlike a lot of '**real life**' modelling where children may know and interact with models such as their parents.
3) Behaviourism and SLT emphasise learning as the cause of behaviour and so are on the '**nurture**' side of the **nature-nurture debate**. This has implications for society. For example, children may imitate aggression from media role models (see pages 71-72). However, potential **genetic influences** are not taken into account.

Practice Questions

Q1 Explain the assumptions made by behaviourism.

Q2 How did Pavlov condition dogs to salivate when he rung a bell?

Q3 What is the difference between negative reinforcement and punishment?

Q4 Why do Bandura's results support SLT?

Q5 What do behaviourism and SLT imply about the nature-nurture debate?

Exam Questions

Q1 Explain the behaviourist approach to learning. [6 marks]

Q2 Describe and evaluate Bandura's 1961 study on observational learning. [8 marks]

Walk away from the Bobo doll with your mallet in the air...

These psychologists are an interesting lot. Pavlov rang a bell over and over again to get a dog to dribble and Bandura and his gang beat up toys in front of children — whatever floats your boat I guess. Anyway, what you need to do is remember what they did — and more importantly what conclusions they drew.

The Effects of Day Care on Child Development

AQA A and OCR. *'Day care' refers to any **temporary care** for a child provided by someone other than the parents or relatives they live with. It includes day **nurseries**, **childminders** and **nannies** but does not include residential nurseries or fostering. Psychologists have been interested in whether day care has any positive or negative effects on development.*

There are Concerns That Day Care May Affect Social Development

It may be necessary for children to have a strong attachment with their main carer before they can learn social skills and form relationships with others (for more information, see pages 26-29).

There has been concern that **day care** may damage social development by disrupting this attachment. However, it could actually help social development by letting children form more friendships and **multiple attachments**.

Several studies have investigated these possibilities:

Belsky and Rovine (1988) — negative effects of day care

Method:	Infants were placed in the '**strange situation**' where different scenarios occurred — a stranger approached, the infant was left alone, the mother returned (see page 23). The strange situation was a test to assess how secure their attachments were. One group had experienced no day care and one had experienced at least 20 hours of day care per week before their first birthday.
Results:	The infants who had received day care were more likely to have an **insecure** attachment type. They were either **'anxious-avoidant' (type A)** — ignored their mother and didn't mind if she left, or **'anxious-resistant' (type C)** — uneasy around their mother and upset if she left. Those who had not had day care were more likely to be **securely attached** (type B).
Conclusion:	Day care has a **negative** effect on an infant's social development.

Comments:

The results from the 'strange situation' may not be **accurate**. Children who are used to separations may not show distress when their mother leaves because they have developed more **independence**.

However, **DiLalla (1998)** also found negative effects — the more day care a child had, the **less prosocially** they behaved, i.e. the less they helped, shared, etc.

Shea (1981) — positive effects of day care

Method:	3-4 year old children were assessed for their social skills during their first 10 weeks of attending a nursery school. One group attended 5 days per week, and the other attended twice a week.
Results:	**Both** groups showed increasing **social skills** (e.g. less aggression and more interaction with others) over the 10 weeks. The group that attended 5 days per week improved more quickly.
Conclusion:	Attending day care has a **positive effect** on social development.

Comments:

This study doesn't tell us whether there were any **long-term effects** on the children. However, **Schweinhart et al (1993)** found long-term positive effects linked to day care in terms of **less involvement in crime**.

There are Many Conflicting Findings on Day Care and Social Development

Many studies show a negative effect, many show a positive effect and some show no effect at all.

It seems that many things influence how day care affects a child, including the child's own **temperament** and the **quality** of the day care that they receive.

For example, **Vandell et al (1988)** found that children who had **good quality** day care were more likely to have **friendly** interactions with others compared to those receiving lower quality day care.

The Effects of Day Care on Child Development

There are Also Concerns That **Day Care** May Affect **Cognitive** Development

For intellectual abilities (e.g. reasoning, problem-solving) to develop, a child needs **stimulation** from the environment — playing with toys, exploring new things. They might get this through day care.

However, if a child doesn't have a **secure attachment** as a 'safe base', it may have less confidence to explore. So, day care may have positive or negative effects.

Ruhm et al (2000) — negative effects on cognitive development

Method: The cognitive abilities of 4000 infants were recorded to compare those who had day care with those who didn't.

Results: Infants who had day care during their first year showed poorer verbal skills at 3-4 years of age. Having day care at some time during the first three years was also linked to poorer maths and reading skills at 5-6 years of age.

Conclusion: Day care has **negative effects** on several aspects of cognitive development.

Baydar and Brooks-Gunn (1991) also found that day care during the first year of life had negative effects on cognitive development. However, these results may be due to poor quality day care. Andersson et al (below) studied this.

Andersson et al (1992) — positive effects on cognitive development

Method: Over 100 Swedish children were followed to investigate the long-term effects of their **high quality** day care. They were assessed for their cognitive and social development using IQ tests and ratings from their teachers.

Results: Children who began day care before one year of age showed the highest scores at age 8 and 13. Those who never had day care showed the lowest scores.

Conclusion: High quality day care can have **long-term positive effects** on cognitive development.

Comment: The children in high quality (therefore expensive) day care may have had **wealthier** families and so also have had a more enriched **home environment**. However, **Project Headstart**, which gave extra day care classes to socially disadvantaged pre-school children, found children in the project later did better in education compared to others. This suggests that positive effects were due to the quality day care rather than the home environment.

There are **Mixed Results** for Day Care's **Effect** on Development

Many things may have an influence on how day care affects development. **Scarr (1998)** identifies several factors — good staff training, adequate space, appropriate toys and activities, having a good ratio of staff to children and trying to minimise staff turnover so children can form stable attachments with carers.

Good quality day care shouldn't have any negative effects and may possibly be beneficial.

Practice Questions

Q1 Describe some evidence showing negative effects of day care on social development.

Q2 What positive effects does Shea's study show?

Q3 Describe some evidence showing positive effects on cognitive development.

Q4 Describe Ruhm et al's findings.

Exam Questions

Q1 Outline research findings on the effects of day care on social development. [6 marks]

Q2 Outline research findings on the effects of day care on cognitive development. [6 marks]

If this is all getting too difficult you can always blame it on your day care...

Let me see if I've got this — if a child is stuck in poor quality day care their social and intellectual skills don't develop so well. If the day care is good and stimulating however, it can have positive effects on the child's development. I don't mean to knock these guys' hard work — but it's not exactly rocket science. Anyway no complaints, it makes it all easier to learn.

The Physiological Approach

These 2 pages are for OCR and Edexcel only. *The physiological psychology approach is all about looking at how physical, squidgy bits cause behaviour and determine experience. Yep, there's a shed-load of biology coming up...*

There Are Three Basic **Assumptions** of the Physiological Approach

1) Human behaviour can be explained by looking at biological stuff such as **hormones**, **genetics**, **evolution** and the **nervous system**. This puts the approach firmly on the **nature** side of the nature-nurture debate.
2) Because all behaviour is explained using biological causes, **unwanted behaviour** can be **modified** or removed using **biological treatments** such as medication for mental illness.
3) Experimental research conducted using **animals** can inform us about human behaviour and physiological influences, because we share a lot of similar biological makeup.

Genetics Is Used to Explain Behaviour

First of all, here's a speedy recap of the basic genetic knowledge that'll be handy in this section:

1) At conception, the egg and sperm join up to give a total of **46 chromosomes**.
2) Each chromosome is made up of a coil of **DNA**, which in turn is made up of loads and loads of **genes**.
3) The genes contain the information that make us **unique** in appearance (e.g. hair, skin and eye colour).

Darwin's theory of evolution suggests that over time, individuals who are **better adapted** to their environment are more likely to survive to reproduce and pass on their more useful genes. Those who are **less well-adapted** will be less likely to survive to reproduce and pass on their genes. Eventually, their genes will be eliminated from the gene pool for that species. Through this process of **natural selection**, early humans **became better adapted** to their environments.

Physiological psychologists reckon that **genetics** can explain "**psychological traits**". These are things like gender behaviour (things that men and women do differently), intelligence, personality and sexual orientation. They also study genetics to see which genes make some people more likely to develop things like mental illness or addictions.

The **Nervous System** Controls What We Do and How We Do It

Biology recap time again – this time for the nervous system:

1) The nervous system allows parts of the body to **communicate** with each other.
2) The **central nervous system** (CNS) consists of the **brain** and the **spinal cord**.
3) The **peripheral nervous system** (PNS) is all the **nerves** connecting the CNS with the rest of the body.
4) The body contains billions of neurones organised into nerves — spinal and cranial nerves.

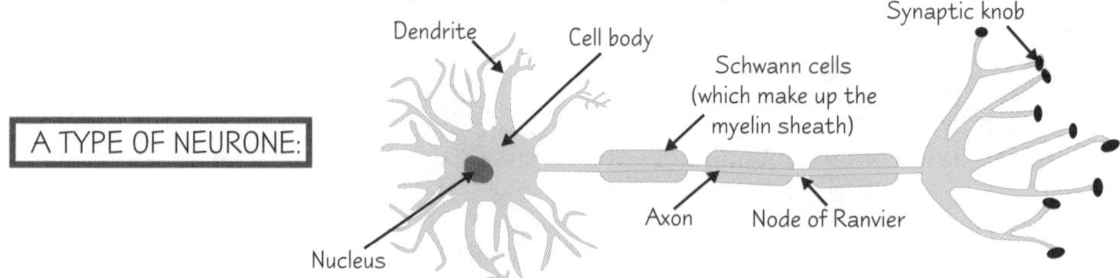

5) The **cell body** has **dendrites** that receive information from other neurones.
6) This info passes along the **axon** in the form of an **electrical charge** and ends up in a **synaptic knob**.
7) There is a small gap before the next neurone called the **synapse**.
8) **Neurotransmitters** are chemicals that are released from the synaptic knob. They pass across the synapse, to pass on info to the dendrites of the next neurone.

Physiological psychologists spend loads of time working out what different neurotransmitters do and how they can be influenced by things like **diet**, **exercise** and **drugs**. They also work out how to manipulate neurotransmitters with **medications**, to control different behaviours. E.g. If a medication or diet was developed to reduce the neurotransmitters that signal stress, this could help people who get stressed out too easily.

The Physiological Approach

Psychologists use Four Methods to Study the **Structure** & **Function** of the Brain

The brain (you know, the big, fat, grey thing at the top of the spinal cord) is what the white-coats really want to work out, so they've come up with quite a few, worrying ways of prodding it about:

1) **Scanning** — Magnetic Resonance Imaging (MRI) uses **magnetic fields** to produce a detailed image of the brain which can show up abnormalities. It also shows brain activity by **monitoring blood flow** to different bits. It's dead handy for showing what's going on during experiments, but it's very **expensive** to use.
2) **Electroencephalograms** (EEGs) involve placing electrodes on the scalp, to measure **electrical activity** in the brain. They show up which sections of the brain are active when performing certain tasks.
3) **Lesioning** (destroying brain tissue). Any resulting change in behaviour suggests what the damaged bit of brain was responsible for. **Animals** are used for this, but the results can't always be accurately applied to humans and some people think it's ethically wrong. Psychologists also study people who've suffered damage to parts of the brain. A few older studies altered people's brains in operations in an attempt to change their personality traits. E.g. In 1935, Moniz pioneered the **frontal lobotomy** in which the frontal lobes are severed. This is very rarely used today.
4) **Electro Brain Stimulation (ESB)**. This is the process of stimulating brain cells by inserting an **electrode** into part of the brain and applying a mild electrical current. It's often done to volunteers while they're fully awake so they can do tasks and answer questions. Apparently it doesn't hurt as the brain has no pain receptors ... yeah like I'm gonna try it!

There are Two Key Ways to Study **Genetic Influences**

The methods below look at the **genetic relationship** between people who **share** certain **characteristics**. Similarities between two people who are genetically close suggests a genetic explanation for the characteristic.

1) **Twin studies**. If there's a genetic explanation for intelligence, for example, we'd expect similar intelligence scores for **identical twins** because they've got identical genes. Although several studies show strong positive correlations, this could be because identical twins also tend to experience very similar upbringing, education and influences.
2) **Adoption and family studies**. Adoption studies are useful because they can look at people with close genetics, but different upbringings. E.g. Research into schizophrenia supports a genetic influence because adopted children are at a higher risk if a biological parent had the disorder, even if no-one in their adoptive family suffers from the disease. Family studies also support this link, as the risk of developing schizophrenia is higher for a person with a closer genetic relationship to a relative with the disorder.

A correlation looks at the relationship between two variables — a positive correlation shows that as one variable increases, so does the other.

Some families are studied more than others.

Practice Questions

Q1 Write down three basic assumptions of the physiological approach.

Q2 What does the CNS consist of?

Q3 What does an EEG measure?

Q4 Name a method used to study genetic influences.

Exam Questions

Q1 Explain how information is passed through the nervous system. [6 marks]

Q2 Outline two methods used to study the structure of the brain. [6 marks]

MRI scans have shown that a student's brain patterns were identical when reading this page and when sleeping — coincidence...

Actually I think this is pretty interesting stuff, I mean the way your brain works must be one of the biggest remaining mysteries in medical science — sure they can start to recognise areas of the brain and stuff — but there's a long way to go.

Stress as a Bodily Response

Just for AQA A. *I'm sure you all know what stress is. It's having 3 hours left to revise before an exam, or visiting your girlfriend's parents — we all feel it, but this is psychology so it needs a proper scientific explanation.*

Stress is a Response to **Stimuli** in the **Environment**

1) Stress can be explained as the **stimulus** in the environment that triggers a stress response. In simpler words, the thing that causes you to act stressed, e.g. a giant cockroach dancing towards you. Psychologists call anything that causes someone to act stressed a '**stressor**'.
2) Stress can also be explained as the **response** to the stimuli — our reaction, e.g. running for the hills.
3) However, the white-coated ones have agreed to explain stress as '**the response that occurs when we think we can't cope with the pressures in our environment**'. This is shown in the diagram below.

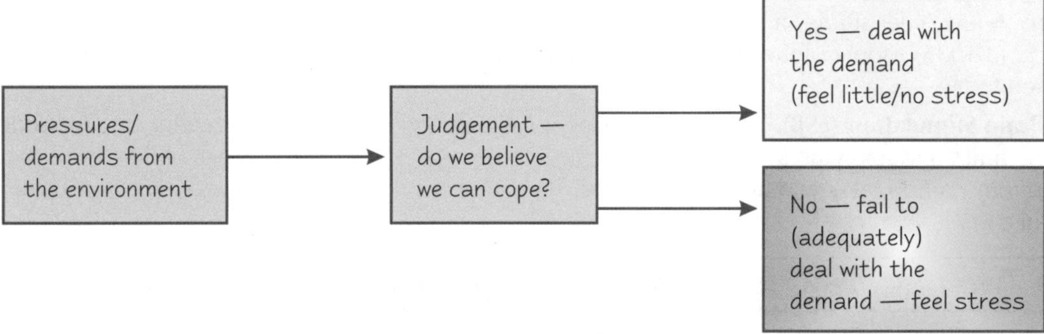

So, stress is the response that occurs when we think the demands being placed on us as are greater than our ability to cope. These are our **own judgements**, so we could over or **underestimate** the demands, or our ability to cope.

Whether the stress is justified or not doesn't matter, if we think we can't cope we get stressed. And when we get stressed something physically changes in us. Hans Selye studied this with stressed-out little rats...

Hans Selye Explained Stress as a **Three Stage Response**

In 1956 Hans Selye was researching the effects of hormones when he noticed that the rats would become ill (e.g. develop stomach ulcers) even when they were given harmless injections.

He concluded that the **stress** of the daily injections **caused the illness** and suggested that all animals and humans react to stressors through a **three stage physiological response**. This is called the **General Adaptation Syndrome (GAS)**.

1) **The Alarm Stage** — when we perceive a stressor our body's first reaction is to increase arousal levels in the body so that we are ready to make any necessary physical response, e.g. if confronted with a big-toothed monster we'd probably run away (the 'fight or flight' response). So our heart rate increases, we breathe more quickly, our muscles tense etc.
2) **The Resistance Stage** — if we are exposed to a stressor for a long time our bodies can adapt to the situation and we seem to be able to cope in a normal way. For example, if we start work in a high pressure situation we would initially be unable to cope and the alarm reaction might frequently occur, but after a while we would seem to adapt. However, even though we might seem to be coping, higher than normal arousal levels would continue in our bodies to deal with the situation.
3) **The Exhaustion Stage** — after long term exposure to a stressor our bodies will eventually be unable to continue to cope with the situation. Alarm signs may return and we may develop illnesses e.g. ulcers, high blood pressure, depression etc. Selye called these 'diseases of adaptation'.

Comment — the stages Selye identified are supported by a lot of scientific research. However, the GAS theory offers a single type of response and so neglects that the body's reaction to stress does vary, e.g. how much adrenaline is released depends on how the stressor is perceived by the person (how frightening etc).
Also, a certain bacteria has been found to be the cause of ulcers. It could still be the case, though, that stress weakens the immune system making ulcers more likely.

Stress as a Bodily Response

The **Hypothalamus** is the Bit of the Brain that **Responds** to **Stress**

When we perceive a stressor the following chain of events is triggered in the body: (for extra exam marks, learn the full name for these events, which is... wait for it, the **hypothalamic-pituitary-adrenal axis**, wow)

1) The evaluation of whether something is a stressor occurs in the higher brain centres (the cerebral cortex).
2) When there is a stressor in the environment, these higher areas send a signal to the **hypothalamus**, which starts two simultaneous processes in the body:
   a) Signals are sent to the **pituitary gland**, which then releases a hormone called **ACTH** (adrenocorticotrophic hormone) into the bloodstream. This stimulates the **adrenal cortex** (a structure above the kidneys) to release corticosteroids which help to give us energy by converting fat and protein.
   b) **The Autonomic Nervous System** (ANS) is also activated. This stimulates the **adrenal medulla** (a structure close to the adrenal cortex) to release adrenaline and noradrenaline into the bloodstream. These lead to an increase in heart rate, blood flow, blood pressure etc.

The result of these changes is that the body is ready to use energy to do whatever action needs to be done, e.g. run away from a dangerous animal.

These **Changes** in the Body Can Be Seen as Having **Survival Value**

1) During our evolution many threats to us would have been from predators or other physical dangers.
2) So, to successfully respond to them would have required energy to fight or run away — the **'fight or flight'** response.
3) However, in **modern society** stressors are more likely to be **psychological** than physical and are more long-term, e.g. the stresses of working at a desk, commuting, noisy neighbours, etc.
4) Therefore the physical stress response is not really needed, but in the long-term it may actually be harmful to our bodies — page 38 explains how.
5) Some stress can be positive and exhilarating — this is known as **eustress**, e.g. a parachute jump might lead to this kind of arousal.

Leo was finding the journey to work increasingly stressful.

Practice Questions

Q1 Outline the different ways of defining stress.

Q2 Describe how Selye discovered the GAS.

Q3 Outline the three stages of the GAS.

Q4 Outline the hypothalamic-pituitary-adrenal axis.

Exam Questions

Q1 Outline the main features of the GAS and give a criticism of it. [6 marks]

Q2 Describe how the body responds to stress. [6 marks]

Well, as bodily responses go, I guess stress isn't so bad...

Stress is a natural reaction by your body to anything which threatens you. In the past, it would have been a lion chasing you. Now it's more likely to be a deadline or late train. So next time you see someone getting stressed about something, try telling them, "relax, it could be worse — at least you're not being chased by a lion" — that'll soon calm them down.

Stress and Physical Illness

Only for people doing AQA A. *The last couple of pages made it blindingly obvious that stress isn't just something in your head, it's a physical response. These pages cover what stress can do to your physical state in the long run.*

Long-Term Stress *Can Affect your* ***Cardiovascular System***

The "cardiovascular system" is a fancy name for the **heart** and **blood vessels**.

A **long-term stress response** may have a direct effect on this system:

1) The stored energy (e.g. glucose) that is released during a stressful event is normally re-absorbed by the body after the stressor has gone. But, if the stress is long-term it will **remain** in the blood stream, which may lead to a **blockage**, producing **heart attacks** or **strokes** (if a blood vessel in the brain is blocked).
2) Stress causes a high **heart rate** and **blood pressure**. Over a long time this pressure can **weaken** blood vessels and form **scars** on them.
3) If blood vessels are weakened or damaged, this increases the risk of one **breaking**, which is called a **haemorrhage** (in technical Casualty-speak).

	Krantz et al (1991) — stress and the heart
Method:	39 participants did one of three stress-inducing tasks (e.g. a maths test) while the **blood flow** to their hearts and their **blood pressure** were measured.
Results:	The stressful tasks caused **less** bloodflow to the heart (a condition called **'myocardial ischemia'**, which is a cause of cardiovascular disorders). The stressful tasks also caused **higher** blood pressure.
Conclusion:	Stress may have a **direct influence** on aspects of body functioning, making cardiovascular disorders more likely.

Comment — Although the effects were clearly linked to stress, it was not shown whether they also occur at other times. They might sometimes happen even if the person feels relaxed and therefore are not simply produced by feeling stressed. Not everybody showed the same reaction, which suggests that differences between the participants may also have a role.

Differences in ***Personality*** *Might Cause Cardiovascular Problems*

Research has shown that as well as stress, certain aspects of personality are linked to cardiovascular disorders.

1) **Friedman and Rosenman (1974)** found that people with a 'type A' personality had an increased risk of heart attack. 'Type A' people are very competitive, always in a hurry and can be very hostile (see page 42 for more detail).
2) **Williams (2000)** also found that feelings of anger are linked to the risk of heart attack:

	Williams (2000) — anger and cardiovascular disorders
Method:	A sample of 13,000 participants completed a questionnaire. This asked questions about their feelings of anger — for example, did they ever feel like hitting someone?
Results:	At the beginning of the study, all of the participants were healthy. It was found that those with a **high** score on the anger questionnaire were much more likely to have had a **heart attack** when the sample was checked six years later.
Conclusion:	People who get angry easily / react more angrily have a higher risk of cardiovascular problems.

Comment — Other influences, apart from personality, must also be considered. For example, participants' diet, their occupations, genetic vulnerability, exercise levels, smoking and consumption of alcohol may also influence the development of cardiovascular disorders.

Stress and Physical Illness

Stress Can Also Affect the ***Immune System***

The immune system is made of cells (e.g. white blood cells) and chemicals that **seek and destroy bacteria** and **viruses**. When someone experiences stress over a long time (a **long term stress response**) their immune system stops functioning properly. Loads of studies have tested whether long-term stress makes us more vulnerable to infection and illness.

Brady et al (1958) — stress and the development of ulcers

Method: Monkeys were put in pairs and given electric shocks every 20 seconds for 6 hour sessions. One monkey of each pair (the 'executive') could push a lever to delay the shocks. The other could not delay them.

Results: The 'executive' monkeys were more likely to develop illness (ulcers) and later die.

Conclusion: The illness and death was not due to the shocks but due to the stress that the executives felt by trying to avoid them. In the long-term, this stress reduced the immune system's ability to fight illness.

Comment — the **ethics** of these methods can be questioned — the experiment was very cruel to the monkeys and would not be allowed today. Also, we cannot generalise results from monkeys to humans. Furthermore, we know that people with little control over their own lives (such as those with low level jobs and the long-term unemployed), experience high levels of stress, which this research cannot explain.

The same ***Immune System Suppression*** happens in Humans

Research on humans has also supported the theory that stress can reduce the effectiveness of the immune system, as shown in the following study.

Kiecolt-Glaser et al (1995) — stress and wound healing

Method: Small samples of skin were taken from 13 women who cared for relatives with Alzheimer's disease. This is a very stressful responsibility. A control group also had samples taken.

Results: The carers took an average of nine days longer than the controls for the wound to heal.

Conclusion: Long-term stress impairs the effectiveness of the immune system to heal wounds.

Comment — this is a reliable finding. **Sweeney (1995)** found that people caring for relatives with dementia also took longer than a control group to heal their wounds. However, for both studies the two groups may have varied in other ways apart from the stress of being a carer. The effects on the carers could be due to poor diet, lack of sleep etc, and not just the stress they experienced.

Practice Questions

Q1 Explain what is meant by 'cardiovascular disorder'.

Q2 Outline how stress can lead to cardiovascular disorder.

Q3 How is personality relevant to cardiovascular disorder?

Q4 What is the role of the immune system?

Exam Questions

Q1 Outline the findings of one study of stress and cardiovascular disorder and give a criticism of this study. [6 marks]

Q2 Explain what is meant by the immune system and outline research findings on how it is affected by stress. [6 marks]

Calmer, fitter, happier — more productive...

If you think about it, it kind of stands to reason that being really stressed out all the time will have some effect on your body. You need to remember the actual physiological facts about how this happens and what criticisms all the studies have. Although do take in the lessons for life on these pages — just chill out dude.

Sources of Stress

These pages are only for AQA A. *There are loads of sources of stress, for some unfortunate individuals it's the thought of peanut butter sticking to their teeth, but for normal folk the two real biggies are* ***major life changes*** *and things at* ***work****.*

Life Changes are a Source of Stress

Throughout our lives, we all experience **major life events**, like the death of a close relative, getting married or moving house. These events and the adjustments they cause us to make can be a major source of stress. When psychologists want to find out what level of stress these events cause, they look at health because it's probably linked to stress.

Holmes and **Rahe** Studied Whether the Stress of Life Changes was Linked to **Illness**

Approximately 5000 hospital patients' records were studied and any major life events that had occurred before the person became ill were noted. It was found that patients were **likely** to have experienced life changes prior to becoming ill and that **more serious life changes** seemed to be more **linked to stress and illness**. A scale was produced to show the importance of life changes in terms of the stress caused.

...They **Ranked** Life Events on the **Social Re-adjustment Rating Scale (SRRS)**

1) **Holmes and Rahe** made a list of 43 common life events and asked loads of people to give a score for each one to say how stressful it was. They called the numbers that made up each score the **Life Change Units (LCU)**. The higher this number of LCUs, the more stressful it was.
2) Then they **ranked** the events from most stressful to least stressful and called it the **Social Re-adjustment Rating Scale (SRRS)**. Examples are shown on the table opposite.
3) And finally, after all that build up, they did a study to see if people who'd experienced more stressful events were more likely to get ill:

Life Event	Rank	Score (LCU)
Death of a spouse	1	100
Divorce	2	73
Retirement	10	45
Death of a friend	17	37
Christmas	42	12

Rahe et al (1970) — LCU score and illness

Method: More than 2500 American Navy seamen were given a form of the SRRS to complete just before they set sail on military duty. They had to indicate all of the events that they had experienced over the previous six months.

Results: Higher LCU scores were found to be linked to a higher incidence of illness over the next seven months. Those who had an LCU score over 150 had a 30% higher risk of illness.

Conclusion: The stress involved in the changes that life events bring is linked to an increased risk of illness.

There are some ***Issues*** *with the SRRS*

1) The link between the **SRRS** and **illness** depends on the accuracy of recall. For example, people might rank recent events higher simply because they can remember them more clearly.
2) The SRRS doesn't separate **positive and negative life events**. Stress and illness might be more linked to negative life changes. For example, a wedding might be stressful, but positive overall, while a funeral might have a very negative stressful effect.
3) Long-term, minor sources of stress, such as everyday **hassles** at work (see page 41), are not considered.

Despite criticisms the SRRS was useful for showing that changes in life may link to stress and illness.

Post-Traumatic Stress Disorder (PTSD) is an example of how major life events can be clearly linked to illness. It is considered to be an **anxiety disorder** and is caused by an extreme life event such as a life-threatening accident. PTSD involves extreme anxiety, difficulties concentrating and sleeping and 'flashbacks' to the event. Some people may need therapy to cope with the disorder, although it's debatable whether therapy does any good.

Sources of Stress

The **Workplace** is a Massive Source of Stress

Most people need to work, but some aspects of the **work they do**, **where they work**, or **who they have to work with**, become a source of stress. This is important because if a person is very stressed at work they may be more likely to get ill. This is not only bad for them, but also for their employer because they will take more days off sick.

Stress in the Workplace comes from **FIVE** Key Areas

1) **Relationships at work** — our relationships with our bosses, colleagues and customers may be stressful, for example if we feel **undervalued** and that we **lack support**.
2) **Work Pressures** — having **too much** work to do, maybe with **strict deadlines**.
3) **The Physical Environment** — where we work may be very noisy, over-crowded or too hot or cold. Also, our work may involve health risks or unsociable working hours.
4) **Stresses linked to our role** — worrying about **job security** or our **prospects for promotion**. Also, the range of our responsibilities may be unclear, and we may experience conflict, e.g. trying to please our bosses and the people who work for us.
5) **Lack of control** — we may not have much **influence over the type and amount of work** we do or where and when we do it. Check out the study by Marmot et al (1997) below:

Marmot et al (1997) — lack of control and illness in the workplace

Method: Over 7000 civil service employees, working in London, were surveyed. Information about their grade of employment, how much control they felt they had, how much support they felt they had etc, was obtained.

Results: When the medical histories of these employees were followed up 5 years later, those on lower employment grades who felt less control over their work (and less social support) were found to be more likely to have cardiovascular disorders.

Conclusion: Believing that you have little control over your work seems to be an important influence on work stress and the development of illness.

Comment — the Marmot lot only looked at 'white collar' work (i.e. office-type jobs), so their results may not apply to other kinds of work. Smoking was also found to be more common in those who developed illnesses. So perhaps those people who felt less control at work were more likely to smoke and the smoking caused the heart problems rather than stress.

Practice Questions

Q1 How did Holmes and Rahe develop their SRRS?

Q2 What did Rahe et al find?

Q3 Explain a criticism of the SRRS.

Q4 What did Marmot et al find?

Exam Questions

Q1 Explain three sources of workplace stress. [6 marks]

Q2 Outline findings of research on life change as a source of stress and give a criticism of this research. [6 marks]

*Stress at work — I don't believe it — I live to work...**

As a quick break, make your own SRRS by putting these stressful situations in order: 1) meeting your girl/boyfriend's parents after one shandy too many, 2) watching England in a major qualifying game, it's 0-0 with ten minutes to go, 3) realising that what you are writing will be read by thousands of cynical A-Level students and you're too hungover to write anything funny.

*they made me write this — someone help me get out, I've been typing for weeks without a break... help me...

Stress — Individual Differences

These 2 pages are just for AQA A. *The last few pages have shown how stress affects the body, but that doesn't mean it affects everyone in the same way. If you stick two people in a pit and drop spiders on them, it's unlikely they're going to react in the exact same way. Psychologists call different personal reactions "individual differences".*

Different ***Personalities*** *Can Lead to Different Stress Levels*

Psychologists love sticking people into groups. One theory about personality is that you can split people into two groups called 'type A' and 'type B'. Type A people are competitive and ambitious. Type Bs are non-competitive, relaxed and easy going. The study below tested how these different types of personality affect the likelihood of CHD (coronary heart disease) — one of the most obvious effects of stress.

Friedman and Rosenman (1974) — 'type A' personality and illness

Method: Approximately 3000, 39-59 year old American males were assessed for their personality characteristics, using interviews and observation.

Results: Eight years later, 257 of them had developed **CHD** (coronary heart disease). 70% of these were classed as 'type A' personality. This includes being 'workaholic', extremely competitive, hostile to others, concerned with time and always in a rush. Type B is the opposite, being less competitive, less impatient and less hostile.

Conclusion: Type A personalities seem to be at a **higher risk** of CHD.

Comments —

1) Only two personality types seems a bit simplistic. Later research also identified **Type C** personalities — mild-mannered, easy-going people who may not react well to stressful situations and suppress their emotions. These people seem to have a higher risk of **cancer**. **Type D** personalities were identified as very negative/pessimistic people who worry too much about things and lack social skills. These people seem more at risk from **heart attacks**.
2) This research doesn't prove that personality characteristics can **cause** stress and illness. It could be the other way round. For example, Type A personality may develop as a **response** to being under stress (from work etc). Also, the samples used in studies have been quite limited — mostly white, middle-class, middle-aged, male Americans.

Stress can be Related to ***Culture***

Culture is a really vague term that is used to group people by **beliefs**, **behaviours**, **morals** or **customs** they share. Culture has a big impact on how people live and how others react to them. So those white-coated people have done different studies to find out how a person's culture affects their level of stress.

Biological Studies — **Cooper et al (1999)** suggested that the higher level of cardiovascular disorder that is found in African-Americans could be due to genes, more commonly found in this group, which may contribute to higher blood-pressure. However, they also found that high blood pressure was more likely in Africans who lived in more urbanised countries (like America) than those who live in more rural countries (like Nigeria). This suggests a **social influence**.

Social Studies — higher stress and blood pressure might be found in people in urban areas because of factors like overcrowding, pollution and high unemployment. However, **Adams-Campbell et al (1993)** found that African-American women had higher blood pressure than white women who were of the same **social-economic group** (i.e. people who have the same lifestyle and money).

Cognitive Studies — African-Americans may experience more prejudice which may lead to more negative thoughts and beliefs ('cognitions'). They encounter more difficulties and threats in society which may lead to more stress and so more illness.

Comment — biological, social and cognitive factors influence the links between culture, stress and illness. It is difficult to identify the exact influence of each of them because we cannot do controlled experiments involving genetics or prejudice due to ethical issues. It is also more likely that cardiovascular disorder is due to a number of factors in combination rather than just one single factor.

Stress — Individual Differences

Stress can also be Related to **Gender**

Men and woman are pretty different in lots of ways, so psychologists (who don't miss a trick) thought that maybe these differences could affect what kinds of thing men and women find stressful and how they cope. They looked at how biological, social and cognitive differences between males and females influence their response to stress.

Biological Explanation — males and females may have **evolved** different physiological responses to stress due to their roles during the early evolution of humans. To be better adapted at their roles of 'hunter-gatherers', males might have evolved a stronger 'fight or flight' response than women, who had the roles of child-carers.

Taylor et al (2000) claim that women's hormones produce a calmer response to stress and make it more likely that they seek social support to help them cope. However, it can be argued that social factors may explain gender differences in coping methods.

Social Explanation — all cultures have developed **stereotyped social roles** for men and women, relating to what beliefs, behaviours and occupations they 'should' have. A western stereotype has been that men are (or should be) less open about their feelings. So, they may be less open about feeling stressed and more likely to use **harmful coping methods** like drinking and smoking.

Carroll (1992) found that women do generally make more use of social support to deal with stress. This healthier way of coping may explain why women have a lower risk of **CHD** (coronary heart disease). However, Carroll (1992) also found there has been an increase in rates of CHD in women. This could relate to changing stereotypes, as more women now also drink and smoke.

Cognitive Explanation — males and females may differ in how they interpret stressful situations and think about ways of reacting. For example, **Vogele et al (1997)** claim that women are better able to control anger and therefore respond more calmly to stressful situations. Men may feel that anger is an acceptable way to respond, and feel stress if they cannot show it. These cognitive differences could be the result of biology **or** the roles we are taught to follow or a bit of both.

Comment — it's dangerous to make sweeping generalisations about **all** men and women responding to stress in particular ways. Someone's response to stress will also be affected by other stuff, like their culture, their personality and their individual coping methods.

Practice Questions

Q1 Explain the differences between personality types A, B, C and D.

Q2 Give a criticism of Friedman and Rosenman's research.

Q3 How are biological, social and cognitive factors relevant to understanding culture differences in stress?

Q4 How are biological, social and cognitive factors relevant to understanding gender differences in stress?

Exam Questions

Q1 Describe one study of stress and personality. [6 marks]

Q2 Consider how culture and/or personality are linked to stress. [18 marks]

We are all individuals, we are all individuals, we are all individuals...

This is an important thing to remember throughout psychology. People are divided into groups to show how different things affect people — but there are also individual differences, which means that when put in the same situation, people will often react differently. This seems pretty obvious but it's easy to forget if you get too wrapped up in all the theories.

Physiological & Psychological Approaches to Stress Management

Again, this one's just for AQA A. *Finally, we've got to a bit where psychologists are trying to actually help people rather than just prodding them. There are 2 main types of treatment... Can you guess what they are from the title?*

Physiological Methods of Stress Management use Drugs and Biofeedback

Both drug therapy and biofeedback help people cope with **stress** by changing the way their body **responds** to it.

1) Drug therapy — the drugs used work in two ways

1) They **slow down** the activity of the **central nervous system** (CNS).
Anti-anxiety drugs called **benzodiazepines** (BZs) help the body react to its own natural anxiety relieving chemical **GABA** (gamma-amino-butyric acid), which slows down the activity of neurones and makes us feel relaxed.

2) They **reduce** the activity of the **sympathetic nervous system** (SNS).
The SNS increases heart rate, blood pressure and levels of the hormone **cortisol**. High levels of cortisol can make our immune system **weak** and also cause heart disease. The group of drugs called **beta-blockers** reduce all these unpleasant symptoms.

2) Biofeedback — the person learns to relax

Biofeedback — The person **learns** how to control and **regulate** the symptoms of stress so that they feel **relaxed** in real-life stressful situations. There are 4 steps involved:

1) The person is attached to a machine that monitors and gives **feedback** on heart rate or blood pressure.
2) The person learns to **control** the symptoms of stress by taking deep breaths which slow down their heart rate. This makes them feel relaxed.
3) Relaxation acts like a **reward** and encourages the person to repeat this as an involuntary activity.
4) The person learns to use this in **real-life** situations.

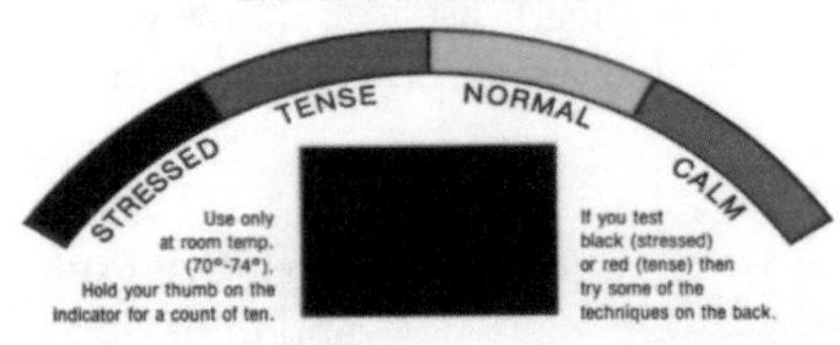

An attempt at making biofeedback a more accessible therapy.

The Physiological Approach Has Strengths and Weaknesses

Both drugs and biofeedback are **effective:**

Drugs are **quick** and **effective** in reducing dangerous symptoms such as high blood pressure. **Kahn et al (1986)** found that BZs were superior to a placebo (sugar pill) when they tracked 250 patients over an 8-week period.

Attanasio et al (1985) found that biofeedback helped teenagers and children with stress related disorders to gain **control** over the symptoms of **migraine** headaches. They also showed an increase in **enthusiasm** and a more positive attitude.

BUT both treat **symptoms** rather than the underlying causes of stress:

Drugs only help with the **symptoms** and only so long as the drugs are taken.

Biofeedback also aims to **reduce** symptoms, but using relaxation techniques can also give the person a sense of **control** and have more long lasting benefits.

Placebos are pills that do nothing at all. They're used to test if any effect happens just because people think they're being treated.

Drugs have **side effects**, biofeedback **doesn't**:

Drugs can have minor **side effects** such as dizziness and tiredness or more serious effects such as blurred vision and changes in sex drive. **Withdrawal symptoms,** such as increased anxiety, seizures, tremors and headaches, when people come off medication can be distressing. BZs can be **addictive**, and are generally limited to a maximum of 4 weeks' use.

There are no side effects of biofeedback, just **relaxation**. This method's advantage is that it is **voluntary** and not invasive.

Drugs are **easier** to use than biofeedback:

Drugs are relatively **easy** to prescribe and use.

Biofeedback needs specialist **equipment** and expert **supervision**. Some argue the benefits of biofeedback could be gained from other relaxation techniques and so this is an unnecessary expense.

Physiological & Psychological Approaches to Stress Management

Psychological Methods Are About Learning to *Think Differently*

The psychological approach helps the person to cope better by **thinking differently** about the stressful situation. These techniques have been shown to be **effective** and deal with the **source** of the problem rather than just the symptoms. They provide **skills** that have more lasting value — like the **confidence** to cope with future problems and the belief of being in **control** and seeing life as a challenge rather than as a threat. (And other cheesy, upbeat things like that).

Meichenbaum's Stress Inoculation Technique (SIT):

This works like immunisation. Just like you might be inoculated against any attack from disease, you can protect yourself from the harmful effects of stress. **Training** involves preparation so that you can deal with stress before it becomes a problem.
3 steps are involved:

1) **Conceptualisation**: Identify fears and concerns with therapist's help.
2) **Skill acquisition and rehearsal**: Train to develop skills like positive thinking and relaxation in order to improve self confidence.
3) **Application and follow-through**: Practice newly acquired skill in real life situations with support and back up from therapist.

Meichenbaum (1977) found that SIT works both with short-term stressors such as preparing for public speaking, and longer-term stressors such as medical illness, divorce or work related stress.

Hardiness Training:

Kobasa suggests that a strong and hardy person shows **3 Cs**: **Control** over their lives, **commitment** (a sense of purpose in life) and **challenge** (life is seen as a challenge and opportunity rather than as a threat).

Maddi introduced a training programme to increase hardiness, arguing that the more hardy the person, the better they cope with stress. This training has 3 steps:

1) **Focusing**: Learn to **recognise** physical symptoms of stress, e.g. increase in heart rate, muscle tension and sweating.
2) **Reliving stressful encounters**: Learn to analyse stressful situations to better understand possible coping strategies.
3) **Self improvement**: Take on **challenges** that can be coped with and build **confidence**, thereby gaining a greater sense of **control**.

Maddi (1998) got 54 managers who went on a hardiness training programme to report back on their progress. They recorded an increase in hardiness and job satisfaction and decrease in strain and illness.

Despite proven effectiveness, there are **weaknesses** with psychological methods:

1) Psychological methods only suit a narrow band of very **determined** individuals.
2) Research is based on white middle class business folk and so can't necessarily be **generalised** to others.
3) The procedures are very lengthy and require considerable **commitment** of time and effort.
4) The **concepts** may be too complex. For example, a lack of hardiness may be just another label for negativity. It might be argued that it is just as effective to relax and think positively.

Practice Questions

Q1 Describe two ways in which drug therapy helps in stress management.

Q2 What are the four steps involved in biofeedback?

Q3 In what way is biofeedback better than drug therapy?

Q4 What does SIT stand for and what three stages does it involve?

Exam Questions

Q1 Describe one physiological approach used in managing the negative effects of stress. [3 marks]

Q2 Give one strength and one weakness of the psychological approach to stress management. [6 marks]

Stress management — quite the opposite of traditional management...

This ridiculously stressed and hectic lifestyle we choose to live is turning us all into ill people. I can't understand it myself — personally I choose the more Caribbean attitude to time management. I'm quite confident I'll never need to take BZs or teach myself to think differently. But then again, I might get into trouble for not finishing this book on time. Hmmm...

The Role of Control in Stress

Just AQA A. *Things are a lot less scary if you're in control — stress isn't any different. You often can't control what causes the stress, but you can control how it affects you. It's all about how you view stress and what you do to cope.*

*How We **View** Stress is More Important Than Stress Itself*

The **transactional model of stress** suggests that people differ in how they **view** a stressful situation. For example, one person being made redundant at work might feel **devastated**, while another might feel **positive** about the opportunities it opens up.

Lazarus (1966) believed that our **perception** of the 'stressor' (the source of stress) is more important than the stressor itself. If we feel we have some **control** in dealing with the demands of a stressful situation, then we are more likely to cope with it than if we feel we have no control over it.

Control *over How we View Stressors Affects How Stressed we Get*

There are 6 studies to learn about how a **lack of control** can either cause or enhance stress:

Perceived locus of control means who or what people think is in control of their lives.

1. **Seligman (1974)** conducted a study where two groups of dogs were given electric shocks. One group could press a lever to stop the shock, the other group couldn't. Both groups received the same amount of shocks, but when later given the chance to escape, the dogs with no previous control didn't even try. This is known as **learned helplessness**. Seligman believed that human **depression** can also be explained in terms of learned helplessness.

2. **Rotter (1966)** believed that the perceived **locus of control** affects how stressed people get. People can be described as one of two types:
   Externalisers — They believe good things happen due to luck and bad things are someone else's fault. Such people are more likely to become **anxious** as they perceive no sense of control over anything.
   Internalisers — This type of person takes **personal responsibility** for both good and bad events in life. Such individuals are more likely to feel a sense of control and therefore take steps to **cope** with stress.

3. **Suls and Mullen (1981)** found that illness was associated more with **uncontrollable** life events than with **controllable** life events.

4. **Marmot (1997)** found that people in jobs with less responsibility showed higher risk of **cardiovascular disease**. These people reported low job **control,** poor social support and no control over decision making processes at work.

   This study used a potentially biased sample — urban civil servants who may be quite job-oriented and ambitious. Additionally, the results could be explained by socio-economic status (SES). People of low SES are statistically more likely to smoke, live in stressful environments and have poor diets — factors which are also related to cardiovascular disease.

5. However, **Schaubroeck (2001)** found that employees who believed that they were responsible for things going wrong at work were more stressed (no shock, Sherlock). This suggests that greater control isn't always better for some people or for some situations.

6. **Glass and Singer (1972) investigated the illusion of control.**

Aim:	To investigate whether the **illusion** of control can reduce stress. The 'illusion of control' means that people think they're in control, but they aren't really.
Method:	Participants in the experimental group were deceived into believing that they could **control** a loud noise by pressing a button. Their stress response was compared with a control group of participants who were simply exposed to the loud noise. Their arousal level was measured using the **galvanic skin response** (GSR). GSR is simply a measure of increased sweating, and hence increased electrical conductivity, which indicates increased stress.
Results:	The experimental group showed **less** stress response (lower arousal level) compared to the control group.
Conclusion:	If people think they are in control (even when they're not), they are less likely to get stressed.

The Role of Control in Stress

Informational and *Cognitive* Control Are Useful Together

Informational control is having some **knowledge** on the nature of the stress so that a person can plan to cope with it.
Cognitive control is control over stress through **relaxation** to avoid negative thinking and increase positive thinking.
Langer et al investigated the effectiveness of these two methods of control:

Langer et al (1975) studied the types of control.

Aim: To compare three groups of patients who were undergoing non-emergency surgeries, investigating the **effectiveness** of **informational** and **cognitive control**.

Method: One group was given informational control — they were **informed** about the nature of the treatment and the effect this would have on them in the days to follow. The second group was given cognitive control — they were prepared to **think** positively and avoid negative thoughts about the surgery. A third group was not prepared in any specific way. This served as the **comparison** group.

Results: The first two groups coped far **better** than the comparison group.

Conclusion: Both informational and cognitive control increase people's ability to cope with stress. For maximum benefit, there is no reason why they should not be used **together**.

Stress Management Techniques Use Cognitive Control

Stress management techniques aim to **increase cognitive control** and minimise the negative effects of stress.
A simple method is to say things to yourself that will help you cope with stressful situations:

Self instructions that can help us to cope better

Preparation	Confronting the situation	Reinforcing self statement
What is the point in worrying?	Take a deep breath.	That worked.
It is not the end of the world.	I can only do one thing at a time.	It was not so bad after all.
What is the worst that could happen?	I will focus on this task for now.	I always knew I could do it.

Practice Questions

Q1 Describe the theory of learned helplessness.
Q2 Why does Rotter think externalisers are less able to cope with stress?
Q3 What did Marmot discover about the link between workplace conditions and stress?
Q4 Name two types of control that are helpful in managing stress.

Exam Questions

Q1 Outline the procedure and findings of any one study on the role of control in stress. [6 marks]

Q2 Describe the findings of research on the role of control in stress. [6 marks]

Aaaaaaaaaaaaaaaaaaaaarrrrrrrrrrrrrrrrrrrrrrgggggggggghhhhhh...

Makes sense doesn't it? You get bossed around, told to write huge essays, told to write them again, told you can't go out until you've done your essay — of course you're going to feel stressed, it's only natural. But if you insist to yourself that it's all your own choice because it's the only path to a good job and lots of money, then you'll feel better. In theory anyway...

Explanations of Aggression

These pages are just for OCR. *Aggression is one of those topics in psychology that throws up a lab-load of theories. Eventually there might be one unified, simple, elegant explanation, but until then you've got to learn the lot I'm afraid.*

*Every Psychological Theory has a **Different Explanation** of Aggression*

Aggression has six theories from social psychology, the usual weirdo one from Freud and a load of biological ones.

***Social Psychology** has Six Very Different Theories*

1) The **social learning theory** of aggression argues that aggression is learned indirectly and directly, through **vicarious reinforcement** (seeing others rewarded for certain behaviours), **vicarious punishment** (seeing someone punished for a behaviour) and **disinhibition** (watching violent behaviour can result in our own learned behaviours being unlearned). (See **Bandura** on p 72 for more on this.)
2) The **frustration-aggression hypothesis (Dollard et al, 1973)** argues that all aggression is caused by frustration and that all frustration causes aggression.
3) The **excitation-transfer theory** suggests aggression aroused by one stimulus can be **transferred** to another. For example, a hot day makes you irritable, then someone bumps into you and you become aggressive. You think you're annoyed because of the bump, but on a cooler day you wouldn't have got mad about it.
4) **Environmental triggers** such as heat, noise, and overcrowding can lead to aggression.
5) **Deindividuation** means losing our sense of personal **identity** (e.g. wearing a uniform or standing in a crowd) can lead to aggression because we feel less constrained by social norms of behaviour. However, people in crowds do not always become aggressive.
6) **Social constructionists** see aggression as a **social behaviour**, not just an expression of anger. For example, at a football match, a foul will affect fans in different ways depending on which team they support. Our view of someone else's behaviour depends on our own **beliefs** and **knowledge**, and our decision to behave aggressively depends on how we view their behaviour.

*The **Psychoanalytic Theory** is About Conflicting Instincts*

Freud argued that we all have innate instincts including the life instinct and the death instinct:

The **death instinct** is a desire to return to lifelessness or the mother's womb.

The **life instinct** has to fight that instinct, by directing aggression that could be directed towards the self, away and outwards towards others. *[Now maybe it's just me, but this one sounds as mad as a badger.]*

***Biological Theories** are more Easily Testable*

Biological theories are more **scientifically testable** than the more psychological theories of aggression above.

Jacobs et al (1965) suggested a genetic theory of aggression

They found that a number of men in prison had an extra Y chromosome, so rather than having XY chromosomes, they had **XYY chromosomes**, which potentially made them more aggressive. However, the abnormality has since been found to be **widespread** in the population, so alone it doesn't explain aggression.

The **evolutionary** or **ethological** perspective sees aggression as a natural function

Animals are biologically **programmed** to fight over resources. Always fighting to the death, however, would risk the species becoming extinct, so animals (including humans) can '**turn off**' their aggression.

There are three aspects to the **physiological** approach:

1) **Hormones** such as testosterone are thought to lead to aggression in males. Castrated male animals (i.e. with no testosterone) tend to fight least. Women with premenstrual syndrome (causing hormone fluctuations) tend to be more irritable and hostile.
2) The **neurotransmitter serotonin** has been linked with aggression. A link has been found between people with low levels of serotonin and a history of criminal behaviour.
3) Another physiological explanation involves **brain anatomy**. There's more on this over there, on the next page...

Explanations of Aggression

Brain Scans Can Help Examine Patterns of Brain Activity and Anatomy

There are five basic techniques used:

1) **PET scans** show which part of the brain is **active** during different tasks. It shows average activity over a 60 second period, not moment by moment.
2) **CAT scans** detect **damaged** parts of the brain, tumours and blood clots. Brain **structure** is shown, not function.
3) **MRI scans** detect small tumours and provide **detailed** information about **structure**.
4) **Functional MRI scans** are **3D** scans providing **structural** and **functional** information.
5) **Squid magnetometry** produces accurate images of brain **activity** by measuring neurones activated by magnetic fields. However, outside sources of magnetism can affect measurements.

Raine et al used PET scans to investigate the differences in **brain activity** of a sample of **violent** offenders:

Raine et al (1997) studied murderers' brains.

OCR Core Study

Method: 41 murderers (39 men, 2 women) pleaded not guilty by reason of insanity (NGRI). They were matched to 41 control subjects by age, sex and schizophrenia. **PET scans** were conducted on the participants.

Results: Murderers pleading NGRI were found to have different brain functioning compared to control subjects. They found the murderers had **reduced** activity in the **prefrontal cortex** and **increased** activity in **subcortical** regions, such as the **thalamus**.

Conclusion: This is quite a large sample of seriously violent offenders, whose differences in brain activity cannot be due to age, sex, schizophrenia or other possible confounding effects . Although it seems likely that violent offenders have **differently active brains**, the results can't claim that violence is solely due to biology or that people claiming NGRI did not know what they were doing. Also, there are people with prefrontal cortex damage who do not commit violent acts, so we cannot and should not use PET scans to find potential murderers.

He's so beautiful, just perfect.
Don't know — looks like a potential murderer to me.

Practice Questions

Q1 What is the psychoanalytic theory of aggression?

Q2 What male hormone is thought to lead to aggression?

Q3 What is deindividuation?

Q4 What did Raine et al conclude from their study of murderers' brains?

Exam Questions

Q1 Describe what effect biology is thought to have on aggression. [6 marks]

Q2 Outline and compare two explanations of aggression. [8 marks]

Grrrrrrrrrrrrrrrrrrrrrrrrrrrrrrrrrrrrrrrrrrrrrrrrrrrrrrrrrrrrrrrrrrrrrrrrrrr...

Well, what an interesting page. Seeing as all our decisions come from the brain, I wouldn't be at all surprised if there were differences in brain activity between murderers and non-violent people. Although I doubt we'll find them properly anytime soon. I mean, brains are pretty darned complicated things. Imagine actually finding the violent bits. Brain surgery time...

Localisation of Function

Just OCR. *Yep, it's a page about brains. Interesting things. I mean, really, they're just a pile of gooey, squidgy, messy bits of meat. They probably taste quite nice, but how on earth can they see, think, feel, create consciousness, play chess...*

Localisation of Function — Certain Bits of Brain Do Certain Things

Certain areas of the brain are thought to be responsible for particular functions, e.g. vision, language, coordination... This is known as **localisation of function**.

The brain is split into two **hemispheres** (halves) — the right hemisphere and the left hemisphere.

View from above

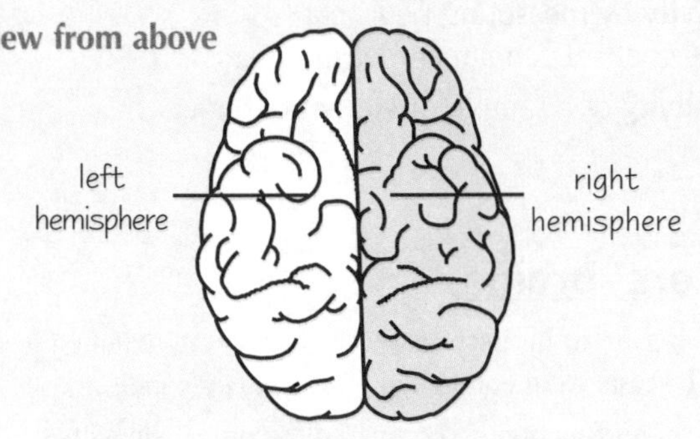

Within each hemisphere, there are four **lobes** — the **frontal** lobe, the **parietal** lobe, the **temporal** lobe and **occipital** lobe.

Side view from left

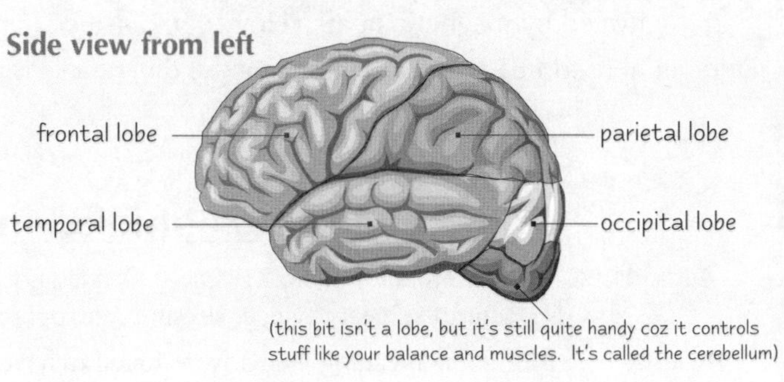

In most people, the **left** hemisphere handles the bulk of the **language** functions, **analysis and problem solving**, and **cognitive capacity**. The **right** hemisphere is more concerned with **spatial** comprehension, **emotions** and the **processing** of language.

The **lobes** are named after their nearest **cranial** (skull) **bones**. Each lobe is responsible for so many different areas of specialised **function** that they are not normally distinguished in terms of function themselves.

Broca's Area and Wernicke's Area Are Associated With Language

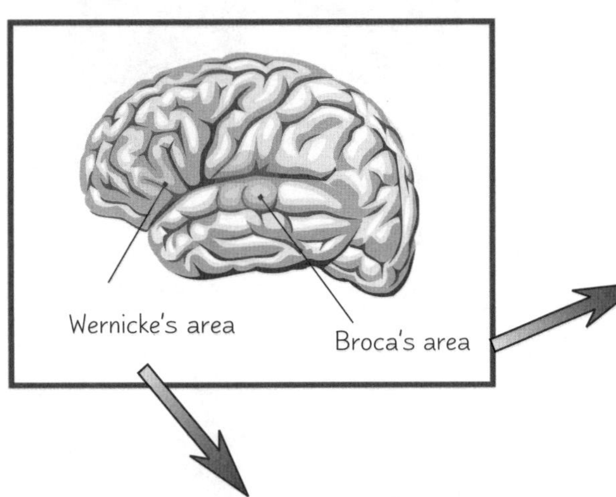

1) **Broca's area** was named after **Paul Broca** who studied brain-damaged patients in the 1860s.
2) The patients had **difficulty speaking** and tended to talk slowly and not fluently.
3) They could **understand** speech, but not as well as someone without brain-damage.
4) He called this **Broca's aphasia** or **expressive aphasia**.
5) Broca concluded that this aphasia was due to a **lesion** in the area now known as Broca's area.
6) This suggested the brain function concerned with speech production was **localised in this area**.
7) Broca was partly correct, but later research has shown that the function is not as localised as it first appeared.

1) **Wernicke's area** was named after **Carl Wernicke** who studied stroke patients who were able to speak, but had poor understanding of language.
2) For example, they had difficulties producing meaningful speech to express their thoughts (they could articulate, but the content was garbled), difficulties understanding word meanings and could not recognise words even though they could recognise sounds.
3) He called it **Wernicke's aphasia** or **receptive aphasia**.
4) The patients had suffered damage to the area of the brain now known as Wernicke's area.
5) This was an example of **localisation** of the brain function concerned with comprehension of speech.
6) However, sometimes the whole of Wernicke's area can be removed without speech being affected, so the function cannot be solely localised in that area. Other brain areas also contribute, particularly areas associated with memories and associations.

Localisation of Function

Split-Brain Surgery Provides more Evidence for the Localisation of Function

Quick biology recap:

The brain is set up so that information from the right visual field goes to the left hemisphere and information from the left visual field goes to the right hemisphere (see diagram). Information passes through the **corpus callosum** to whichever side of the brain needs to deal with it.

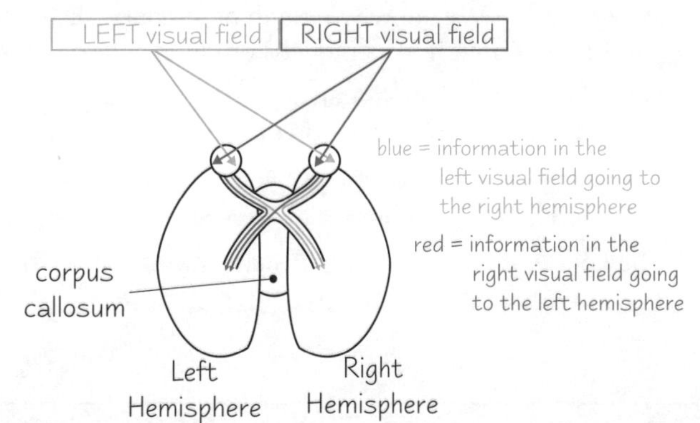

The effect of split-brain surgery:

1) In very severe cases of **epilepsy**, the only treatment available is to sever the corpus callosum and literally split the brain in two, to stop seizures spreading across the brain.
2) But a side-effect of splitting the hemispheres is that information can no longer move between them.
3) Sperry used patients of split-brain surgery to study whether different sides of the brain process speech and writing.

Sperry (1968) studied individuals after split-brain surgery.

OCR Core Study

Method: Participants covered one eye and looked at a fixed point on a projection screen. Pictures were projected onto the **right** or **left** of the screen at high speeds.

Results: If the picture was shown in the right visual field, they could say or write what it was without a problem. But if the image was flashed onto the left they couldn't say or write what they'd seen and often reported seeing nothing.

Conclusion: This shows that the left hemisphere (which receives visual information from the right visual field) can convert sight into spoken and written language. Usually information entering the right hemisphere crosses over to be processed in the left. As the results show, this can't happen in split brains, so the information going to the right hemisphere can't be converted into language at all.

Comment: Epilepsy is usually caused by brain damage. The patients had also been on medication which may have affected their brains. Therefore, it is hard to conclude that the ways they processed information would be the same as for people without epilepsy or split-brain treatment.

Practice Questions

Q1 Define 'localisation of function'.

Q2 What function is Wernicke's area thought to be associated with?

Q3 What function is Broca's area thought to be associated with?

Q4 What is split-brain surgery?

Exam Questions

Q1 Discuss Broca's and Wernicke's research on the localisation of brain function for language. [6 marks]

Q2 What does Sperry's research on split-brain patients tell us about brain function? [6 marks]

Brings a whole new perspective to being in two minds about things...

I heard a story about a man who got attacked with a machete. Very nasty story — read no further if you're at all squeamish. Anyway, someone chopped right through the middle of his head with the machete. Blood everywhere, but the guy was absolutely fine. It'd gone right between the two hemispheres and not touched a single brain cell. Lucky man eh?

Emotion

Another couple of pages just for OCR people. *Emotion's a great topic, it's what makes us human. But then we go and study it and find that emotion's a pretty basic thing, nothing to be so proud of...*

Emotions Exist in a **Variety of Forms**

When an emotion is triggered it can be expressed and experienced in a variety of ways:

1) **Cognitive** — We know we are in an emotional situation because we are **consciously aware** of the situation and **think** about it. Cognitively, emotions are **directed** at people or things, e.g. being angry **at** someone.
2) **Physiological** — Emotional situations lead to arousal of the autonomic nervous system (**ANS**) or to hormonal activity in the **endocrine system**. These cause increases in blood pressure, heart rate, respiration rate and sweating.
3) **Experiential** — In an emotional situation, we **feel** the sensations of our physiological response.
4) **Expressive** — Emotions are **expressed** through bodily gestures, facial expressions and other non-verbal behaviour.
5) **Behavioural** — An emotional state causes a pattern of **behaviour** e.g. crying, frowning or laughing.

The **James-Lange Theory** Was One of the First Theories of Emotion

William James and **Carl Lange** independently developed one of the first major theories of emotion, which later became known as the **James-Lange** theory. There are three stages to this theory:

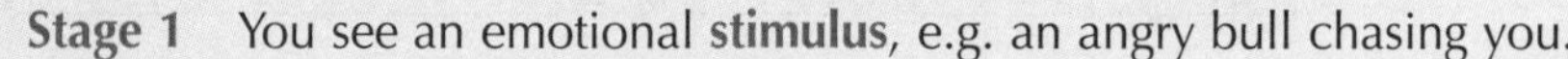

Stage 1 You see an emotional **stimulus**, e.g. an angry bull chasing you.

Stage 2 This triggers a **bodily change**, e.g. arousal of the ANS and thus a pounding heart.

Stage 3 Bodily changes cause **feedback**. The **awareness** of the bodily response is what we know as **emotion**, e.g. fear.

The **Cannon-Bard Theory** Was an Alternative to the James-Lange Theory

Although physiological changes can lead to emotion, sometimes we experience emotion **before** any physiological changes. Also, we can experience bodily changes **without** emotion, e.g. running increases our heart rate, respiration and sweating, but does not usually make us feel emotion. Therefore, there must be more to emotion than just the result of physiological changes.

The **Cannon-Bard theory** suggested that:

1) When we are in an emotional situation, the **thalamus** is activated.
2) The thalamus then sends signals to both the **hypothalamus** and the **cerebral cortex**. The hypothalamus triggers the **physiological changes**, while the cortex registers an **emotion**, e.g. fear.
3) Therefore, feelings are not determined solely by physiological arousal.

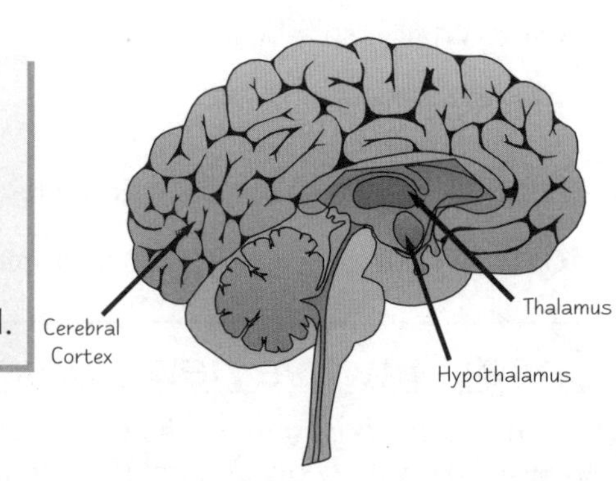

However, research does suggest that emotion is **partly dependent** on physiological arousal. Also, the theory does not explain how we **know** when a situation is an emotional one.

Emotion

Maranon (1924) investigated arousal without emotion.

Method: Participants were injected with **adrenaline**, which has an effect similar to natural arousal. Participants were asked how they **felt**.

Results: **71%** reported physical symptoms with **no emotional arousal**. The majority of the remaining participants reported feeling emotions, but they were emotions without their usual intensity.

Conclusion: Physiological arousal is **not enough** for an emotional experience. This contradicts the James-Lange theory.

Comment: The participants could have interpreted their emotions as related to the drug, explaining why they did not attach an emotional label to the feeling. Therefore, this experiment lacks **ecological validity**.

*Schacter and Singer Developed the **Cognitive Labelling Theory** of Emotion*

Schacter and Singer argued that there are two essential factors for emotion — **high physiological arousal** and a **cognitive interpretation** (label) of the arousal. They argued that emotion can't be experienced without both of these factors. Using this theory, **Maranon**'s study shows that participants did not attach an emotional label to the feeling as they knew it was due to the drug. Schacter and Singer did an expanded version of the study:

Schacter and Singer (1962) tested their theory.

OCR Core Study

Method: Participants were told they were being given a vitamin injection. They were actually injected with **adrenaline**. There were three conditions –

1) They were told the **true side-effects** of the injection. (informed)
2) They were told there would be **mild side-effects**. (mis-informed)
3) They were told there would be **no side-effects**. (uninformed)

After the injection, participants were put into the same room with a confederate who was either acting **joyfully** or **angrily**. The intention was to give the participant a **'label'** for what they were feeling — joy or anger.

Results: The group who were given adrenaline, and either misinformed or uninformed, experienced the most emotion. But the effects were small.

Conclusion: The group who were given adrenaline, but who did not know their arousal was due to the drug, felt emotional. This supports the cognitive labelling theory. However, the effects were small, so it doesn't lend as much support as expected.

Comment: The study has been **criticised**. Adrenaline produces different effects on different people. Arousal created by drugs may not be the same as real-life emotion. The data from participants who felt no physiological sensations of the drug were excluded, affecting the findings. Also, it may have been perfectly normal to feel emotional when put into the emotional situation with the confederate, even without adrenaline, which was not considered.

Practice Questions

Q1 Outline the three stages of the James-Lange theory of emotion.

Q2 List three physiological changes that can occur due to high arousal.

Q3 What two factors did Schacter and Singer say are necessary for emotion?

Exam Questions

Q1 Outline and compare the James-Lange theory and Canon-Bard theory. [10 marks]

Q2 Critically consider Schacter and Singer's (1962) research on emotion. [10 marks]

*Emotional?!? Don't you call me ****ing emotional!*

Phew. What a lot of theories. I personally prefer the Cognitive Labelling theory. I mean, it makes sense. Emotion wouldn't be emotion without some sort of arousal. But then, the same arousal can lead to different emotions or even no emotion, so we need a little cognitive labelling to get the right sort. But then, I do sometimes get emotional without bothering to label...

Sleep and Dreaming

OCR and Edexcel. *We've all got biological rhythms that affect our behaviour. They regulate things like eating, temperature changes and blood pressure, but the big daddy of body rhythms is the daily sleep/wake cycle.*

Circadian Rhythms are Daily Biological Cycles

1) A **biological rhythm** is a cycle of behaviour or bodily functioning that keeps repeating itself.
2) **Circadian rhythms** are biological rhythms that take place once a day (e.g. the sleep/wake cycle).
3) We have **internal body clocks** (called endogenous pacemakers), telling us when to get up, go to bed, eat etc.
4) Body clocks are influenced by **external cues** (called exogenous zeitgebers), e.g. sunset, cockerels and man-made clocks. **Light** is the most important cue — without it our bodies actually work on a **25 hour** circadian rhythm.
5) The sleep/wake cycle is the circadian rhythm that's been studied the most by physiological psychologists because it's **extremely powerful**. People can override the urge to eat and actually starve themselves to death, but they can't escape sleep for long. *(Which is a little annoying for those kids in Nightmare on Elm Street).*

Sleep Can Be Split into Stages of Different Brain Activity

This table shows the types of brain activity found in different stages of sleep, as recorded by an EEG (see page 79).

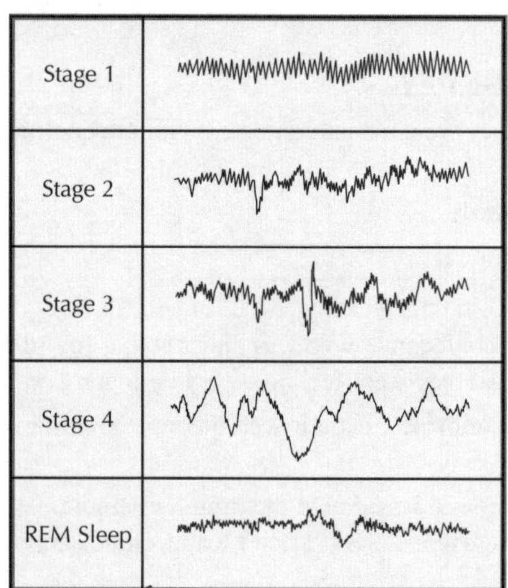

1) Adults pass through the stages about five times a night, taking about 30 minutes to reach stage 4.
2) As you fall into deeper sleep from stages 1 to 4, the activity becomes **higher voltage** and **lower frequency**.
   - **Stage 1** is a bit like deep relaxation, with lowered heart rate, muscle tension and body temperature. It's quite easy to wake people from this stage.
   - **Stage 2** has slower and larger EEG waves, with some quick bursts of high frequency waves called **sleep spindles**.
   - **Stage 3** has even larger, slower waves.
   - **Stage 4** has the largest, slowest waves of all, because it's the deepest stage of sleep. Metabolic activity is pretty low in general, and the sleeper is very hard to wake.
3) After stage 4, the cycle reverses and goes back through stages 3 and 2. Then instead of stage 1, a period of '**active sleep**' occurs.
4) During the active stage, metabolic activity increases, and the body appears almost paralysed except for **rapid eye movement (REM)**. The EEG pattern is almost like when you're awake.

There are Two Big Physiological Theories about Sleep

Evolutionary theory says different types of animals have evolved sleep patterns that fit in with their hunting behaviour and need for **survival**. Grazing animals don't need much sleep because they need to be awake to eat and to watch out for predators. Those who hunt can sleep for longer as they don't need to look for food as often and they're at less risk from predators.

Meddis (1975) claims that sleep helps to keep animals **safe**, because they're less likely to attract predators. Other people have pointed out that sleeping might make animals an easier target and so more **vulnerable**. One problem with any type of evolutionary theory is that it's very **difficult to test** and prove or disprove.

Restoration theory says that sleep allows the body to **restore** itself after a tiring day of biological processes.

Oswald (1980) says that REM sleep (see next page) allows the **brain** to be restored and non-REM sleep allows the **body** to be restored. Oswald's idea is supported by the sleeping patterns of babies, who sleep much more than adults and spend a longer proportion of time in REM sleep. Their brains are going through a huge surge of development, so they'll need to spend more time in REM.

An alternative explanation of sleep is that the brain needs time to **consolidate** all the information it's absorbed during the day, and sleep is an opportunity to prevent any new information **interfering** with this process.

Sleep and Dreaming

Sleep Research Supports **Restoration Theory**

Shapiro et al (1981) — sleep and exercise

In this study, Shapiro figured out that **exercise** resulted in changes in sleep patterns.
People were able to get to sleep more easily and felt that they slept better if they'd exercised first.
This backs up **restoration theory** — you'd expect that after exercise, the body would have an increased need to restore itself.

Huber-Weidman (1976) — sleep deprivation

Huber-Weidman investigated the effects of **sleep deprivation** and found that people lacking in sleep have problems such as delusions, confusion and impaired attention. However, the problems are not permanent and disappear once people get enough sleep. This supports the restoration theory — it suggests that the brain is struggling to cope with its normal activities without sleep. That's because it hasn't had an opportunity to restore itself, so it's **tired out**.

Physiological Research Has Also Attempted to Understand **Dreaming**

OCR Core Study

Dement and Kleitman (1957) woke people up during different stages of sleep and found that dreaming was much more likely to take place during **REM** sleep. However, it could be that you **recall** dreams better if you're woken from REM rather than non-REM sleep. They also found that the **content** of dreams sometimes corresponded to **eye movement** — one participant had vertical eye movements when dreaming about climbing up ladders and looking up and down them. These findings don't necessarily mean that you only dream in REM sleep, and they also don't tell you anything about the **purpose** of dreaming.

The **activation-synthesis model** by **Hobson and McCarley (1977)** suggests that **random neural activity** is muddled up with **existing knowledge** and memories, and expressed in the form of a **dream**. It's a **by-product** of the brain sorting out what to keep and what to forget — and it explains why dreams are often about recent events.

Winson (1993) linked together psychological and evolutionary theories of sleep and dreaming and used them **together** to get a better understanding. He said that REM sleep in humans **evolved** so that humans could dream, to work on information that they needed for **survival**, such as hunting and hiding from predators.
Today, our brains use dreams to work on our **current problems** such as jobs, relationships and money.

Practice Questions

Q1 Give an example of a circadian rhythm.

Q2 What's the role of external cues in our daily biological rhythms?

Q3 According to evolutionary theory, why do different types of animals have different sleeping patterns?

Q4 What are the effects of sleep deprivation according to Huber-Weidman?

Exam Questions

Q1 Discuss the evolutionary theory of sleep. [4 marks]

Q2 Describe two theories of dreaming. [6 marks]

Zzzzzzzzzz... *snort* — Wha? Oh... yeah, sleeping... nice... Zzzzzzzzzz...

*I think it's amazing that we spend about a third of our lives just switched off, and yet we have no idea why. Something to think about is whether we really **need** sleep. I mean, if we didn't eat or drink, we'd eventually die, but what would happen if we didn't sleep? We'd not function very well, but would we kick the bucket? Something for David Blaine to try next...*

Physiological Psychology in the Real World

Just Edexcel. *Every now and then a pale, white-coated psychologist stumbles outside, rubbing the lab dust from its eyes and squinting at all the big, fat, real-world problems. And occasionally it tries to solve a problem, with its theory-dust.*

Shift Work Causes Problems with Circadian Rhythms

1) **Shift working** means working hours outside the traditional hours of about **9am to 5pm**.
2) Shift workers include people who work in hospitals, factories, bars and restaurants, and even some shops.
3) The problem that shift workers have is that their **circadian rhythms** are disrupted by confusing **exogenous zeitgebers** — the external cues that we use to set our body clocks.
4) If a person is working night shifts, they'll arrive home as the day becomes lighter rather than darker so their brain thinks the day is starting rather than finishing.
5) On days off, the body becomes more **confused** as people tend to revert back to sleeping at night time.
6) If a person constantly works a particular shift, their body will **adapt**, but this can take between 7 and 14 days.
7) Adapting to a new shift pattern can be **unpleasant** — **symptoms** can include tiredness, irritability, impaired performance, difficulty getting to sleep, stomach problems and headaches.

Jet Lag Also Affects Circadian Rhythms

1) **Jet lag** is a sleep disorder caused by travelling across time zones, resulting in the internal body clock **not matching** the actual time where you are. E.g. your body might think it's bedtime when it's 10am.
2) **Symptoms** are similar to those experienced by shift workers — tiredness, irritability, impaired performance and sleep problems.
3) The symptoms are **inconvenient** for people travelling on holiday. It is more worrying for those who work in the travel industry and need to be alert and react quickly, like **pilots**.
4) The hormone **melatonin**, which is produced in the pineal gland in the brain during darkness, is involved in setting our circadian rhythms. It can therefore help prevent jet lag if administered in line with the new time zone.

Well, she may be tired, but at least she has nice shoes.

Jet lag is **worse** when travelling from the **west** to the **east** because the actual day becomes **shorter** — so when our body wants to sleep it is time to get up. Travelling from the **east** to the **west** is less disruptive because our day becomes longer and we can cope by just going to bed early.

There are Consequences of the 24-Hour Society

1) We are becoming a **24-hour society** where many services are available day and night.
2) It is more **economical** to keep factories active 24 hours a day than to shut them down at night.
3) People working **antisocial shifts** still want to use services, so supermarkets and food outlets also extend their hours.
4) The **Internet** means that people are more used to shopping when they want, so **cultural changes** are taking place.

There are **consequences** of the 24-hour society in terms of **health and safety**:

Studies of **shift workers** have found that they have higher levels of **sick leave** and use health-care facilities more often than day workers. They report more problems with **sleeping** and **stomach problems**, are more vulnerable to **depression** and **anxiety**, and there is increasing evidence that they have more **cardiovascular** (heart) problems.

The negative **symptoms** of shift work have been blamed for several famous disasters which all involved an **emergency** happening during the night shift. The devastating effects of the nuclear accidents at **Chernobyl** in the Ukraine and **Three Mile Island** in the USA, and the toxic chemical accident at **Bhopal** were all caused by mistakes made by shift workers.

Physiological Psychology in the Real World

Developments in **Genetics** Have Created Ethical Problems

The development of **eugenics** (**selective breeding** in humans to choose certain characteristics) is an example of an **ethical problem** faced by psychologists. The world's past experience of selective genetics is pretty nasty and gruesome:

1) Historically, laws existed in some countries allowing them to **forcibly sterilise** those identified as 'feeble minded' or 'morons'.
2) For example, between 1931 and the 1970s, nearly 36,000 people were sterilised in the USA. Sweden sterilised 62,000 people before the law was abolished in 1976.
3) In 1930s Germany, the Nazis sterilised 400,000 people before making it legal to **kill** those who were 'mentally retarded'. 70,000 people were then killed in Germany and the occupied territories by 1941. The next step was the mass murder of thousands of people in **concentration camps**. Being Jewish, Romany, gay, mentally ill, physically deformed or a Jehovah's Witness was seen as a **genetic flaw**, and these people were killed for the creation of a **master race**.

Recent scientific advances have opened up many beneficial possibilities, but have also created new **ethical problems**:

1) It is now possible to **screen** unborn babies for many genetic defects, including **cystic fibrosis** and **Down's syndrome**. Pregnancies can be **terminated** in cases of severe defects, but people often disagree on what counts as a 'severe defect'.
2) Direct **genetic manipulation** and the **screening** of eggs, sperm and early embryos will soon make it possible to **select** many features of a baby, to create so-called '**designer babies**'. It's already possible to select the **sex** of a baby, but many people find this ethically unacceptable, and it has been banned in many countries.
3) The **screening** of **adults** will soon allow the creation of **genetic profiles** of people. There are worries that people with certain genetic defects might be discriminated against (e.g. they could be refused life insurance, or not given a job). This could result in a '**genetic underclass**' of people who are denied opportunities because of their genes.
4) Advances in **cloning technology** mean it might soon be possible to clone humans. Some people have suggested creating clones to provide people in need with **replacement tissues** and **organs**. The cloning of humans has been widely condemned and it has been banned in many countries.

Maybe robotic humans are the way forward...

Practice Questions

Q1 Give three examples of occupations that require shift work.

Q2 What are the symptoms that can result from shift work?

Q3 What is melatonin?

Q4 Why are more people working non-traditional hours?

Q5 What ethical problems have advances in human genetics thrown up?

Exam Questions

Q1 Discuss the effects of shift work. [6 marks]

Q2 Discuss the ethical debate concerning new developments in genetics. [8 marks]

I'm a shift-worker and I'm OK... I work all night and I sleep all day...

You should start to see how all the theoretical stuff can be applied to actual problems in the real world. Psychologists have a part to play in some of the major questions facing society today, like how will we cope with changing work patterns and the question of genetic engineering — pretty interesting, better than those endless abstract theories.

The Individual Differences Approach

These couple of pages are just for OCR, and nobody else. *Section four is all about individual differences — basically the fact that everyone is different. What psychologists want to know is how, and why.*

*Individuals **Differ** in their Psychological Characteristics*

The **individual differences approach** studies how psychological characteristics, like aggression and degree of conformity, differ from person to person.

Psychologists argued for ages about whether an individual's personality is influenced by **nature** (inherited factors) or **nurture** (environmental factors). This is known as the **nature-nurture debate**. It's now thought most likely that **both** have an effect and interact with one another, so there shouldn't be much more debate over which one is solely to blame.

***Intelligence** is One Area Where We are All Different*

You've heard of the IQ test — well that's an intelligence test. But it's just one of many and they all have problems.

*Intelligence Tests Can Only Test **Current Intellectual Performance***

Intelligence tests only test the person's intellectual ability at the time they're taking the test. They work on the principle that this will **predict** how people will perform **generally**.

Intelligence Tests

1) They are the most common **measure of intelligence**.
2) They can help identify **learning disabilities** or **intellectually gifted** children, and help academic planning and neuropsychological evaluations (e.g. dementia).

However...

3) They only measure what is considered important by the **particular psychologist** who invented the test.
4) They may not be valid when used with a **cultural group** different from the one the test was designed for.
5) They do not take account of the fact that some people are very intelligent in **some areas**, but not others.

So... they're useful tests, but they're **not universal tests** which can be used on anyone, anywhere, at any time.

OCR Core Study

***Gould** Wrote a Book Called 'A Nation of Morons'*

In 'A Nation of Morons', **Gould (1982)** discussed IQ test devised by **Yerkes** (another psychologist) to test the abilities of army recruits for World War I in the USA.

Gould on Yerkes' test:

1) The test was mainly based on knowledge of **American society**.
2) It was a three part test — the **alpha test** taken by literate recruits, the **beta test** by illiterate recruits or those who failed the alpha test and an **individual interview** for those who failed the beta test.
3) Gould argued that **procedures** were **not followed**. For example, many recruits failing the alpha test were not allowed to take the beta test, tests were rushed and no allowance was made for language difficulties.
4) From the results, Yerkes' assistant, **Boring**, studied 160,000 cases and argued that —
   - The average mental age of white American adults was 13 years.
   - Darker skinned southern and eastern Europeans were less intelligent than western and northern Europeans.
   - Black people had an average mental age of 10.41, and the darker their skin, the less intelligent they were.
5) These arguments led in part to a strict **immigration law** in 1924 that prevented many Jewish refugees coming to America in the 1930s.
6) It's now generally believed that the tests were obviously **culturally biased** —
   - Recent immigrants scored poorly because they didn't know much about American society.
   - Many recruits couldn't write well, and didn't know what the exam was for, which made them **nervous**.
   - There was a **correlation** between how long a person had **lived in America** and how well they did in the test. This wouldn't happen if the test just tested intelligence.

Gould's work shows how IQ tests can be **culturally biased**.

The Individual Differences Approach

*Psychologists Try to **Classify** People*

The **DSM IV** is the fourth edition of the American Psychiatric Association's Diagnostic and Statistical Manual. It offers a new **method of classification** — a **multiaxial classification**:

1) Individuals can be rated on **multiple axes/dimensions**. Diagnostic categories are used, for example organic mental disorders, personality disorders etc.
2) DSM IV made diagnosis more **concrete and descriptive** than previously.
3) Classifications are useful to acquire new information about a disorder, which can help to form new **treatments** and medication.
4) This type of classification has been criticised for **stigmatising** people and ignoring their "uniqueness" by putting them in artificial groups.

Rosenhan (1973) — psychiatric classification can be inaccurate.

OCR Core Study

Method: Eight 'normal' people tried to be admitted to twelve different psychiatric hospitals around the USA, with only one symptom — claiming they heard voices, saying 'empty', 'hollow' and 'thud'.

Results: Seven were diagnosed with **schizophrenia** and all eight were **admitted** to psychiatric hospital. On admission, they said they were sane and had faked symptoms to get admitted, but this was seen as a symptom itself. It took, on average, 19 days before they were released, usually with a diagnosis of 'schizophrenia in remission'. Other, real patients could tell that these people were not mentally ill.

Method 2: Rosenhan later told staff at a psychiatric hospital that one or more **pseudopatients** (normal people pretending to have schizophrenia) were trying to be admitted to the hospital.

Results 2: No pseudopatients appeared, but 41 genuine patients were judged to be pseudopatients by staff.

Conclusion: Medical staff could not distinguish the sane from the insane (although the patients could).

Comment: Staff would probably not expect 'normal' people to try to gain admission to a psychiatric hospital. 'Schizophrenia in remission' is a diagnosis that is rarely used, which suggests the psychiatrists concerned may not have believed they were really suffering from schizophrenia. There are **ethical** considerations in this study — people had their freedom taken away, they may have received treatments, professionals were deceived, and they may have risked genuine patients not being treated.

Remember — it's the medical staff here who are the sample being studied, not the pseudopatients.

Practice Questions

Q1 What are IQ tests designed to measure?

Q2 Who devised IQ tests for Americans in World War I?

Q3 Who was Gould?

Q4 What is DSM IV?

Q5 Describe Rosenhan's study.

Exam Questions

Q1 Critically discuss the use of IQ tests developed by Yerkes in World War I. [8 marks]

Q2 Critically discuss Rosenhan's study of psychiatric hospital admission. [8 marks]

Get me out of here, I'm not crazy — I'm as sane as any other rabbit...

Remember, intelligence tests are designed to measure intelligence, but that doesn't mean that they actually do measure intelligence — they just measure whatever it is they're testing. Like most psychology, it's a grey area full of theories, not facts.

Defining Abnormality

Skip these pages if you're doing Edexcel.
Defining what's abnormal is easy — it's just what's not normal — but what's normal...?

Some Behaviours are **Rare** Within a Population

The concept of deviation from the majority is expressed in terms of **normal distribution**:

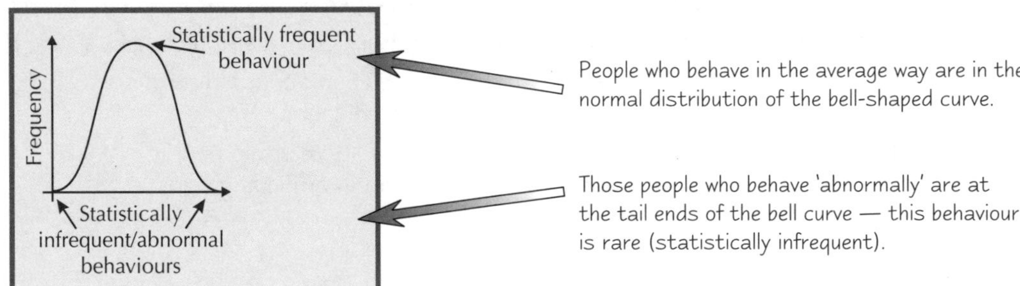
Frequency
Statistically frequent behaviour
Statistically infrequent/abnormal behaviours
People who behave in the average way are in the normal distribution of the bell-shaped curve.
Those people who behave 'abnormally' are at the tail ends of the bell curve — this behaviour is rare (statistically infrequent).

However there are **problems** with defining abnormality simply in terms of statistical infrequency —

1) It doesn't take account of the **desirability of behaviour**, just its frequency. For example, a very high IQ is abnormal, as is a very low one, but the high IQ is desirable and the low IQ is undesirable.
2) There is **no distinction** between **rare, slightly odd** behaviour and **rare, psychologically abnormal** behaviour.
3) There is **no definite cut-off point** of where normal behaviour becomes abnormal behaviour.
4) Some behaviours are psychologically abnormal, but quite common, e.g. mild depression. **Hasset and White (1989)** argue that you cannot use statistical infrequency to define abnormality because of this. Using the statistical infrequency idea, some disorders would not be classed as anything unusual.

Interestingly, as recently as the 80s, homosexuality was considered a **clinical syndrome**. It was described as a **sexual deviation** and was only dropped from a diagnostic category in DSM in 1987. The diagnosis was dropped because it was found that homosexuality was **not as infrequent** as previously thought and that homosexuals did not differ from heterosexuals in terms of **psychological wellbeing**.

Abnormality Can Also be Described as **Deviation From Social Norms**

1) All societies have their **standards** of behaviour and attitudes. Deviating from these can be seen as abnormal. This can also be described as 'departing from the expected'.
2) But **cultures vary**, so there isn't one universal set of social 'rules'.
3) The problem with defining abnormality as deviation from social norms is that it can be used to justify the removal of some people from a society. For example, people opposing a particular political regime could be said to be abnormal.

Malinowski provided an example of how behaviours that would be considered abnormal in our western culture, can be considered perfectly normal and functional in others:

Malinowski observed the hunter-gatherer Trobriand islanders.

1) He observed how they satisfied their **basic needs** (food, shelter), their **derived needs** (defence, social control) and their **integrative needs** (psychological security, social harmony etc.).
2) He found that the islanders used **magic** and **ritual** before embarking on dangerous deep sea fishing, but not before safe lagoon fishing.
3) He viewed this superstition or magic as perfectly **rational**.
4) He thought that the magic functioned to **reduce anxiety** and tension associated with the dangers of deep sea fishing.
5) In modern western society, the use of magic in this way would possibly be considered '**abnormal**'. In the culture of the Trobriand islands, however, Malinowski did not consider it unusual, but as serving a need for the islanders. In western society, praying might be seen as serving a similar purpose.

Defining Abnormality

Jahoda (1958) *Identified* ***Six Conditions*** *Associated With* ***Good Mental Health***

Jahoda's six conditions were:

1) Positive self attitude
2) Self-actualisation (realising your potential, being fulfilled)
3) Resistance to stress
4) Personal autonomy (making your own decisions, being in control)
5) Accurate perception of reality
6) Adaptation to the environment

However, it would be **hard to meet** all the standards set in this list, and they are **subjective** (ideas of what is required for each will differ from person to person).

Also, a violent offender, for example, may have a positive self attitude and be resistant to stress etc, yet society would not consider them to be in good mental health.

The Idea of Ideal Mental Health ***Varies*** *Across Time and Between Cultures*

What is considered mentally 'healthy' at one time, would not be at another.
For example, in some cultures today, it is considered **abnormal** for women to **enjoy sex** and they may be forced to have their clitoris surgically removed to prevent their enjoyment. In Victorian times here, women who enjoyed sex were deemed abnormal and hence Freud coined the term '**nymphomania**'. There is still influence from this and so today there are still **double standards** about male and female sexual activity.

But the idea of 'ideal' mental health can be a useful one because it moves away from focusing on mental 'illness'.

Some ***Symptoms*** *are Associated With Mental Illness*

The Department of Health provides a guide to assess symptoms associated with mental illness.
To be classified as a mental illness, there should be **one or more** of the following (**not temporary**) symptoms:

1) Impairment of **intellectual functions** that is not temporary, such as memory and comprehension.
2) Alterations to **mood** that lead to **delusional appraisals** of the past or future, or lack of any appraisal.
3) Delusional **beliefs**, such as persecution or jealousy.
4) Disordered **thinking** — the person may be unable to appraise their situation or communicate with others.

Practice Questions

Q1 What is the statistical infrequency definition of abnormality?

Q2 What does Jahoda (1958) say are the six conditions associated with mental health?

Q3 Define abnormality using the deviation from social norms explanation.

Q4 Describe Malinowski's findings.

Exam Questions

Q1 Discuss the idea of mental health in relation to different cultures. [8 marks]

Q2 Compare the deviation from social norms definition and the statistical infrequency definition of abnormality. [12 marks]

I'm not abnormal — I'm just a little statistically infrequent

The fact that homosexuality was, until very recently, classed as a sexual deviation and a form of abnormality goes to show just how difficult defining normal and abnormal is. It varies with culture and time and is very difficult to define in any scientific way. What's important is that you understand why and how people have attempted to define it.

Defining Abnormality

No need to bother with these two pages if you're doing Edexcel.
I'm beginning to think it's just wrong to try and define abnormality. I mean, for starters, calling someone 'abnormal' just isn't very nice. More to the point, it seems almost impossible to define.

The Concept of Abnormality **Varies** From One Culture and Time to Another

1) **Cultural relativism** means that judgements we make in relation to abnormality are relative to individual cultures. That's because what's normal in one culture is sometimes abnormal in another. So definitions of abnormality are **limited** because they're **culturally specific**.
2) It's important to work out whether the abnormality is **absolute**, **universal**, or **culturally relative**.

   a) **Absolute** — occurring in the same way and frequency across cultures.
   b) **Universal** — present in all cultures, but not with the same frequency.
   c) **Culturally relative** — unique to that particular culture.

3) Many **physical** conditions are **absolute**, as are some mental conditions e.g. **schizophrenia**. However, **social norms** vary from one culture to another. This can affect how these conditions are **perceived**. For example, in some countries such as Puerto Rica it is considered **normal** to experience hallucinations, but in the western world it can be seen as a symptom of schizophrenia.
4) Some abnormal behaviours are **universal**, e.g. **depression** occurs in all cultures, but is more common in women and in industrial societies.
5) Some abnormal behaviours are **culturally relative** — these are known as **culture-bound syndromes**.

'**Witiko**' is an example of culturally relative behaviour. It is a culture-bound syndrome, suffered by native Canadians, who **lose their appetite** for ordinary food, feel **depressed** and believe they are **possessed by the Witiko**, who is a **giant man-eating monster**. This can result in cannibalism, murder or pleas for death from the sufferer. It is thought to be an extreme form of **starvation anxiety**.

Attempts to **Define** Abnormality May Be **Biased**

There are often problems when it comes to defining abnormality — these often relate to **stereotypes**.

Gender...

Factors such as **biological** or hormonal differences, and the different ways that men and women are **brought up**, could lead to gender differences in the frequencies of disorders.

However, the **gender stereotype** can lead people to believe that women are generally moodier, and men generally more violent and anti-social. This could be a factor in clinicians tending to diagnose more **mood** disorders in women and more **anti-social** disorders in men — the clinicians expect to find them.

Race...

Several studies have found that very large numbers of **black people** in Britain are being diagnosed with **schizophrenia**. Surveys of inpatients by **Bagley (1971)** and **Cochrane (1977)** found that immigrant groups in Britain are more likely to be diagnosed as schizophrenic than native-born people. This is particularly so for people originating in Africa, the Caribbean and Asia. It was thought at first that this could be explained in terms of genetic or biological factors, except that the same rates of occurrence were not found in the countries of origin.

Therefore, possible reasons include **racial stereotypes** in diagnosis and **greater stress**. Stress could be due to poorer living conditions, prejudice, or the general stress of living in a new culture.

Even if stereotypes alone are to blame for a diagnosis, the person could 'develop' the disorder: Once a person is **labelled** with a mental disorder, they may begin to behave in the expected way due to the label. The diagnosis then becomes a **self-fulfilling prophecy**.

Defining Abnormality

Classification Systems **Pigeon-hole** People

A major **problem** with classification systems of abnormality is that they can lead to pigeon-holing people into **certain categories**. This leads to **practical**, **theoretical** and **ethical considerations**, which **you need to know**.

1) **Diagnosis** — When people report how they feel 'psychologically', these are **subjective** feelings. One person's "I'm extremely depressed" may mean the same as someone else's, 'I'm fed up'. A more **idiographic approach** would be useful — that is, focusing on each unique case and viewing patients on their merits.
2) There are many **different theories** — psychodynamic, learning, cognitive theory etc. They all have their own definitions and ideas on what causes abnormality.
3) There is little evidence of **validity** — how much the classification system measures what it's supposed to. It is hard to find a central cause (**aetiology**) for most disorders. If patients have more than one disorder it can be difficult to spot symptoms of one disorder.
4) Psychiatrists may not always agree from category to category, so classification systems may not always be **reliable**.
5) **Treatment** — Grouping patients can help to find treatments, but treatment often depends on diagnosis. Therefore, if the diagnosis is subjective initially, treatment may not be correct.
6) **Labelling theory** (**Scheff, 1966**) argues that if people are treated as mentally ill, their behaviour will change and become more like that expected from their diagnosis.
7) **Szasz (1974)** said that psychiatric labels were **meaningless**. He said illness was a bodily problem, so 'mental' illness could not exist. He believed the term was used to exclude non-conformists from society.
8) Finally, it is hard to say where normality ends and abnormality starts anyway.

In my culture, this isn't just normal, it's goooooorgeous.

Practice Questions

Q1 What is cultural relativism?

Q2 What are culture-bound syndromes?

Q3 Give an example of a culture-bound syndrome.

Q4 Briefly define labelling theory.

Q5 What is an idiographic approach to abnormality?

Exam Questions

Q1 Discuss the concept of cultural relativism in relation to abnormality. [8 marks]

Q2 Discuss the drawbacks of the use of classification systems for defining abnormality. [10 marks]

In the seventies people even thought men with huge perms were normal...

You've got to know all the stuff on these pages if you're going to answer a "defining abnormality" question in the exam. I reckon the best way is to read the pages and make a list of all the main points in note form. Then cover the pages up, and just try to write them out again from the notes you've just made. I know it's tough and dull, but it'll help you learn.

The Biological Model of Abnormality

These pages are pretty useful for everyone, I reckon.
There are many different models of abnormality that describe symptoms and treatments differently.
You need to know the biological model's explanations of causes and treatments, and its strengths and weaknesses.

The Biological Model Assumes Psychological Disorders are **Physical Illnesses**

The **biological (or medical or somatic) model** assumes that psychological disorders are **physical illnesses** with physical causes, in principle no different from physical illnesses like flu, except they have major psychological symptoms.

When the same symptoms frequently occur together, they represent a reliable **syndrome** or **disorder**.
The cause or '**aetiology**' may be one or more of the following:

1) **Genetics** — Faulty genes are known to cause some diseases that have psychological effects e.g. Huntington's disease that leads to a deterioration of mental abilities.
2) **Neurotransmitters** — These are chemicals that allow brain cells to send signals to each other (see page 34). Too much or too little of a particular neurotransmitter may produce psychological disorders, e.g. an increased level of **dopamine** is linked to schizophrenia — **drugs** like cocaine, which increase dopamine levels, can lead to schizophrenia-like symptoms.
3) **Infection** — Disorders may be caused by infection. **General paresis** is a condition involving delusions and mood swings, leading to paralysis and death. It is caused by **syphilis**, and can now be treated.
4) **Brain injury** — Accidental brain damage may produce psychological disorders. For example, **Phineas Gage** was involved in building a railway line in 1800s America. Dynamite accidentally exploded, sending an iron rod through his head, destroying parts of his frontal lobes. He miraculously survived, but he became more impulsive, disorganised, couldn't plan for the future and had a strangely different personality.

Biological Disorders Can Be **Treated** With Biological Therapies

The biological model says that once the physical cause of a psychological disorder has been identified, a physical (biological) therapy is needed to treat the physical problem. One or more of the following may be used:

1) **Drugs** — Drugs can be used to change **neurotransmitter levels** in the brain. For example, **phenothiazines** reduce levels of dopamine and can therefore relieve symptoms of schizophrenia.
2) **Psychosurgery** — Psychosurgery is brain surgery involving destruction or separation of parts of the brain. **Moniz** developed the '**frontal lobotomy**' in the 1930s to separate the frontal lobes from the rest of the brain. This reduced aggression and generally made people more placid. However, it is **not a cure,** it's a change — the **irreversible** changes to personality may have just made patients easier to manage. Psychosurgery is now only a last resort treatment for some disorders, e.g. very serious depression.
3) **Electro-convulsive therapy (ECT)** — ECT is an electric shock of about 100-150 volts given to a person's brain. This can help relieve depression, but can also produce memory loss. Although quite commonly used in the past, it's now only a last resort therapy.

The **Biological Model** Has **Strengths** and **Weaknesses**

Strengths:

a) It has a **scientific** basis in biology and a lot of evidence shows that biological causes **can** produce psychological symptoms.
b) It can be seen as **ethical** because people are **not to blame** for their disorders. They just have an illness.
c) Biological **therapies** have helped relieve conditions (e.g. schizophrenia) that could not be treated previously.

Weaknesses:

a) Biological therapies raise **ethical** concerns. Drugs can produce addiction and may only suppress symptoms, not cure the disorder. The effects of psychosurgery are irreversible.
b) Psychological disorders may not be linked to any physical problem and **psychological therapies** can be just as effective as biological treatments, without any interference to biological structures.

The Psychodynamic Model of Abnormality

The Psychodynamic Model is Based On **Conflict in Development**

1) According to the **psychodynamic model**, abnormality is the result of problems in childhood.
2) The model is based on **Freud's** division of personality into the id, ego and superego.
3) It also uses his stages of development — the oral, anal, phallic, latency and genital stages (see page 21).
4) The model suggests that conflict and anxiety may occur during childhood because the **ego** is not yet **developed** enough to deal with the id's desires, understand real-world issues or cope with the super-ego's moral demands.
5) Psychological disorders may also come from **conflict** or anxiety which happens in a certain stage of development. For example, during the anal stage, conflict may occur during potty training.
6) Anxiety from the conflicts is repressed into the **unconscious mind**.
7) **Stress** or **trauma** in adulthood may 'trigger' the repressed conflicts, leading to **psychological disorders**.

The **Psychodynamic Model** Also Has **Strengths** and **Weaknesses**

Strengths:

1) It's quite a unique approach to abnormality, suggesting that childhood experiences are important and that disorders may be linked to unresolved conflicts related to biological needs.
2) It offers a method of therapy. **Psychoanalysis** uses **dream analysis** to reveal unconscious desires. They also use '**free association**', to analyse what the person freely says. This may also uncover unconscious conflicts. The client can then understand the causes of their problems and so resolve them and release their anxieties (see also pages 74-75).

Weaknesses:

1) Freud's claims are based on his subjective interpretations of his patients' dreams etc. Therefore they are hard to **scientifically test** and so cannot be proven right or wrong.
2) **Psychoanalysis** may take a long time and so be very expensive. The childhood conflicts that are 'uncovered' may be emotionally distressing and possibly inaccurate, depending on the reliability of the patient's memory and the analyst's interpretations.

If you're doing Edexcel, you need to learn a load more about this topic — see pages 74 and 75.

Practice Questions

Q1 What causes psychological disorders according to the biological model?

Q2 What methods of therapy are used in the biological model?

Q3 Provide a strength and a weakness of the biological model.

Q4 Why are the id, ego and super-ego in conflict with each other?

Q5 Explain the methods used in psychoanalysis.

Exam Questions

Q1 Outline the assumptions of the biological model in terms of the causes of abnormality. [6 marks]

Q2 Outline the assumptions of the psychodynamic model in terms of the treatment of abnormality. [6 marks]

So it's either electric shocks, or chatting about your childhood...

These are very different approaches to dealing with abnormality — the biological model suggests psychological illness is much the same as any other illness and can be treated with medicine. The psychodynamic model, by contrast, concentrates on vague psychological effects of events in your childhood — now that's as different as chalk and cheese.

The Behavioural Model of Abnormality

This is all you need to know on the behavioural model of abnormality if you're doing AQA or OCR — but if you're Edexcel, there's more on pages 70 and 71.

The Behavioural Model of Abnormality says **Behaviours** are all **Learnt**

Behaviourists argue that abnormal behaviours are learnt in the same way that all behaviours are learnt — through classical and operant conditioning. This page is all about their take on the matter.

1) Behaviourists reckon that classical conditioning (see page 30) can be used to explain the development of many abnormal behaviours, including **phobias** and **taste aversions**. In classical conditioning, a certain stimulus (**unconditioned stimulus** or **UCS**) triggers a natural reflex (**unconditioned response** or **UCR**). When some other stimulus (**conditioned stimulus** or **CS**) is repeatedly presented with the UCS, over time it will elicit the UCR by itself. The response is then called the **conditioned response**, or **CR**.

Phobias can be created when the natural fear response is associated with a particular stimulus.

Watson and Rayner (1920) experimented with an 11 month old boy, **'Little Albert'**, producing fear of a white rat by associating it with a loud, scary noise.

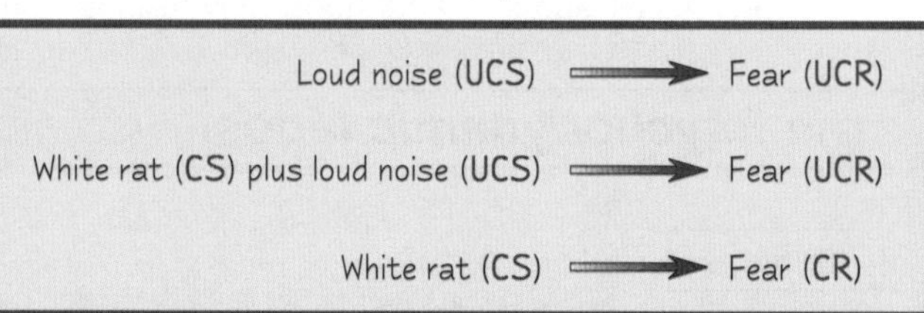

Taste aversions are often created if a person is ill after a certain food or drink. Its taste will become a CS, producing a CR of nausea. So, if you were ill after eating a curry with bad meat, the taste of curry might always make you feel ill.

2) **Operant conditioning** (see page 30) — Operant conditioning is learning from the **consequences** of actions. Actions which have a good outcome through **positive** (reward) or **negative** (removal of something bad) **reinforcement** will be repeated. Actions which have a bad outcome (**punishment**) will not be repeated. Some examples include:

a) Maintaining **phobias** — we get anxious around phobic stimuli (heights, spiders etc) and avoid them. This removes the anxiety, which acts as negative reinforcement.
b) **Bulimics** feel guilt and disgust, so make themselves sick, removing these feelings in negative reinforcement.
c) **Anorexics** desire to lose weight, or to have more control of their life, so not eating is positive reinforcement.

Behavioural Therapies are Based on **Changes** Through **Conditioning**

Behaviourists try to identify what **reinforces** current behaviours and try to change this through conditioning.

1) Behavioural therapies can use **classical conditioning** to change behaviour:

Aversion therapy — An undesirable behaviour or stimulus can be associated with an **unpleasant response.**

Systematic desensitisation — A phobic can be **gradually** introduced to the feared object.

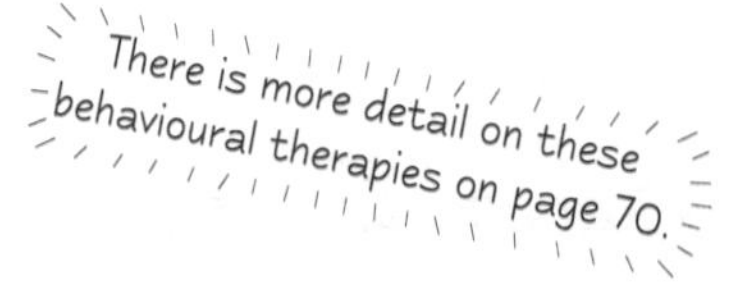

There is more detail on these behavioural therapies on page 70.

2) **Operant conditioning therapies** are often used in psychiatric hospitals. They control abnormal behaviour by removing the reinforcements which maintain the behaviour, and giving new reinforcements for better behaviour.

The Behavioural Model Has **Strengths** and **Weaknesses**

Strengths:

1) It is a **scientific** approach — it has clear **testable** concepts, which have been supported in many experiments.
2) Behavioural **therapies** can be very **effective** for treating phobias, eating disorders, obsessions and compulsions.

Weaknesses:

1) It cannot explain all behaviours because it neglects:
   a) The influence of **genetics** and **biology** — how survival value and brain functioning affect behaviour.
   b) The influence of **cognitions** — how thought processes contribute to disorders (see page 67).
2) Behavioural therapies are **not effective** for **all** disorders, e.g. conditioning does not cure schizophrenia. Also, the procedures sometimes raise **ethical** issues, e.g. aversion therapy may be quite distressing.

The Cognitive Model of Abnormality

Another model you've got to learn. And if more models are right, that means they're all a bit wrong...

The Cognitive Model of Abnormality Concentrates on **Thoughts** and **Beliefs**

The cognitive model assumes that behaviours are controlled by thoughts and beliefs. So, irrational thoughts and beliefs cause abnormal behaviours. A few different versions of the model have been suggested:

Ellis (1991) — The '**ABC model**' claims that disorders begin with an **activating event (A)** (e.g. a failed exam), leading to a **belief (B)** about why this happened. This may be rational (e.g. 'I didn't prepare well enough'), or irrational (e.g. 'I'm too stupid to pass exams'). The belief leads to a **consequence (C)**. Rational beliefs produce adaptive (appropriate) consequences (e.g. more revision). Irrational beliefs produce maladaptive (bad and inappropriate) consequences (e.g. getting depressed).

Beck (1963) — Beck identified a '**cognitive triad**' of negative, automatic thoughts linked to **depression**: negative views about **themselves** (e.g. that they can't succeed at anything), about the **world** (e.g. that they must be successful to be a good person) and about the **future** (e.g. that nothing will change).

Cognitive Therapies Try to Change **Faulty Cognitions**

Cognitive therapies assume that we can treat psychological disorders by changing the original faulty thoughts and beliefs.

1) The therapist and client **identify** the client's faulty **cognitions** (thoughts and beliefs).
2) They then try to work out whether the cognitions are true, e.g. is it true that they always fail at what they do?
3) Together, they then set **goals** to think in more positive or adaptive ways, e.g. focusing on things the client has succeeded at and trying to build on them.

An example of this is Meichenbaum's **Stress Inoculation Training (S.I.T)**, developed to reduce stress (see page 45).

The Cognitive Model, Surprise Surprise, Has **Strengths** and **Weaknesses**

Strengths:

1) The cognitive model offers a **useful** approach to disorders like depression and anorexia. This is because it considers the role of **thoughts** and **beliefs**, which are greatly involved in problems like depression.
2) Cognitive therapies have often **successfully treated** depression, anxiety, stress and eating disorders.

Weaknesses:

1) Faulty cognitions may simply be the **consequence** of a disorder rather than its cause. For example, depression may be caused by a chemical imbalance in the brain, which causes people to think very negatively.
2) Cognitive therapies may take a long **time** and be **costly**. They may be more effective when **combined** with other approaches, e.g. cognitive-behavioural methods.

Practice Questions

Q1 How may classical conditioning explain abnormal behaviour?

Q2 Give an example of how operant conditioning could explain behaviour.

Q3 Explain a criticism of the behaviourist model of abnormality.

Q4 Explain the ABC model of abnormality.

Q5 Describe what happens in cognitive therapy.

Exam Questions

Q1 Explain an assumption of the behaviourist approach to abnormality and give a criticism of this approach. [6 marks]

Q2 Outline the assumptions of the cognitive approach to the causes and treatment of abnormality. [6 marks]

I think I'm mentally ill, therefore I am...

What's a bit confusing is that all these theories make some sense — you read them and think, 'So that's what it's all about, I get it now!' But then you read the next one and think the same thing... A second later you realise they can't both be true. Well, they can sort of both be true, but just not universally.

The Behaviourist Approach

This bit's for Edexcel, so ignore it if you're not Edexcel.

Behaviourism tries to understand how we learn behaviour — and from that how we can deal with abnormal behaviour.

Behaviourism is Also Known as '**Learning Theory**'

1) Behaviourism ('**learning theory**') started in America in the early 1900s, mainly through the ideas of **John Watson**.
2) Watson felt that earlier psychological research wasn't as scientific as it should be.
3) For example, Wilhelm Wundt tried to study consciousness using **introspection**. This is about analysing your own experiences. However, there's no way of finding out whether what a person said is true or not, so introspection can never be properly scientific.
4) Watson came up with some assumptions on which to base a **scientific** approach to psychology.

There are **Three** Main **Assumptions** of Behaviourism

Remember — this is theory, not fact.

1) **Nearly all behaviour is learnt.**
The only exceptions are a few inborn **reflexes** (e.g. blinking when we get dirt in our eyes) and a few inborn **instincts** (e.g. instinctively running when in some types of danger).
However, evidence now shows that **genetics** can influence psychological features, e.g. genetics may contribute to the cause of schizophrenia. Behaviourism still claims, though, that learning, and not genetics, is the cause of the **majority** of behaviours, even if some vague genetic causes can be found.

2) **Animals and humans learn in the same ways.**
Humans can do much more complex things than other animals, but the **principles** by which we learn are the **same**. So, we learn to drive a car through the same principles as a cat learns to use a cat-flap. These principles are based on the idea that we can form **stimulus-response associations** between stimuli and our actions.
However, although we may both use conditioning, humans can be said to use other forms of learning as well, such as **social learning** (see pages 72-73).

3) **The 'mind' is irrelevant.**
We can't directly observe and measure a person's thinking.
So we can only obtain **testable scientific data** by studying behaviour.
However, although **cognitive abilities** cannot be directly, scientifically measured, they may give a more complete explanation of behaviour — as shown by **Social Learning Theory** (see pages 72-73).

'All learnt through stimulus-response associations'. Pretty impressive, but does beg the question 'why?'

The **Environment** and **Learning** are Important in Behaviourism

The environment's important...
The **nature-nurture debate** is the question of whether our characteristics are caused by genetic influences ('nature') or by our environment and learning experiences ('nurture'). Behaviourists are on the **nurture** side of the debate. They claim that the **environment** is the main, if not the only, cause of our behaviour.

...and learning's important...
If all our behaviour is due to the environment, it must be **learnt** (as opposed to being inborn). This idea also makes sense in terms of **Darwin's** theory of **evolution**. This claims that the characteristics which evolve are those that make us '**fitter**' to survive in our environment, and so more likely to pass on the genes which cause these features. An animal that is able to **learn** from the environment will be more able to adapt to it, and so more likely to survive and pass on its genes.

The Behaviourist Approach

*Behaviourists Use Their **Assumptions** to Design **Research Methods***

The research methods used by the behaviourists follow directly from their **assumptions**, as follows:

1 — Nearly all behaviour is learnt.
So, understanding the principles of **learning** is the main research goal.

2 — Animals and humans learn in the same ways.
Animals can be used as research subjects because what is true for them should also be true for humans. Using animals has **practical advantages**, e.g. they are easy to keep, in many circumstances don't know they are being studied and so behave 'naturally', and procedures can be used with them which would be illegal with humans (e.g. giving electric shocks).

3 — The 'mind' is irrelevant.
Behaviourists only observe **quantifiable behaviour** — e.g. how many times a lever is pressed, how long it takes to solve a puzzle. Typical research therefore involves **laboratory experiments** on animals, to see how they learn.

*Behaviourist Research Has Provided Great **Insights** Into Learning*

1) **Pavlov's research on classical conditioning.** Pavlov wasn't a behaviourist, but his work was useful to them. He showed how dogs could be '**conditioned**' to produce a reflexive response (e.g. salivation) to a stimulus that would not normally trigger that response (e.g. a bell). Pavlov **precisely measured** how much saliva his dogs produced and showed that it increased each time the bell was rung before feeding (see page 30).

2) **Skinner's research on operant conditioning.** Skinner placed rats into boxes containing a lever. He varied the **consequence** of pressing the lever. The consequence was either something good (a reinforcement, e.g. food) or something bad (a punishment, e.g. an electric shock). This influenced whether or not the lever was pushed again. This showed that the rats learnt from the consequences of their actions (see page 30).

3) **Human research**. Some experiments were done on humans, e.g. Watson and Rayner's experiment on '**Little Albert**' (see page 66). This experiment was extremely **unethical**, but it showed how easily a phobia can develop.

Comment — Behaviourists are often criticised for focusing research on animals.
Research on humans shows things that animal research hasn't:
e.g. that our **genes** influence our behaviour, that we can **learn in ways other than conditioning** and that **mental, cognitive processes are relevant** to understanding behaviour.

Practice Questions

Q1 Who pioneered behaviourism?

Q2 Outline the assumptions of behaviourism.

Q3 Explain whether behaviourists support the nature or nurture side of the nature-nurture debate.

Q4 Why may the assumptions of behaviourism be questioned?

Exam Questions

Q1 Describe two assumptions of behaviourism. [6 marks]

Q2 Describe research methods used by behaviourists. [6 marks]

Learn like a dolphin — lob live fish in the air and catch them in your mouth...

The behaviourist assumption is that we learn like animals... so you can study the way animals learn and apply the results to people. I'm not so sure that we learn exactly like animals, but then I suppose the basic principles are the same. Whether you like the idea or not, you need to understand the assumptions and how behaviourist research methods follow from them.

Behaviourist Therapy

Edexcel only again. Behaviourists developed therapies based on the findings of their research. You've got to know it all.

Learning Theory Assumes Behaviour is Shaped Through Conditioning

Learning theory assumes that virtually all behaviour is learnt, so the principles of conditioning should explain most things.

Skinner (1971) claimed that we are constantly being conditioned by the environment. So '**free will**' is an illusion — our behaviours are shaped by the desire to obtain reinforcement (eat the cake) and avoid punishment (dodge the sick). He reckoned our patterns of behaviour are completely due to our individual '**reinforcement histories**'.

Classical Conditioning Can Be Used in Therapy

The principles of classical conditioning (see page 68) have been used in therapy to deliberately change behaviour.

Systematic desensitisation. This is a treatment for **phobias**.

1) First, the phobic person makes a 'fear hierarchy'. This is a list of feared events, showing what they fear least (e.g. seeing a picture of a spider) through to their most feared event (e.g. holding a spider).
2) When put in the situation of their least feared event, they are anxious.
3) Then they are encouraged to use a **relaxation** technique.
4) Relaxation and anxiety can't happen at the same time, so when they become relaxed and calm, they are no longer scared.
5) This is repeated until the feared event is only linked with relaxation.
6) This whole process is repeated until the end of the hierarchy is reached, and they are calm through their most feared event.

Aversion therapy.
This removes an undesired behaviour by associating it with **unpleasant feelings**. For example, alcoholics are given alcohol at the same time as a drug that naturally produces nausea. Nausea becomes a conditioned response to alcohol, so they should then feel no urge to drink, but instead feel sick at the idea of it.

Operant Conditioning Can Be Used in Therapy

Parents and teachers use operant conditioning without realising it. Whenever a child is praised (**reinforcement**) or told off (**punishment**), operant conditioning is happening. It has also been specially used as a treatment for some disorders.

Token economy. Ayllon and Azrin (1968) reported how operant conditioning was used to change the behaviour of psychiatric patients. **Tokens** were given to them whenever they behaved 'normally' or 'adaptively'. These tokens could then be exchanged for reinforcements such as sweets or TV watching. It was found that most patients, even schizophrenics, showed much more 'normal' behaviour.

Autism is a disorder involving extreme social skill impairment. Children show little or no interest in interacting with others, weak attachments and little language development. **Lovaas (1968)** gave autistic children reinforcement (e.g. chocolate) for any **pro-social** act (e.g. making eye contact, imitating a behaviour, making speech sounds). In time, they had to show more of these responses to get reinforcement. Much improvement in their social behaviour was seen.

There are Problems with Behaviour Change Through Conditioning

1) Evidence shows that behaviour change is possible through these therapies, but they do have **limitations**.
   - Systematic desensitisation cannot help with **severe** disorders.
   - Aversion therapy may only produce **short-term** improvement.
   - Operant conditioning therapies won't produce long-lasting change if the reinforcements aren't **maintained**.
   - Conditioning may not be able to change **genetic influences** on behaviour.
2) The therapies also raise **ethical issues** — they may be distressing (e.g. aversion therapy) or involve withholding things of value to later use as reinforcements (e.g. token economy), perhaps violating human rights.
3) **Deliberate attempts** at behaviour change raise ethical issues about **free will and choice**. There may not be such an issue if an individual wanted the behaviour change (e.g. curing a phobia), but there would be a problem if those in power used conditioning to make us behave in more '**socially desirable**' ways.
   This would reduce our free will. Also those in power might have biased views of what is 'socially desirable'.

Contemporary Issues

There's Debate Over Whether its Right to **Punish** and Whether it **Works**

Punishment is used to try and reduce undesirable behaviour.
Many people claim punishment to be very **effective**, but there are also criticisms:

1) It doesn't '**remove**' a behaviour, it only '**suppresses**' it — so an undesirable behaviour may still occur if someone thinks they won't be caught, especially if there's possible reinforcement (e.g. from stealing).
2) It tells us what not to do but doesn't suggest a more desirable **alternative**.
3) For punishment to work, it needs to be given **straight after** the undesirable behaviour, **every time** it occurs. So, punishing a child only when you find out what they've done might not be effective.

These criticisms could explain why punishment sometimes doesn't work, and why some criminals reoffend.

There are some issues with **smacking** as a punishment:

1) Children who are smacked may associate the unpleasant feelings with the **person** who punished them, and become frightened of them.
2) Children may **imitate** aggressive acts involved in punishment, and become **aggressive** themselves.
3) Causing **distress** to the child is an obvious ethical concern.

There's Also Debate About **Violence on TV**

There's debate over whether children **imitate** the violence they see on TV. (See also page 72.)
Various methods have been used to study this possibility, leading to mixed results:

1) **Correlational studies** — e.g. **Robinson and Bachman (1972)** found that children who watched more TV had **higher** levels of aggression. However, correlation **doesn't show cause and effect** — so these findings don't necessarily mean that TV caused aggression. It could be that a certain parenting style leads to both aggression and increased TV watching.
2) **Laboratory experiments** — e.g. **Bandura's 'Bobo doll' studies** (see pages 31 and 72). Children were found to imitate violence they saw on a video. However, these studies lack **ecological validity** (they were experiments, not real life) and were unlikely to show long-lasting changes.
3) **Natural experiments** — e.g. **Williams (1986)** found that when TV was introduced to a community previously without TV, children later showed significantly **more** aggression. However, full **control** of variables is not possible in 'real life' studies. Other things may also have caused the change in the children.

Conclusions...

The evidence is **mixed** and all methods have **limitations**. Overall, there appears to be a **link** between watching violent TV and behaving more violently. However, many things will affect how much a child is **influenced** by the violence they see on TV (e.g. their personality, home environment, peer group).

Practice Questions

Q1 Explain one way that behaviour change can occur through classical conditioning.
Q2 Explain one way that behaviour change can occur through operant conditioning.
Q3 Outline three limitations of the use of punishment.
Q4 What methods have been used to study the influence of violence on TV?

Exam Questions

Q1 Describe one example of the deliberate alteration of human behaviour using learning theory. [4 marks]

Q2 Explain how learning theory can help the understanding of one contemporary issue or debate. [10 marks]

Big Issue Sir, Big Issue Miss, Big Issue, Big Issuuuue....

There are so many big issues in psychology — smacking's a huge one. It's illegal in lots of countries, and maybe one day it will be here too. On the other hand, lots of people say it's important to teach children discipline and smacking is a key way to do this. You need to know some of the arguments for and against it.

Social Learning Theory

Edexcel and AQA A only... *Social learning theory is a development of the behaviourist theory which can be used to explain abnormality. The main difference is that social learning theory also takes into account social factors (big surprise).*

Social Learning Theory (SLT) Takes Account of Cognitive Processes

SLT developed in America during the 1950s. Like behaviourism, it accepts that humans can learn by classical and operant conditioning, but SLT emphasises that humans learn a lot by **observation** and **imitation** of role models (models). So social learning isn't just stimulus-response learning — **cognitive processes** are involved too.
For example, someone must pay **attention** and **perceive** what their role model does, **think** about the purpose of the behaviour they observe, and **remember** it to accurately **reproduce** it later (although this doesn't necessarily happen at a conscious level).

Various Factors Influence Social Learning

We don't imitate everything we see, so there must be some factors helping us decide what to copy and what to ignore.

1) The consequences of the model's actions have an important influence on us — this is **vicarious conditioning**. So if someone in your class asked the teacher for doughnuts, and then got them, you'd be likely to do the same. **Vicarious reinforcement** is when the model's actions have a desirable consequence — we are more likely to imitate the action. **Vicarious punishment** is when there was an undesirable outcome — we are then less likely to imitate.
2) The **characteristics of the role model** are also important. We are more likely to imitate models who we see have **desirable qualities** (e.g. power, status, talent) and also who are **similar** to us in important ways (e.g. people of the same gender or cultural group).

SLT Can Explain the Learning of Aggression

The idea is that **aggression** may be learnt by direct **conditioning**, e.g., if we find through trial and error that aggression can get us what we want (so the aggression is reinforced). However, we may also learn particular actions by watching role models. This was shown by Albert **Bandura**.

Bandura (1965) — observational learning of aggression

Method: Children watched a video of an adult being aggressive to a 'Bobo doll' (an inflatable toy doll).
They were in three groups, each seeing a different consequence of the aggression:
Group 1 saw the adult being praised (**reinforcement**).
Group 2 saw the adult being told off (**punishment**).
Group 3 saw a **neutral** ending (**no praise or punishment**).
Later, the children individually played with the doll.

Results: Group 2 (the ones who saw the adult being punished) were the **least aggressive** towards the doll.
However, there was little difference between groups 1 and 3.

Conclusion: If we see a model's actions having an unpleasant outcome, we are less likely to imitate them.
But seeing them get praise or no praise makes little difference.

Learn these comments about the Bandura experiment —

1) The children in group 2 (who saw the adult punished) may have paid less attention to the model. However, when they were later asked to imitate as many of the model's actions as they could remember, there was no difference between the three groups. So, they had all seen and remembered the same behaviours, but **vicarious punishment** (the adult role model being punished) had made group 2 less likely to imitate.
2) It is not known if there were any **long-lasting** effects from the learning or whether it was only **short-term**.
3) The children may not really have been aggressive — they may have thought that they were just playing with the doll in the **appropriate** way.
4) The study encouraged aggression in children — this could be an **ethical problem**.
5) **Summary:** There may be important **implications** from the study. Children may imitate aggression shown on TV if it is not seen to result in negative consequences. But there are (as ever) some problems with the study.

Social Learning Theory

*Studies of **Aggression in the Home** should be More Ecologically Valid*

In Bandura's 1965 'Bobo doll' study, the children only watched the model on film — so there wasn't any interaction. This may be relevant to children imitating violence on TV, but children may be more influenced by '**real life**' models, such as their parents.
Patterson et al produced evidence showing that children may imitate aggression observed in the home:

	Patterson et al (1989) — aggression and home environment
Method:	Families with at least one **very aggressive child** were compared with families without such a child. They were matched for family size, socio-economic status and other factors. Observations were made in the home and family members, peers and teachers were also surveyed.
Results:	Aggressive children were more likely to be from homes where **less affection** was shown, more **arguments** occurred and more **punishment** was used.
Conclusion:	The children may have become more aggressive by **imitating** the aggression of their parents.

Comment — The evidence is only **correlational**, so doesn't **prove** that aggression is learnt by modelling. There may be **genetic influences**. However, conditioning may help reduce violence in the home. For example, **Lore and Schultz (1993)** found that men arrested for beating their wives were less likely to beat them again.

*Social Learning Theory Has Been **Criticised***

1) SLT says that **reinforcement** is **not essential** for learning and that learning can happen just through observation. However, reinforcement is an important influence on whether or not we **perform** the behaviour. If we think we might be punished we are less likely to perform the behaviour (see that Bandura experiment on the opposite page). This means that the role of reinforcement is **underestimated** by SLT.
2) SLT neglects the influence of **genetics** and so supports the '**nurture**' side of the **nature-nurture debate**. But some behaviours may be more influenced by genes than learning. For example, in all cultures, aggression is more common in males than females. So it may be more linked to genetics than to learning. Males may have **evolved** to be more aggressive because this has helped them survive (e.g. by being better hunters or better at competing with other males).
3) There is **mixed evidence** that violence on TV will influence children.

Practice Questions

Q1 What type of learning is emphasised in SLT?
Q2 Explain what is meant by 'vicarious conditioning'.
Q3 Explain two limitations of the 'Bobo doll' study.
Q4 What does the study by Patterson et al show?

Exam Questions

Q1 Describe one example of social learning in humans. [6 marks]

Q2 Assess one strength and one limitation of the social learning approach. [6 marks]

For some quality social learning, watch 'Itchy and Scratchy'...

Big debate, this. Does watching violence on TV lead to kids being violent? It seems more likely that kids use their parents as role models than TV. But then would a kid who grew up watching 'Lethal, Gory, Alien Attack IV' grow up more violent than one who only watched Blue Peter? It's difficult to say one way or the other.

Psychodynamic Theories of Abnormality

This bit's just for Edexcel and AQA A again.
Psychodynamic theories like to explain abnormality by talking about unconscious causes — talk about abnormal...

Freud Developed The **Psychodynamic** Approach

'**Psycho**' refers to the mind and '**dynamic**' refers to change or activity.
So, this approach emphasises the **active nature** of mental processes and their role in shaping personality and behaviour.
This approach was developed by **Sigmund Freud** (1856-1939), in the late 1800s/early 1900s. It assumes:

1) Human behaviour has **unconscious causes** that we are not aware of.
2) From birth, humans have a need to fulfil basic biological **motivations** — for food, sleep, warmth etc.
3) **Childhood experiences** are a really important influence on the development of adult personality and psychological disorders.

Freud Said There Are Three **Levels of Consciousness**

Freud was interested in '**hysteria**', a disorder involving physical symptoms such as headaches, paralysis and blindness, but with no apparent physical cause. As his patients couldn't give any **conscious** reasons, Freud concluded they had an **unconscious** mind and that's where the cause of the hysteria was. He identified three levels of consciousness:

1) **Conscious**. This is what we are **aware** of at any given time, e.g. what we are seeing, hearing, smelling or thinking.
2) **Pre-conscious**. This is made up of **memories** that we can recall when want to, e.g. we can recall our address, phone number, childhood memories or what we did at the weekend.
3) **Unconscious**. This is made up of memories, desires and fears which cause us extreme anxiety and have therefore been '**repressed**' or forced out of conscious awareness. However, the unconscious still influences behaviour. For example, it causes 'Freudian slips' and influences the content of our dreams. This part of our mind can be accessed with the help of a **psychoanalyst**, using the methods that Freud developed (see the next page).

There Are Two **Instincts** That Motivate Our Behaviour

Freud claimed that from birth, two types of **instinct** motivate our behaviour.
The two instincts are in constant **conflict** with each other, and one may **dominate** in a person:

1) **The Life Instinct ('Eros').**
This is the need to fulfil basic biological needs, such as warmth, food or sleep.
However, Freud also claimed that infants have the need for **sexual pleasure**, i.e. they obtain pleasure through **erogenous zones** — parts of the body that are sensitive to stimulation. Although this does not involve mature sexual needs, Freud claimed that '**infantile sexuality**' is a major motivation as we progress through the stages of **psychosexual development** (see page 21).
The energy of the life instinct is called '**libido**'.
2) **The Death Instinct ('Thanatos').**
The death instinct involves the urge to be **aggressive** and **destructive** to others and/or ourselves. This causes violence, war and suicide.

Freud Reckoned **Early Experiences** Influence Development

1) Each stage of psychosexual development focuses on **obtaining pleasure** through that stage's erogenous zone.
2) How parents raise a child affects how much pleasure is obtained through that stage (e.g. how strict they are when potty training, and what type of role models they are).
3) If a child experiences a lot of **conflict** or **anxiety** during a stage of development it becomes '**fixated**' with that stage and will remain, to some extent, attached to that erogenous zone.
4) This experience is all **repressed into the unconscious**, but influences adult personality. Severe fixation could lead to a psychological **disorder**.

Psychodynamic Theories of Abnormality

Clinical Interviews and Symbol Analysis Reveal Unconscious Problems

Freud did **case studies** on each of his patients using several **methods** to reveal the **conflicts**, **fears** and **desires** buried in the patient's unconscious mind. These unconscious problems could then be faced, allowing the patient to understand and resolve them.

Clinical interviews and **symbol analysis** are the main methods of studying the unconscious mind:

1) **Clinical interviews.**
These are flexible, informal interviews allowing the analyst to explore issues most relevant to the patient. This may involve:
   a) **Free association**. This is where the patient is given a cue and then asked to say whatever comes into their mind, however silly or embarrassing. By analysing what a person does and doesn't talk about, the psychoanalyst can identify unconscious influences, e.g. I say 'revision', and you say 'night out'.
   b) **'Freudian slips'**. These occur when we do or say something that we consciously think are mistakes, but which really show our unconscious true feelings. An example given by Freud was how an MP once said 'the honourable member from Hell' when he really meant 'from Hull'. You get the idea.

2) **Analysis of symbols in dreams and culture.**
Freud believed that the unconscious can reveal itself in the form of symbols. They allow the unconscious fears, desires and conflicts to show themselves or be 'fulfilled'. However we don't become consciously aware of them, and therefore don't feel anxious or guilty:
   a) **Dream analysis**. Freud claimed that dreams involve '**disguised wish fulfilment**'. This means that we use them to 'play out' our repressed wishes — ones which would produce guilt or anxiety if we were consciously aware of them. The images we can recall are the '**manifest content**' (the superficial stuff), but the analyst can interpret the '**latent content**' — the true meaning.
   b) **Culture**. Freud claimed that cultural art, theatre and literature are 'manifest content' which symbolically represents the 'latent content' of universal human needs and conflicts. Hmmm... all that sex and violence on TV...

Comment — All these methods depend on the interpretations of the analyst, so, they are **subjective** and **not truly scientific**. Having said that, they still may be useful.

Practice Questions

Q1 Explain the difference between the 'pre-conscious' and the 'unconscious'.

Q2 Why is early experience important, according to the psychodynamic approach?

Q3 What happens in 'free association'?

Q4 What is the difference between 'manifest content' and 'latent content'?

Exam Questions

Q1 Describe one assumption of the psychodynamic approach. [6 marks]

Q2 Describe one advantage and one disadvantage of the methods used in the psychodynamic approach. [6 marks]

My favourite subject is (insert Freudian slip here)... Oops — I mean art...

If you've ever called your teacher Mum, or boyfriend Dad, you probably just thought it was a simple mistake. According to psychodynamic theory, you're actually showing your deep felt desires. Remember it's not just what you say, but what you think about and what you dream that shows your unconscious mind peeking through — hands up who's scared now.

Psychodynamic Theories of Abnormality

Just Edexcel again.

Freud's theory, like most theories, had a lot of problems. So other people came up with their own psychodynamic theories. Which means you have to learn more stuff — great.

There Are Many **Problems** With Freud's Theory

1) A major problem with Freud's work is that it **can't be tested**. This is because most activity takes place in the unconscious mind, which we have little access to.
2) So we **can't prove** Freud's theories and we **can't disprove** them either.
3) Freud developed his theories based on a small number of case studies and observations about his own family and his childhood. The case studies were mostly of middle-class women. This small sample is very **unrepresentative**.
4) The techniques used (such as dream interpretation) are **subjective** so they are vulnerable to personal bias and inconsistency. They're hardly strict lab conditions.

Freud Wasn't the **Only** Psychodynamic Theorist

Erikson, **Jung** and **Klein** followed in Freud's psychodynamic way of thinking, but developed their own psychodynamic theories.

Erikson's theory had eight stages.

1) Erikson also suggested a developmental approach. His theory consisted of **eight psychosocial stages**.
2) Each stage gives us an opportunity to **develop** qualities that will influence our relationships with others and our success in life.
3) The theory assumes that all of our progressions through life are the **same** and that we all want the same things like marriage, a family and an occupation at the same points.
4) But this idea that we are all the same makes it difficult to apply the theory to **individuals**.

Key point: Erikson sees personality as continuing to **develop** in **adulthood** whereas Freud doesn't.

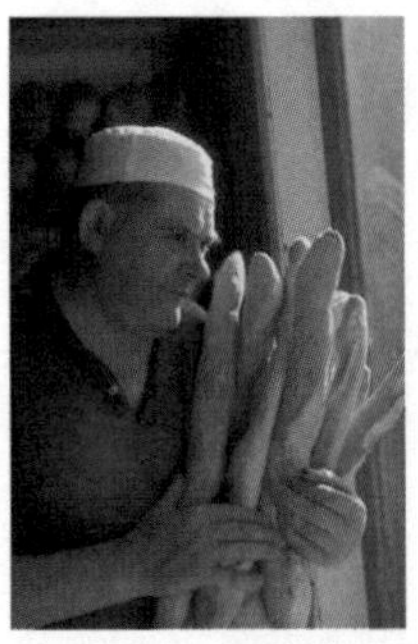

Freud tried to explain Billy's obsession with French bread. It wasn't pretty...

Jung said personality has three parts.

1) Jung suggested that the personality, which he called the **psyche**, is made up of **three parts** and is **complete** from birth.
2) A person has to **strengthen** their psyche to prevent the parts from breaking away from each other.

Key point: Unlike Freud, Jung emphasised **social influences** and suggested that part of the psyche is made up of **cultural** information inherited from our ancestors.

Klein's theory was a bit different.

1) Klein focused on interpreting children's **play** to find out about underlying fears and desires.
2) For example, Klein suggested that if a child didn't have a **nurturing** relationship with their carer they might create an **imaginary world** with fantasy objects to compensate.

Psychodynamic Theories of Abnormality

Freud Mainly Based His Theories on **Case Studies**

As I've said before, Freud based much of his psychodynamic theory on a small number of case studies of his patients:

	Freud's case studies
Little Hans (1905):	Although much of Freud's theory relates to childhood, Little Hans (1905) was his only case study of a child. Little Hans was a five-year-old boy with a phobia of being bitten by a **horse**. Freud interpreted his fear as a representation of his fear of his **father**. According to Freud, Little Hans was afraid of his father because at this stage, the male child develops the **Oedipus complex**, which means he is sexually attracted to his mother and sees his father as competition.
There's proper detail on page 21	
Dora (1900):	Dora was a young woman with symptoms of **hysteria**. Freud attributed these symptoms to anxiety caused by her troubled family, and her sexual attraction towards her father's mistress. Freud said she used **defence mechanisms** to avoid having to deal with her situation and feelings, which in turn were causing her distress.
'Rat-man' (1909):	The 'rat-man' was a man with **obsessive** thoughts. He had been sexually abused by his father as a child, and later in life still feared his father who had been dead for many years. Freud interpreted the obsessive thoughts as the ego's way of **reducing** the **anxiety** caused by the differing needs of the id and superego (see page 2). He said other events in the rat-man's life such as new relationships and time in the military had triggered the onset of symptoms.

The Psychodynamic Approach Can be Used to Explain **Unplanned Pregnancy**

Harris and Campbell (1999) compared a group of women who had experienced unplanned pregnancies with a group who had planned pregnancies. They found that the group with unplanned pregnancies were significantly more likely to have **gained** something extra from parenthood, e.g.

1) Giving up an unsatisfactory job.
2) Maintaining an unstable relationship, or increasing power in one.
3) Ending rifts with a partner or parents.
4) Keeping up with friends and family who already had children.

A **psychodynamic explanation** is that unconsciously, the women were **motivated** by these gains to try and become pregnant. They were not consciously aware of their motivations, so finding out they were pregnant was still distressing. This study supports Freud's suggestion that we do not understand why we behave in certain ways because the cause is hidden from our conscious thought.

Practice Questions

Q1 Make one evaluation comment about Freud's psychodynamic theory.

Q2 Explain how Jung's theory differs from Freud's.

Q3 How did Freud explain the rat-man's obsessions?

Q4 What type of gains were women able to make from pregnancy as shown in Harris and Campbell's study?

Exam Questions

Q1 Compare two different psychodynamic theories. [6 marks]

Q2 Describe and evaluate how two of Freud's case studies support his theory. [8 marks]

*I'm the rat-man — shibby dibby dibby dibby doo bop bop**

*I know I've said it before, but I'm not convinced by Freud's ideas. A lot of what he said makes sense — I'm sure traumatic childhood events **will** lead to later issues, and dreams probably **do** symbolise some sort of inner conflict. It's just that I like my theories to be testable and scientific. We're never going to be able to prove Freud's ideas, and that just makes me mad.*

*This gag refers to the early 90s hit, 'I'm the Scat Man', by the thankfully little known Scat Man John. If you don't know his work I suggest you be grateful.

Psychodynamic Theories of Abnormality

Another two pages just for Edexcel.
Freud really had a good go at sorting mental health out with his theories. He developed quite an effective therapy too. Whether it works because his theory is right, or just because it's therapeutic to talk, well that's up to you...

The Psychodynamic Approach Can Explain **Mental Health Problems**

Several different types of mental illness (including anxiety, depression, eating disorders and schizophrenia) can be explained using a psychodynamic approach.

1) The psychodynamic perspective focuses on **unconscious conflicts** starting in early childhood. That's how it tries to deal with mental health problems.
2) Early experiences are seen as very influential, so therapists look for examples of **childhood trauma** to explain adult disorders.
3) Treatment involves bringing the unconscious conflict into the **conscious mind** to remove the **anxiety** that has been created, e.g. remembering how a trauma felt and talking about it.

Freud Said **Repression** and **Regression** Can Cause **Depression**

Repression is where distressing information is pushed out of the conscious mind into the unconscious mind — it's a way of coping with it. There are **two possible psychodynamic explanations** for depression, repression or regression:

Explanation 1

1) Negative, distressing memories and information are pushed into the unconscious mind to protect the conscious. This is **repression**.
2) This negativity and distress is **turned inwards** and aimed at the **self**.
3) An example might be a woman whose husband cheats on her:
   She represses her feelings about this and turns the hostility she feels towards him onto herself.
   She then becomes depressed, thinking that if she were a better person he would have stayed faithful.
4) Feelings of **low self-esteem** are common in depressed people, which gives this theory some support.

Explanation 2

1) People have strong reactions to **loss** because it reminds them of childhood experiences of loss.
2) Adult losses in employment, friendships and relationships trigger **regression**.
3) The depressed person will revert back to a similar childhood experience of loss, and experience the feelings of **dependency** and **helplessness** that they originally felt at that stage of development.
4) Feelings of a lack of control over life and an inability to help themselves are **symptoms** of depression, which lends this theory support — children have little control over their lives and can't help themselves.

Anxiety Can Also Be Explained From a Psychodynamic Perspective

Anxiety is a mental health problem characterised by feelings of stress, fear and apprehension that are **out of proportion** to the threat involved. Three anxiety-related disorders can be explained using psychodynamic theories:

General anxiety disorder (GAD) can be explained by the **conflict** between the **id** and the **superego** in the unconscious mind. This conflict results in general feelings of anxiety in the conscious mind, which is troubling for the person involved as they are **unaware** of the underlying conflict.

Phobias can be explained using the defence mechanism of **displacement**.
Displacement means **redirecting** emotions from their source to another object or person.
For example, **Little Hans** was afraid of his father but it wasn't appropriate for him to show this fear. So he displaced the fear of his father onto horses as an outlet for his feelings.

Obsessive-compulsive disorder is explained through **overly strict toilet-training** — the person is stuck in the anal stage. So, someone might be afraid of soiling themselves, which appears as an obsession about being clean. This could result in compulsive washing.

Psychodynamic Theories of Abnormality

Psychoanalytic Therapies have been Shown to Work

See page 75 for what psychoanalytic therapies actually consist of.

There was originally debate over the **effectiveness** of psychoanalytic therapies. However, they have been found to be just as effective as other therapies, for example:

Smith et al (1980) — effectiveness of therapies

475 studies were compared, looking at the **effectiveness** of a range of therapies, including psychoanalytical types.

They found that those **receiving treatment** had better outcomes than **80%** of those who didn't receive treatment. They suggested that psychoanalytical treatments generally work just as well as other types such as client-centred therapy and behavioural therapies.
However, they believed that effectiveness did depend on the **individual** and **disorder** involved.

Psychoanalytic therapy doesn't work for everyone.

Psychoanalytic Therapies Have a Number of Criticisms

Despite finding psychoanalytic therapies to be **effective**, there are a number of **problems**:

1) The effectiveness of the therapy depends on the **disorder** — schizophrenia doesn't respond well to psychoanalytical therapy, but disorders such as anxiety and depression often do.
2) Freud said himself that psychoanalytical therapy would **only** work if the person was **willing to change**, **appreciated** that they had a problem and entered into treatment **voluntarily**.
3) Therapists find it hard to know when to **end** treatment, as the symptoms may have disappeared, but could easily return next time there's a problem.
4) It's hard for the therapist to know whether improvement is actually happening in the person's **everyday life**.
5) At the beginning of therapy, many people **overestimate** their problems to justify needing therapy. At the end, they **underestimate** them to feel like improvement has occurred, to justify the time and expense of therapy. This is the **hello-goodbye effect** — it makes improvement look greater than it really is.

Practice Questions

Q1 Name three mental health problems that can be explained using a psychodynamic approach.

Q2 What is meant by repression?

Q3 What is meant by displacement?

Q4 What is the function of obsessive thoughts in the psychodynamic approach to obsessive-compulsive disorder?

Q5 Name a mental health disorder that does not respond well to psychoanalytic therapy.

Q6 What is meant by the hello-goodbye effect in therapy?

Exam Questions

Q1 Describe how depression can be explained using a psychodynamic approach. [5 marks]

Q2 Discuss issues in evaluating the effectiveness of psychoanalytic therapies. [5 marks]

One minute you like washing — next you're in love with your mother...

Psychoanalytic therapy can actually work. But that doesn't mean all of Freud's theories are right. I mean, who wouldn't feel a bit better if they got to lie on a couch and talk about themselves for an hour three times a week... And another thing, seeing as Freud suggested a reason for schizophrenia, you'd think his therapy would have some sort of effect... But no.

Eating Disorders

You can ignore these pages if you're doing OCR or Edexcel.
Eating disorders are examples of psychological abnormalities. These pages show how different theories deal with them.

***Anorexia Nervosa** is an Eating Disorder*

There are four main characteristics of anorexia:

1) **Anxiety** about getting fat, even when very underweight.
2) A **distorted body image** — **feeling fat**, even when they are very thin.
3) **Body weight** is less than 85% of what it should be for the person's age, height and build.
4) Female sufferers have further problems — their **periods stop**, or never start, depending on their age. The absence of **three or more** consecutive periods can indicate anorexia.

*There are Loads of Suggested **Causes** for Anorexia*

***Genetic Factors** Have Been Suggested*

Holland et al investigated the possibility of **genetics** playing a part in anorexia:

	Holland et al (1988) — genetic vulnerability to anorexia nervosa.
Method:	The participants were 45 sets of twins where at least one twin had had anorexia. They were interviewed on eating habits, body satisfaction and eating disorders in relatives.
Results:	In identical twins, **56%** both suffered from anorexia, whereas in non-identical twins, **5%** were both sufferers. There was also significantly more anorexia in the twins' **relatives** than in the normal population.
Conclusion:	There may be a **genetic vulnerability** for anorexia nervosa, which is triggered by environmental conditions.
Evaluation:	The results could perhaps be explained by the **environment** instead of genetics — maybe identical twins are treated more similarly than non-identical twins. It is also possible that twins **imitate** each other's behaviour, which might be more common in identical twins.

***Biochemical Factors** Have Been Suggested*

1) **Fava et al (1989)** suggested a link between anorexia and increase in the levels of the neurotransmitters **serotonin** and **noradrenaline**.
2) **Antidepressants** work on people with eating disorders, suggesting an underlying **biochemical** problem.

But... It has been suggested that biochemical changes are actually a **consequence** of self-starvation, rather than a cause of it. **Fichter and Pirke (1995)** starved normal individuals and found changes in neurotransmitter and hormone levels, thus suggesting that they are a consequence, not a cause.

***Brain Abnormalities** Have Been Suggested*

1) Parts of the **hypothalamus** control the release of hormones that regulate **hunger**.
2) **Garfinkel and Garner (1982)** suggested that anorexics have disturbed functioning in the hypothalamus.

But... This disturbed functioning may be a **consequence** rather than a cause of the anorexia. Also, **post-mortems** have not shown any problems or lesions in this area.

***Psychological Factors** Have Been Suggested*

1) Freud's **psychodynamic theory** suggests that anorexics stop eating in order to avoid the adult body shape and so remain pre-pubescent. In this way, they can avoid the anxieties related to adulthood and sexual maturity.
2) **Bruch (1980)** suggested a psychodynamic approach based on **poor parenting**. If the child's signals are never properly responded to, the child never feels in control. Anorexia is a way of exerting control over his/her life.
3) Anorexia can be explained through **classical conditioning**. Eating might become associated with anxiety, as eating too much leads to unattractiveness. So losing weight reduces anxiety. It could also be **operant conditioning** — there might be reinforcement in the form of more attention for being slimmer.
4) The **cognitive approach** blames anorexia on **faulty belief systems** — simply not 'seeing' the huge weight loss.
5) **Becker (1999)** interviewed Fijians 3 years after they started receiving TV. She found that there was a strong increase in teenage girls who thought they were too fat. There was also an increase in eating disorders which she believed were due to the prevalence of **western media images**, linking beauty with slimness.

Eating Disorders

***Bulimia Nervosa** is Also an Eating Disorder*

There are **four main characteristics** of bulimia:

1) The sufferer will **binge eat** — eating excessively without self-control (e.g. eating ten bars of chocolate non-stop).
2) The sufferer then tries to prevent weight gain by certain unhealthy behaviours, e.g. **self-induced vomiting**, **excessive exercise**, **laxative use**, **missing meals**.
3) They will **evaluate** themselves excessively on their **body image.**
4) The **binge-purging** behaviour will happen at least **twice a week** or more, over a three month period.

Bulimia is a **different condition** from anorexia — bingeing and purging are not the same as starving.

*There are also Loads of Suggested **Causes** for Bulimia*

***Biological Factors** Have Been Suggested*

1) Bulimia has been linked to **low serotonin** levels (as opposed to high levels in anorexia). Being the opposite to levels in anorexics makes sense seeing as anorexics starve themselves and bulimics **binge**.
2) Eating lots of carbohydrate-rich, starchy foods can improve the **mood** of people with **low serotonin** levels. But, **Barlow and Durand (1995)** found that when bulimics binge, they did not focus specifically on carbohydrate-rich foods.
3) There might be a genetic link — **Kendler et al (1991)** carried out a twin-study and found that when one twin was bulimic, the other twin was also bulimic in **23%** of identical twins, and **9%** of non-identical twins.

***Psychological Factors** Have Been Suggested*

1) The **behaviourist approach** suggests that bingeing is reinforcing because it provides a sense of indulgence. However, it causes anxiety which purging then reduces, so both bingeing and purging are **reinforced**.
2) A **cognitive theory** suggests that people with bulimia tend to **overestimate** their actual body size and want their body to be smaller than most people do. This is **distorted thinking** and **cognitive bias**.
3) The **psychodynamic theory** suggests that bulimia may be a result of repressed **childhood abuse**. Bulimia is therefore a way of both **punishing** the body and expressing **self-disgust**.
4) **Ruderman's (1986) disinhibition hypothesis** is about losing restraint. If bulimics feel they've overeaten, they think they've done the damage so they may as well carry on eating, and so binge — they've lost control. Afterwards, they feel guilt and disgust and so to get control back, they purge the food from their bodies.

Practice Questions

Q1 List four characteristics of anorexia nervosa.

Q2 Describe the findings of Holland et al.

Q3 Explain Freud's theory of anorexia.

Q4 List four characteristics of bulimia nervosa.

Q5 What is the disinhibition hypothesis?

Exam Questions

Q1 Critically evaluate biological explanations for anorexia nervosa. [18 marks]

Q2 Critically evaluate biological and psychological explanations for bulimia nervosa. [18 marks]

Every branch of psychology has a different explanation — great...

Anorexia and bulimia are very serious disorders. If untreated, anorexics can eventually starve themselves to death. We all want to look good, and a lot of us want to be thinner, but that doesn't mean there's anything wrong with us. It's when things get out of hand, when thoughts and feelings get too extreme and we start risking our health that it's wrong.

Multiple Personality Disorder

Right, these are for OCR only. Do what you want with them if you're AQA or Edexcel.
This is a scary topic. Imagine if one day you woke up with no memory of the previous night, but everyone said you were acting like a different person... but you'd not had a drop to drink...

Multiple Personality Disorder (MPD) is Very Rare

1) **Multiple personality disorder**, or **dissociative identity disorder** (DID) is where a person develops different personalities (no surprise there then).
2) These different personalities may have different memories, behaviours, attitudes and cognitive functioning, and may or may not be aware of each other.
3) But there has been debate over whether such a condition actually **exists**. Having said that, now people generally believe that it does, and that it is a consequence of **extreme abuse** in childhood.
4) It's suggested that a **dissociation** (a lack of **connection**) happens as a form of **mental escape** from trauma. This will produce changes in memory and perhaps if this happens often, the person's whole sense of history and identity will change.

The **clinical characteristics** of MPD include:

1) The person is **unable to recall personal information** which would not normally be forgotten.
2) Two or more **distinct personalities** exist, each with their own perceptions of the environment and themselves.
3) These personalities take turns at **controlling** the behaviour of the person.
4) The disturbance is **not due** to other physiological effects, such as alcohol abuse or epilepsy.

Eve White Was the First Convincing Account of MPD

Yeah, I know this looks bad, but it's actually quite interesting. Actually, I don't know why I'm hyping it up — you've got to learn it whether it's as dull as Darius and David Gray all rolled into one, or not.

OCR Core Study

Thigpen and Cleckly (1954) — case study of Eve White

Eve White's real name was Christine Sizemore. She was a 25-year-old married woman, who after suffering from **headaches**, **blackouts** and **memory loss**, was referred to a psychiatrist.

Her psychiatrist received a letter with the final lines written in a different handwriting and tone. Eve White said she had started a letter but not finished it. In a therapy session, she asked if hearing voices was a sign of insanity. Then she put her hands to her head as if in pain — another personality who called herself **'Eve Black'** appeared. Eve White was **not aware** of Eve Black until informed, but Eve Black was **aware** and critical of Eve White.

A number of Eve's **life events** suggested that she was suffering from **MPD**:
Eve White recalled being punished for things she didn't remember doing in childhood.
Her parents confirmed this. Eve Black claimed responsibility for many childhood pranks.
Additionally, Eve Black claimed no knowledge of Eve White's husband and child. She claimed to be married to someone else, who beat her for not having sex with him — a husband who Eve White claimed no knowledge of. A relative revealed that there had been a previous marriage, and later, Eve Black admitted that this had been a time when she was in control, not Eve White.

Psychometric tests revealed the extent of the two personalities' differences:
Eve White had a **slightly higher IQ** and **memory** function in tests. Eve White was found to be serious, anxious, conscientious and emotionally **repressed**.
Eve Black, by comparison, was hedonistic, shallow, irresponsible, less anxious, lacked compassion and often **regressed** to childlike behaviour. Only Eve White could be hypnotised and was thought to be the **dominant** personality. 'Black' was Eve White's maiden name, which suggested that Eve Black was not a different personality as such, but the same personality at an earlier stage of life, perhaps brought about by a desire to return to this earlier, more irresponsible time of life.

During the progress of therapy, improvements seemed to occur. Eve White stopped having headaches and blackouts and hearing voices. Eve Black also caused less trouble, although still acted quite irresponsibly. Later, a third personality, **Jane**, appeared who was more mature, capable and interesting than Eve White, yet lacked Eve Black's faults. Jane was seen as a compromise between the two previous personalities. In the following years, over 20 different personalities appeared. The final one was **Mrs Christine Sizemore** (her real name), who said she had **assimilated** her different selves.

Multiple Personality Disorder

There is Debate Over Whether Some MPD Cases are **Genuine**

1) At the time of Thigpen and Cleckly's case study, **very few** cases of MPD had been reported.
2) Today, up to **2%** of the American population are believed to have MPD, mostly women.
3) A rash of reported cases followed a popular book and film called **Sybil** about a case of MPD.
4) It has been suggested that this book led to a trend among therapists to **inadvertently suggest** that their patients were developing symptoms of MPD.
5) People now sometimes use MPD as a **defence** for committing crimes, claiming they did not do the crimes, another personality did. It would be easy to **fake** a case of MPD — little more than good acting skills would be required.
6) However, even if this trend in therapists once existed, and faking now occurs, these are not reasons to dispute that the condition **does exist**.

Case Studies Can Be **Unreliable**

There are a number of weaknesses of the Eve White case study:

1) The case study was reliant on **interviews**, so we have lots of 'rich' information that wouldn't be available through any other method.

BUT

2) Only one individual was studied, so it can't tell us anything about general trends in people, only about one person's individual **quirks**.
3) Case studies are more likely to be **retrospective**, relying on personal accounts from memory, which can be **biased**.
4) Case studies also suffer the possibility of **biased** information through the individual trying to **impress** the therapist, or say what they think he/she **wants to hear**.
5) Case studies are also likely to become **biased** because of the **therapist** or interviewer — they might only record what they want to hear, miss out important information, or skew the information to fit with their diagnosis or expectations.

Since watching *Many Limbed Dancing People*, everyone wanted to get in on the action.

Watch *The Three Faces of Eve* about Eve White, and watch *Sybil*... but don't watch *Me, Myself and Irene* — it's rubbish.

Practice Questions

Q1 What are the clinical characteristics of MPD?

Q2 What is DID?

Q3 Who studied Eve White?

Q4 Which film is thought to have led to increased diagnosis of MPD?

Q5 List four criticisms of case studies as a research method.

Exam Questions

Q1 Critically evaluate Thigpen and Cleckly's 'Eve White' study of MPD. [8 marks]

Q2 Does MPD really exist? Discuss the evidence for and against. [12 marks]

The best thing about me is there's so many of me...

A common misconception about MPD is that it leads to the typical mental illness stereotype of talking to yourself. It's not that there's different people inside you, all wanting to argue and shout at once, it's that different aspects of the personality arise independently and are sometimes unaware of each other — not that that makes anything less confusing.

Cultural Variations in Behaviour & Experience

These pages are for OCR only, and nobody else.
We're not all the same, I hope you're grasping that now — and another thing that affects behaviour is cultural background.

*Different **Cultural Groups** May Have Different Levels of **Self-Esteem***

1) **Self-identity** is the sense you have of **who you are** and the things that are special to you. So you know what you look like and that you like playing sport, for example.
2) **Self-esteem** is how highly you think of yourself — it's the **value** you attach to your self-identity. So if you feel that it's important to do well at something, or belong to a particular group, but you don't, this could make you **feel bad** about **yourself** and **lower** your self-esteem.
3) People **identify** with the **groups** they belong to, which has an impact on **self-esteem**. Therefore feeling that your social group is not looked upon highly will often lead to low self-esteem.
4) This is particularly relevant with **cultural groups**:

> **Clark and Clark (1939)** found that black children in the USA preferred to play with white dolls, claiming that the black doll on offer didn't look as good.
> They mostly correctly identified their own race and the race of the doll (although black children with a lighter skin tone were more likely to identify themselves as white).
> This study suggests that, at the time, many black children had **negative attitudes** about their own race.

***Hraba and Grant (1970)** Studied Racial Preference and Identification*

Ah great... a load more about an experiment for you to learn.

OCR Core Study

Hraba and Grant (1970) — racial preference and identification

Method: 160 black and white children from schools in Nebraska, USA, aged between 4 and 8, were interviewed. There were two black and two white dolls used.
The children were given instructions, such as 'Give me.......:
1) the doll that you want to play with, 2) the nice doll, 3) the doll that looks bad, 4) the doll that is a nice colour, 5) the doll that looks like a white child, 6) the doll that looks like a 'coloured' child, 7) the doll that looks like a 'negro' child, 8) the doll that looks like you'.
The first 4 instructions were to measure **racial preference**, instructions 5-7 were to measure **racial awareness**, and the last instruction was to measure **racial self-identification**.
The children (and their teachers) were also asked to name and identify their best friend and their best friend's race. This was to measure the way racial preference affects behaviour (such as choosing friends).

Results: In **racial preference** (1-4), black and white children generally preferred the doll belonging to their **own race**. This tendency increased with age.
In **racial awareness** (5-7), they found that over **85%** of the children correctly identified the race of the dolls. The older the children got, the more accurate their identification was.
In **racial self-identification** (8), they found that **15%** of the black children with lighter skin identified themselves as white (which is considerably less than in Clark and Clark's study).
The race of the interviewer had no effect, and there was no relationship between the choice of doll and the race of their best friend.

Conclusion: The **social changes** in the USA that took place between Clark and Clark's study in 1939 and this one in 1970 may be the reason behind these changes in black children's racial preference and racial self-identification. For example, more positive black role models, positive inter-racial contact and positive racial attitudes in the media and general public will have led to black children's more positive attitudes about their own race.

Evaluation: 1) The study assumes that doll preference is the same as racial preference. However, the lack of relationship between doll preference and friend choice suggests this might not be justified. **Friend choice** is more complicated than **doll choice**. A child may choose a doll simply on colour, but friends may be chosen for a number of different reasons.
2) This study highlights how research can become **out of date** fairly quickly.
Perhaps there are many other studies where results would be different if they were repeated today.

Cultural Variations in Behaviour & Experience

Social Changes *Affect Discrimination and Prejudice*

Prejudice is a set of fixed ideas, beliefs and opinions — about a group of people, for example. Prejudice is often used to justify **discrimination**. Normally, this prejudice will be a **negative attitude** about a particular group of people.

There has been a lot of prejudice and discrimination in history, and a lot still exists today.
Social changes, however, mean that many parts of the world, are becoming gradually less prejudiced, and much more integrated.

Some of the changes that have happened in the US since Clark and Clark's study include:

1954: **Segregation** in US state schools was **banned**.

1955: Black people in Montgomery, Alabama, **boycotted** public buses after a black woman was arrested for not giving up her seat to a white person.

1956: The boycott worked and buses in Montgomery **stopped segregation**.

1961: '**Freedom rides**' occurred where black and white people from northern US states travelled through the **southern states** to challenge segregation that was still in force there.

1963: '**March on Washington**' was a peaceful mass protest — it tried to increase support for new civil rights legislation. This is where Martin Luther King made his 'I have a dream' speech.

1964: President Johnson signed the **Civil Rights Act**.

1965: President Johnson signed the **Voting Rights Act**.

1978: The US Supreme Court **outlawed racial quotas**, meaning that employers and courses no longer had to take a certain proportion of people from ethnic minorities.
Instead, people were to be offered jobs entirely on the basis of merit.

1989: Douglas Wilder became the first **black state governor** in the US.

Of course, all these changes didn't happen peacefully. There were, and still are, many **riots** and **murders**.
Martin Luther King was **assassinated**, as was the equal rights activist **Malcolm X**.

I have a dream that my four children will one day live in a nation where they will not be judged by the colour of their skin but by the content of their character.

Practice Questions

Q1 What is self-identity?

Q2 What is self-esteem?

Q3 Describe the main findings of Hraba and Grant's study.

Q4 How did Hraba and Grant's findings differ to those of Clark and Clark?

Q5 What was the 'March on Washington'?

Exam Questions

Q1 Outline the findings of Hraba and Grant's (1970) study. [12 marks]

Q2 Critically evaluate research on racial preference in children. [8 marks]

Prejudice. Not a nice word. Not a nice thing.

I bet loads of studies, especially social psychology ones, would have different results if they were repeated today. So many studies are about attitudes and tendencies that change with time like any other social trend. Nowadays, kids are being taught how important it is to think for themselves, so I wonder if Milgram, Asch and all those guys would get the same results...

Psychometric Tests

Two more pages to skip if you're doing AQA A or Edexcel.
Psychometric tests are pretty fun to do. You can learn a lot about yourself. Whether you believe what you learn, though, is up to you. I believe only the good scores — those tests were obviously designed by a professional.

Psychometric Tests Measure Psychological Factors

The idea with **psychometric tests** is that if things like personality or intelligence (psychological factors) exist, then we should be able to **measure** them. The **problems** are whether these things really do exist, and whether it's possible to measure them if they do.

Traits are aspects of personality — like punctuality, or liveliness, or laziness. Psychometric tests try to measure traits — with enough of the right kinds of traits you can describe a **personality**.

Psychometric theorists are responsible for the development of standardised tests:

1) Standardised tests provide information about how certain **groups** of people generally perform. The scores of an **individual** can then be compared to the scores of these groups. This is called **standardisation.**
2) In these tests, everyone has the **same** set of instructions and the **same** task to do. This makes sure that differences in results are not due to differences in the test.
3) There are detailed **instructions** for administrators and people scoring the tests.
4) The tests, in theory, allow us to make **objective**, **statistically based judgements** on things like:

   a) people's **capacities** and **potentials** to act or behave in certain ways.
   b) the **severity** of psychological problems.
   c) the likelihood that they will **cope** with a training course.
   d) the potential aptitude for certain types of **job**.

Designing a Psychometric Test Isn't Easy

Learn these things that you've got to think about when **designing** a psychometric test:

1) When designing a test, it's important to carefully choose questions that **represent** what you hope to measure. So in a test of motivation, for example, questions should centre around themes like drive, energy and goals.
2) You've also got to think about:

   a) **scope** (who the test is for, e.g. children, adults or both?)
   b) **accuracy** (how correctly the test measures the factor)
   c) **fairness** (whether everyone it's designed for will be able to use it equally easily)
   d) **practicality** (how easy it is to use, in general)

3) Sometimes the thing you want to measure will turn out to be made up of a number of **factors**, and so won't be so easy to measure. D'oh.
4) For example, **intelligence** may not be just a single trait, but be made up of variations such as problem solving, lateral thinking, social intelligence, spatial reasoning, memory, imagination and many others.
5) However, **factor analysis** has shown **correlations** between different types of intelligence. This suggests that although intelligence can be split up into different traits, they are not as independent as first thought.

Psychometric Tests

*Psychometric Tests are **Not Perfect***

Never mind not perfect — often they're a bit shoddy. Learn why:

1) Tests only measure what the person developing the test thinks they should measure. If there aren't **agreed definitions** of what is actually being measured, there can be difficulties.
2) There is also the difficulty of whether personality traits are **stable attributes**. It is difficult to know whether an individual will perform the same on a test on different days.
3) Many factors from age to ethnicity can affect test performance, so **fairness** should be considered carefully.

***Reliability** and **Validity** are Important*

Reliability and **validity** are very important concepts in psychometric test design. There's no point in using a test if it can't be agreed to be reliable and valid:

Reliability

Reliability is about whether the test measures the trait **consistently**. To **test** reliability, the same person can be given the same test **twice** to see how the scores **correlate** (i.e. if they're the same).

When tests don't measure consistently, it could be because people may administer or score it differently, for example.

Sometimes being the reliable one got too much for Jim.

Validity

Validity is about whether the test really measures what it **claims** it's measuring. It's hard to say whether many psychometric tests are valid as there might be no agreed **definition** for the trait anyway.

Practice Questions

Q1 What are psychometric tests designed to measure?

Q2 What type of attributes do psychometric tests aim to measure?

Q3 What is reliability?

Q4 What is validity?

Exam Questions

Q1 Critically discuss the use of psychometric tests. [8 marks]

Q2 Discuss the issues which should be considered when constructing psychometric tests. [12 marks]

Testing, testing... Hello?

This is quite a boring page to end the section on, sorry. It's pretty important though. Testing aspects of personality is really useful for diagnosing disorders and measuring progress in therapy. And if psychology's going to keep claiming that it's a science, it definitely needs some good, dry scientific tests to keep everyone busy. It's better than learning Freud anyway...

The Social Approach

This page is for y'all. Yes ma'am.

Social psychology is another branch of psychology — this time it's not about how we develop, or physiological differences — what's important in social psychology is interactions, and how people affect each other...

Social Psychology is Concerned With How **People** Affect Each Other

People's influence can be seen in many different forms — like conformity, leadership, prosocial (i.e. helpful) behaviour...

1) Social psychologists consider the importance of **groups** and the influence groups can have on individuals. (Groups are defined as collections of individuals who interact and communicate with each other over time.)
2) Social psychology also considers the influence of **society**. For example, prosocial behaviour is any behaviour which is seen as helpful or cooperative, and what is prosocial depends on the society.
3) Individuals **conform** when they change their behaviour so it matches other members of a group. People may conform due to **social pressures**, e.g. being shunned by a group for acting out of line.
4) **Obedience** to authority means doing what you are told by someone in a position of more power than you. It is often a desirable trait, except when the authority being obeyed is not a just and fair one.

Field Experiments *and* ***Surveys*** *are Often Used in Social Psychology*

Field experiments are experimental studies conducted in an everyday setting, such as a school or street.

1) Like laboratory experiments, field experiments can control an **independent variable** and can put participants in different **conditions**.
2) Because of this, they can be **replicated**.
3) Unlike surveys and case studies, they can be used to establish **cause and effect**.
4) A **disadvantage** is that they can only be used to test **certain things**, e.g. they can't be used to test cognitive factors like perception.
5) Also, if too much effort is made to get information from participants, they may realise they are being studied, and the study will no longer be '**natural**'.

Surveys are a way of gathering data from individuals, rather than testing them experimentally. Surveys can be either **face-to-face (interviews)** or **written (questionnaires)**.

1) **Interview surveys** can be:
   a) **Non-directive** — Relatively unstructured — the interviewee can discuss almost anything they wish with the interviewer guiding the discussion.
   b) **Informal** — Similar to non-directive, but the interviewer has a range of topics they wish to explore.
   c) **Guided** — More structured — the interviewer will tell the interviewee what is going to be discussed. Interviews are still open-ended, but they will usually follow a set of questions in the same order, which stops the interviewer losing control of the interview.
   d) **Clinical interviews** — Structured but open-ended interviews, often used by clinical psychologists.
   e) **Fully structured interviews** — A standard set of questions in a fixed order, with restricted sets of answers (e.g. yes, no, don't know).
2) In **questionnaire surveys**, there can either be a set of answers to choose from (i.e. closed questions), or more open-ended questions.

Some **features of surveys** include:

a) A researcher can **choose** the type of survey to suit their research needs.
b) Unstructured interviews are useful as they produce **qualitative data**, allowing the interviewee's personality, motivation and interests to be revealed. They can therefore reveal **more information** than structured interviews.
c) Structured interviews tend to produce **quantitative data**, which can then be more easily **analysed** to uncover trends.
d) Surveys are usually **reliable**, i.e. two interviewers asking the same question will normally get the same answer.

The Social Approach

*The Social Psychological Approach Has Been **Criticised***

Some **research methods** have been heavily criticised as **unethical**.
It's hard to determine the psychological effect some experiments would have on subjects. For example, thinking you had given an electric shock to someone might cause quite a bit of anxiety and upset, or it might be dealt with quite calmly.

The Trouble with Field Experiments is...

1) **Ethics** — you're often **deceiving** people, which can be a bit dodgy. It's got to be thought about.
2) **Informed consent** (where the participant understands what they're doing, and agrees to it) is important in psychological research. Yet in field experiments, the subject is **not meant to know they are being studied**, as this will mean the study is no longer 'natural'. It's a tricky one.
3) There is no opportunity to **debrief** participants, which is normally important, especially if participants found the situation upsetting.
4) Field experiments tend to have **high external validity** (the results will apply to other people at other times) and **low internal validity** (it's hard to tell whether the experimental manipulation caused the results or not).

The Trouble with Surveys is...

1) Non-directive surveys aren't very useful for experimental research — it's difficult to compare one with another.
2) Questionnaires **depend on people being literate** and wanting to spend time answering the questionnaire. As a result, data are often **biased** towards a certain kind of person.
3) Unstructured interviews tend to be **unsystematic**, so the data can be hard to analyse.
4) **Interviewer bias** means that the information collected during interviews is affected by the interviewer (e.g. the interviewer may only record what they want to hear and miss out important details).
5) Interviewees may wish to present themselves in the best light, so may give distorted answers. This is known as **social desirability bias.**
6) Interviewers can only find out information that the interviewee is consciously aware of, so they can't directly discover Freudian unconscious desires etc.
7) **Confidentiality** is an important consideration, as the interviewer will have access to information about the interviewee they may not want made public.

You've got to learn all these research methods, and the problems and advantages of each one. Learn...

Practice Questions

Q1 Define social psychology.

Q2 What is social desirability bias?

Q3 Define interviewer bias, field experiments and closed questions.

Q4 Outline one criticism of surveys.

Exam Questions

Q1 Critically discuss the use of field experiments in social psychology. [12 marks]

Q2 Critically discuss the use of surveys in social psychology. [12 marks]

Remember — social psychology is all about how people affect each other

With all these different branches of psychology, you need to get the basics clear in your head — everything else follows on from that. In this case it's the idea that people affect each other through the effects of groups, or individual influence. Remember that social influence can also come from less direct sources, like through the media.

Conformity and Minority Influence

Ignore this bit if you're doing Edexcel.
A few quick definitions to get you started — don't read on till you know them. ***Conformity*** *and majority influence mean the same thing — a small group or individual being influenced by a larger or dominant group.* ***Compliance*** *means publicly changing behaviour in line with the majority.* ***Acceptance*** *means changing your beliefs and internalising the majority's views.*

Many **Studies** Have Been Carried Out into **Conformity**

1) Sherif researched whether people are influenced by others in **an ambiguous task** (where the answer isn't clear):

Sherif (1935) — conformity and the autokinetic effect

Method: The autokinetic effect (where a still point of light in the dark appears to move) was used in this experiment. Participants were shown a still point of light in the dark, and estimated how far it moved, first on their own and then in groups.

Results: When alone, participants developed their own stable estimates (personal norms). In the group, judgements gradually became closer and closer until a **group norm** developed — an estimate they agreed on.

Conclusion: Participants were influenced by the estimates of other people.
Estimates converged because participants used information from others to help them.

2) Psychologists therefore wondered whether people conform to a majority's incorrect answer in **an unambiguous task**:

Asch (1956) — conformity on an unambiguous task

Method: In groups of 7, participants judged line lengths (shown below) by saying out loud which comparison line (1, 2 or 3) matched the standard line. Each group contained only one real participant. The others were confederates (who acted like real participants but were really helping the experimenter). The real participant always went last or last but one, so they heard the others' answers before giving theirs. Each participant did 18 trials. On 12 of these (the **critical trials**) the confederates all gave the same wrong answer.

Results: In the control trials, participants gave the wrong answer **0.7%** of the time. In the critical trials, participants **conformed** to the majority (gave the same wrong answer) **37%** of the time. **75%** conformed at least once. Afterwards, some participants said they didn't really believe their answers, but didn't want to look different.

Conclusion: In the control group (where no confederates gave wrong answers) the error rate was 0.7%, so the task was easy to get right. But 37% were wrong on the critical trials — because they conformed to the majority to fit in.

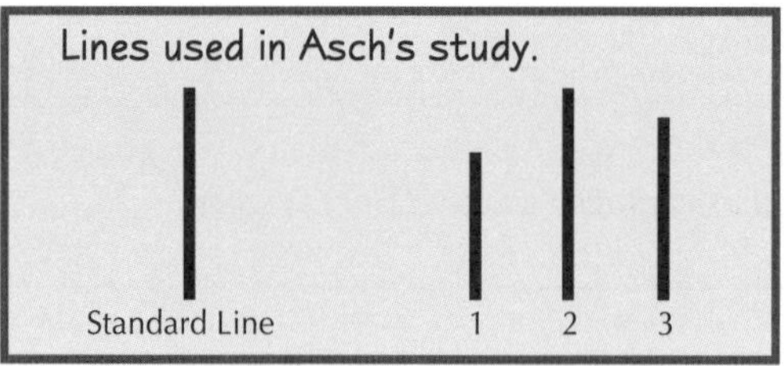

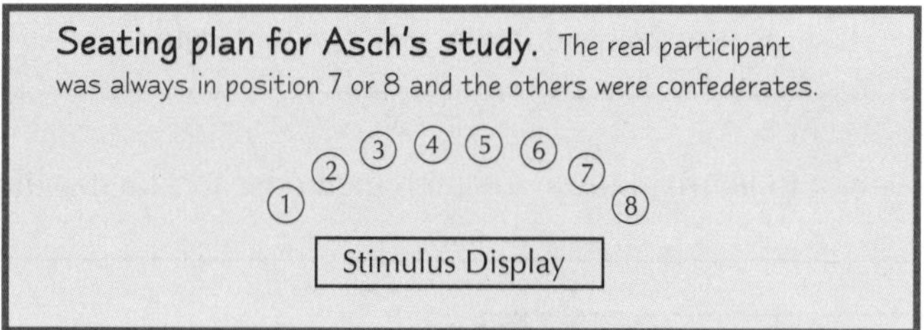

3) A very interesting experiment was carried out to see if people conformed to **assigned roles** (prisoner or guard):

OCR Core Study

Zimbardo et al (1973) — Stanford prison experiment

Method: Male students were recruited to act as either guards or prisoners in a mock prison.
Volunteers were screened and only 'well-balanced' people took part.
They were randomly given the roles of prisoner or guard.

Results: Initially, guards tried to assert their authority and prisoners resisted by sticking together.
The prisoners became more passive and obedient, demonstrating 'learned helplessness' (see p46), and guards invented nastier punishments. The experiment was abandoned early because some prisoners became very distressed.

Conclusion: Guards and prisoners adopted their social roles quickly. Zimbardo claims this shows **that our social role can influence our behaviour**, because well-balanced men became unpleasant and aggressive in the role of guard. However, individual differences played a part as not all the participants behaved according to their social roles.

Conformity and Minority Influence

*In **Minority Influence** the Majority are Influenced by the Ideas of a Small Group*

An example of minority influence is the **Suffragettes**, a group campaigning for women's right to vote.
At the time, they didn't have widespread support, but gradually they influenced the majority to accept their ideas.

***Moscovici et al (1969)** Investigated Minority Influence*

Moscovici et al (1969) — When is a blue slide green?

Method:
This study is a bit like Asch's study (on the previous page).
There were 6 women in each group and 2 of these (the minority) were confederates (people who acted like real participants but were really helping the experimenter).
They were all given eye-tests, so participants knew the others weren't colour-blind.
Each person made a judgement out loud about the colour of 36 slides, which were various intensities of blue.
The error rate in the control group (where there were no confederates) was only 0.25% — so the task was really easy and the slides did look blue.
There were two experimental conditions:
— The '**inconsistent**' condition where confederates said 'green' for 24 of the 36 slides.
— The '**consistent**' condition where confederates said 'green' for all 36 slides.

Results:
Inconsistent condition — real participants said green like the confederates for **1.25%** of the slides.
Consistent condition — real participants said green for **8.42%** of the answers.
32% conformed at least once in this condition.

Conclusion:
Minorities can influence majorities. When the minority gave incorrect answers the majority were more likely to give 'green' as their answer too.
The effect is much smaller than in majority influence (conformity) studies, but there **is** an effect.
A consistent minority (both of them always said 'green') were more influential than an inconsistent one.

Evaluating the study:

1) **Ecological validity:** This study uses an **artificial task** and also the participants' **decisions don't have any major consequences**. Therefore the behaviour we see might not reflect how people are influenced by minorities in real life.
2) **Unrepresentative sample:** Moscovici et al used female students as participants, so it would be **wrong to generalise** these findings to all people — they only tell us about the behaviour of female students.

Practice Questions

Q1 What is the difference between compliance and acceptance?
Q2 In Sherif's study, what happened to the participants' judgements when making their estimates in a group?
Q3 What was the percentage of conformity on the critical trials in Asch's study?
Q4 What is a confederate?
Q5 In the study by Moscovici et al, in what condition were the minority most influential?
Q6 Why was the sample in the study by Moscovici et al unrepresentative?

Exam Questions

Q1 Explain the terms 'majority influence' and 'minority influence'. [6 marks]

Q2 Describe the findings and conclusions of one study of majority influence. [6 marks]

If enough people say this page is good — you'll start to believe it...

It seems unbelievable that just by hearing a few people say a blue tile is green, you will actually start to go along with them and say it is green yourself. Mind you, we've all been there — bands you hate that everyone else likes, people who annoy you but everyone else thinks is cool... we all feel that need once in a while to conform to the majority — or even a minority.

Conformity and Minority Influence

These pages are for AQA A only.
How much we conform and the influence of different groups on us is affected by lots of factors. And here are some lists of those factors — it may not make the most exciting reading, but it should be quite easy to learn.

Four *Factors Affect Conformity*

1) **Group Size**

You might **expect** that the bigger the majority is, the more influential it will be. To test this, **Asch (1951)** conducted his conformity experiment with different numbers of confederates as the majority.

With only **two confederates**, the real participant **conformed on only 13%** of the critical trials. With **three confederates**, conformity rose to **33%**. There was little change to conformity rates after that — no matter how big the majority group got. So, the **size of the majority does affect conformity, but only up to a point.**

2) **Gender**

Research findings have suggested that **females conform more than males.** It has been suggested that this is because **women** tend, more than men, to be **socially orientated** and focus on **interpersonal goals** (like getting on with people).

However, **Eadly & Carli (1981)** argue that it may be because **male researchers** use tasks that are more familiar to men (so they don't need to look to others as much for help). This could explain their finding that male researchers are more likely than female researchers to find female participants higher on conformity. This is an example of **gender bias.**

3) **Personality**

It seems plausible that some people are **more confident** and **resist conforming** to the majority more than others. **Asch (1956)** suggested that people with **low self-esteem** (few positive feelings about themselves) **conform more.** He also found that students in his studies conformed less than non-students, and suggested that **higher IQ might be related to lower levels of conformity.**

4) **Status and knowledge**

If someone is of **high status** (e.g. your boss) or has **lots of knowledge** (e.g. a professor), they might be more influential, and so people will conform to their opinions more. Adverts often use this technique so that their message has more influence — for example, getting a scientist to explain how good a washing powder is. Their **expertise** is influential.

People ***Conform*** *for Two Main Reasons*

1) **Informational influence:**

This is where a person looks to others for **information** when they're not sure how to behave. If you're in an unfamiliar situation or aren't sure of the answer, you might be influenced by someone else's behaviour or opinion.

This is the sort of social influence we saw in **Sherif's study**, where the task was ambiguous. Participants were informed by other people's estimates, which helped them with their judgements.

2) **Normative influence:**

This is where a person conforms to the **group norms**, so that they fit in and **appear 'normal'**.

Going against the majority might lead to exclusion or rejection from the group. They don't have to believe the majority's opinion or agree with their behaviour — they just have to appear 'normal'. People conform to normative influence so that they don't look different or stand out in a crowd.

This is the sort of influence we saw in **Asch's study**, where the right answer was obvious — an unambiguous task. Giving the wrong answer meant the participant didn't look different in the group.

Conformity and Minority Influence

Moscovici *Identified Four Factors That Affect Minority Influence*

Minority influence works by **converting the majority** to the **minority's belief**.
Moscovici (1985) said **conversion** (or **acceptance**) is more likely under the following conditions:

1) **Consistency** — A minority that consistently sticks to its belief is more influential. We saw this effect in Moscovici et al's blue slide study (see page 91).
2) **Flexibility** — A minority must **not seem too rigid** or stubborn. If a minority is unwilling to listen to alternative viewpoints, their own opinions are less likely to be influential.
3) **Commitment** — A minority must be **committed to its opinion and act on it**. For example, the Suffragettes showed commitment to their cause and made sacrifices for it. They were more influential because of this.
4) **Relevance** — A minority whose views are **in line with the general social trend** are more influential than a minority who are 'going against the grain'.
   For example, the current social trend is towards recycling and preserving resources. So these days it would be easier to influence your friends to recycle glass, cans and paper, than for someone to influence their friends to be 'green' 30 years ago.

Other ***Factors*** *Also Make People* ***Give In*** *to Minority Influence*

Group Identification *— We Identify With Someone* ***More*** *When We Have Something in Common*

You might feel you are more similar to a person who goes to the same school as you, who is the same sex or who supports the same team. You will therefore be more likely to accept an opinion from them than from someone very different.

Maass et al (1982) asked a straight audience to listen to a message on gay rights.
It was **more influential** if the message came from a **straight minority** and **less influential** coming from a **gay minority**. They concluded that the audience **identified** more with the straight minority than with the gay minority.

Social Cryptoamnesia *Explains how a* ***Minority Opinion*** *Can Become a* ***Majority Opinion***

Even when people convert their opinion to the minority's belief, they may not express it publicly, because they don't want to stand out from the majority. A minority opinion might become a majority opinion by **social cryptoamnesia**:

1) The minority's view may change people's minds **privately**, but until the **social climate** changes too, these people may not become a majority group.
2) Minority views take time to affect things. During this time people forget where the opinion came from in the first place (the strange or deviant minority) and so the ideas themselves seem less extreme or strange.
3) They become **accepted** and ultimately end up as the **majority view**.

Practice Questions

Q1 According to Asch's findings, how does the size of the majority group affect the level of conformity?

Q2 What aspects of personality make a person more likely to conform?

Q3 Which study showed informational influence, and what is it?

Q4 Which study showed normative influence, and what is it?

Q5 What are the four factors, identified by Moscovici, that make conversion to a minority view more likely?

Q6 How might group identification affect minority influence?

Exam Questions

Q1 Outline two explanations of why people conform to a majority. [6 marks]

Q2 Outline two ways in which a minority can become more influential. [6 marks]

Imagine a bald man on a shampoo ad — no expertise, no influence...

You were warned that there were going to be a lot of lists. At least the facts broken down like this should be easier to understand. The main point to learn is that the influence of different groups and whether people conform to these views depends on lots of different factors — then you just need to learn all those different lists of factors.

Obedience to Authority

These pages are for everyone — hooray. *Obedience means acting in response to a direct order (usually from authority). Some people have problems doing this, but if an organisation or society is to work, many believe obedience is necessary.*

Many Psychologists Have **Investigated** Obedience

1) Milgram studied how far people will obey authority, even when that means hurting someone else:

OCR Core Study

Milgram (1963) — the original 'remote learner' experiment

Method: 40 men from a range of occupations volunteered for a study about 'learning and memory'. The participant and a confederate (acting like a participant, but really helping the experimenter) drew lots to decide who would be the teacher and learner. The draw was fixed — the participant was always the teacher.

In the next room, the confederate was seemingly wired to an electric shock generator. The participant experienced an example shock of 45 volts before the experiment began. The participant taught the learner word-pairs. Every time the learner answered incorrectly the participant had to administer an increasing level of shock, from 15 V up to 450 V. (N.B. The learner didn't actually receive any shocks — he just acted like he did.) By each voltage level, there was a description of the shock, with things like 'slight shock', 'moderate shock' and 'danger: severe shock'. On 450 V, there was 'XXX'. At 300 V, the learner asked to be let out, and said he couldn't stand the pain. Above 300 V, the learner didn't respond.

If the participant stopped, they were ordered to continue by the experimenter in a lab-coat.

Results: It was predicted that around 1% would administer the highest shock. In fact, 65% of participants administered 450 V ('XXX') and none stopped before 300 V. Many participants showed signs of stress during the experiment.

Conclusion: Ordinary people obey orders even when they are acting against their conscience and hurting someone else.

Some of Milgram's variations on this experiment	Percentage administering 450 volts
Male participants	65%
Female participants	65%
Learner's protests can be heard	62.5%
Experiment run in seedy offices	48%
Learner in same room as particpant	40%
Authority (experimenter) in another room, communicating by phone	23%
Other teachers (confederates) refuse to give shock	10%
Other participant (a confederate) gives shock instead	92.5%

2) Hofling investigated whether nurses would break hospital rules to obey a doctor:

Hofling et al (1966) — obedience in nurses

Method: Nurses working in a hospital were phoned by an unknown doctor and asked to administer a drug to a patient. The doctor said he'd sign the paperwork when he arrived. To obey this request, nurses would have to break some hospital rules — taking telephone instructions from unknown doctors and administering drugs without completed paperwork were not permitted. Also, the dosage requested was twice the maximum on the label.

Results: 21 out of the 22 nurses obeyed the doctor and prepared the medication (they were stopped before they administered it). They said they were often given telephone instructions and doctors got annoyed if they refused.

Conclusion: In this real-life setting, levels of obedience to authority were high.

3) Meeus and Raaijmakers used interviews to test obedience:

Meeus & Raaijmakers (1995)

Method: Participants were asked to conduct interviews to test job applicants' reactions to stress. The applicants were really trained confederates. During the interview, the participants were prompted to deliver 15 'stress remarks', designed to inflict increasing levels of psychological harm. The confederates acted confidently at first, but then broke down as the stress remarks were delivered, eventually begging the interviewer to stop.

Results: Despite recognising the distress of the applicant, 22 of the 24 participants delivered all 15 stress remarks.

Conclusion: A high percentage were prepared to inflict psychological harm in this realistic, face-to-face situation.

Obedience to Authority

*Obedience Research Has Been **Questioned***

1) **Ethical issues:**

Meeus and Raaijmakers caused their participants **psychological distress.**

All the experiments on the opposite page used **deception** (not telling participants what the study was really about or that they are in a study at all), so participants couldn't give **informed consent.**

If deceived, it is important to **debrief** participants (tell them the true nature of the study). Milgram's debrief was quite extensive, including being reunited with the 'learner'. Maybe he wasn't such a swine after all.

And no participants in these studies were informed of their **right to withdraw** from the experiment. In fact, in Milgram's and Meeus & Raaijmakers' procedure, participants were prompted to continue when they wanted to stop. I take it back, Milgram was a monster.

2) **Issues of validity:**

Experimental (internal) validity:

Whether Milgram's experiment really measured obedience is debatable. Some people claim that participants didn't really believe they were inflicting electric shocks — that they were just playing along with the **experimenter's expectations** (showing **demand characteristics**). But Milgram claimed participants' **stressed reactions** showed they believed the experimental set-up.

Hofling et al's nurses didn't know they were in an experiment, so it measured real obedience — this study has high experimental validity.

Ecological (external) validity:

Milgram's participants did a task that they were unlikely to encounter in real life (shocking someone). This is not real-life behaviour, therefore the study **lacks ecological validity.**

Real-life obedience is seen in Hofling et al's study — it has **more ecological validity.**

*Milgram's Experiment Showed **Factors Affecting Obedience***

Proximity of the victim: Milgram's results suggest an important factor was the **proximity (closeness) of the learner**. In the 'remote learner' condition, 65% gave the maximum shock. This dropped to 40% with the learner in the same room and 30% when the participant had to put the learner's hand onto the shock plate. Proximity makes the learner's suffering harder to ignore.

Proximity of the authority: When the authority figure gave prompts by phone from another room, obedience rates dropped to 23%. When the authority isn't close by, their orders are easier to resist.

Presence of allies: When there were 3 teachers (1 participant and 2 confederates), the real participant was less likely to obey if the other two refused to obey. Having allies can make it easier to resist orders than when you're on your own.

Practice Questions

Q1 What is obedience?

Q2 Outline the procedure of Milgram's experiment.

Q3 In Milgram's original ('remote learner') experiment, what percentage of participants gave the maximum shock?

Q4 What is meant by 'proximity' and why is it a factor in obedience?

Q5 Outline the ethical issues of obedience research.

Exam Questions

Q1 Explain what is meant by ecological validity. [6 marks]

Q2 Describe **two** criticisms of **one** study of obedience. [6 marks]

Pretty shocking results, don't you think?

There's a lot packed into these two pages, but it's pretty interesting stuff. If you were in a room and a scientist told you to give an electric shock to a guinea pig, would you do it — and would it be because you were obeying authority, or just cos you quite like the idea of shocking a guinea pig... these questions all affect the validity of psychological testing.

Obedience to Authority

These pages are for everyone — except for Edexcel. So not everyone then.

Milgram's Findings Tell Us About the **Psychological Processes** Of Obedience

Gradual Commitment Can Make Us More Obedient

1) Gradual commitment means agreeing to something gradually — in **small steps**. It makes it **harder to refuse** the next request. In Milgram's study, participants were asked to deliver only a 15 volt shock at the start. This was gradually built up to very large shocks.
2) Participants might have been more **reluctant** to obey **if** they had been asked to deliver the 450 volt shock at the start. They obeyed at the lower levels, so it was harder for them to justify disobeying the later requests. They could have thought, 'I've already delivered a 300 volt shock and 315 isn't much more'.
3) Gradual commitment is also known as the '**foot-in-the-door effect**'. Once you've gone along with a minor request, the request could be gradually increased until you're doing something you might never have agreed to in the first place.

An **Agentic State** is When You're Acting For Someone Else

1) Milgram suggested that when we feel we're acting out the wishes of another person (being their agent), we feel **less responsible** for our own actions than if we were behaving normally — for ourselves.
2) This effect is seen in Milgram's studies. Some participants were concerned for the **welfare** of the learner and asked who would take **responsibility** if he were harmed. The experimenter (authority) took responsibility — often the participant would continue.
3) This **agentic state** was also in the experiment's set-up. The participants voluntarily entered a **social contract** (an obligation) with the experimenter to take part and follow the procedure of the study.

Mr Ramsbottom, the new chemistry teacher, naturally exuded the persona of a justified authority figure.

We See Some People as a **Justified Authority**

We are socialised to recognise the authority of people like **parents**, **police officers**, **doctors**, **teachers** etc.

These kinds of people are **justified authorities** — people who have the **right** to **tell us what to do** and so we are more likely to obey them.

We are more likely to act as the agent for someone who we think of as a justified authority.

When Milgram reran his study in some **run-down offices**, obedience rates were lower than when the study was run in the university.

So in the university situation, the experimenter's authority was higher because of the status of the university location.

Some Things Can Act as **Buffers**

1) **Buffers** are things that **protect us** — in this case **from the consequences of our actions**.
2) Milgram's participants were **more obedient** in conditions where they **could not see or hear** the victim receiving the shocks. When in the same room as the learner, there wasn't any buffer.
3) So... losing the buffer made it harder for Milgram's participants to act against their conscience and go along with someone's unjust orders to hurt the learner.

Obedience to Authority

We Can Draw **Conclusions** About the Factors Affecting **Resistance** to Obedience

The **situation** Can Make People **More** Resistant

More of Milgram's participants resisted orders if there were **other teachers present** who refused to obey.

> **Gamson et al (1982)** found that support can help people resist authority, particularly if the request is unreasonable or unjust. They studied a **group** of participants **who felt they were being manipulated**. Participants rebelled against the unjust authority figure. This happened through a process of **minority influence** (see page 91) — with one or two people resisting the authority's requests at first. This rebellion then spread to the whole group.
>
> **Conclusion:** The presence of **allies** and **collective action** seemed to help the participants in their resistance.

Things About the **Individual** Can Make People **More** Resistant

1) If an individual has a high level of **moral reasoning** (thinking about right and wrong) they may be more able to resist an order that goes against their conscience.
2) One of Milgram's participants had experienced a Second World War concentration camp. She **refused** to administer any level of shock, because she didn't want to inflict pain on another person.
3) Those who resisted may have still felt personally responsible — they weren't in an agentic state.
4) As individuals we can also feel that when we are **pushed too far** to obey we can resist by defying the authority.
5) If we feel that someone is trying to control us, or that a rule unjustly restricts our freedom, we may react by doing the opposite. This is also known as the '**boomerang effect**'.

Proximity is an Important Factor

Proximity means closeness.

1) **Proximity of victim:**
It was **harder** for Milgram's participants to ignore the consequences of their actions when the learner was nearby. They were more likely to resist an order that went against their conscience.
2) **Proximity of authority:**
It is **easier** to resist the orders from an authority figure if they are **not close by**. When Milgram's experimenter gave prompts over the phone, obedience rates were lower than when they were face to face with the participant.
3) **Presence of allies:**
Milgram and Gamson et al have shown that the presence of someone else who is resisting orders makes it easier to resist obedience yourself. Supporters or allies can help us resist obedience.

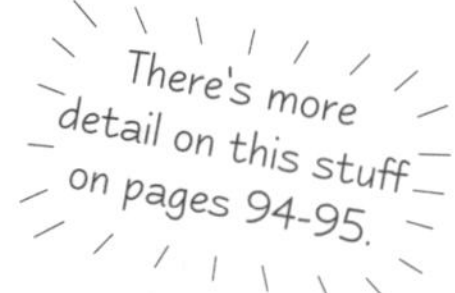

There's more detail on this stuff on pages 94-95.

Practice Questions

Q1 What is another name for the 'foot-in-the-door effect'?

Q2 Why did obedience rates drop when Milgram's study took place in run-down offices?

Q3 What term describes when you act on someone else's behalf and don't feel as responsible for your actions?

Q4 Give an example of a buffer that reduced obedience rates in one of Milgram's studies.

Q5 What did Gamson et al conclude from their research on independent behaviour?

Exam Questions

Q1 Give two explanations of why people obey authority. [6 marks]

Q2 Describe two factors that may help people resist obedience. [6 marks]

My local nightclub is in the local train station — it's called Buffers*...

Some people may resist obedience because they decide that what authority is telling them to do is not the right thing to do morally. Others rebel because they just don't like people telling them what to do. In that respect, disobedience can be a positive or negative thing. Most people would agree however, that setting your teacher on fire is more negative than positive.

*This sounds like a rubbish joke about railway buffers — but it's actually true and represents a terrible reflection on the state of rural night clubbing.

Ethical Issues in Psychological Research

These pages are for AQA A and OCR only. *Ethics are standards about what is right and wrong, so an ethical issue is some dilemma about whether a study is acceptable and justified. Try to imagine yourself as a participant in the studies — if you would've been happy about taking part, how you'd have felt and if it would've had long-term effects on you.*

The British Psychological Society (BPS) produces **Ethical Guidelines**

The British Psychological Society (BPS) has developed ethical guidelines to help psychologists resolve ethical issues in research and protect participants. They include advice on **deception**, **consent** and **psychological harm**.

Deception Means Misleading or Withholding Information from Participants

Asch (see page 90) deceived participants about his study's purpose and about the confederates who pretended to be real participants. He justified this — without deception the aim of this study could not be achieved. If deception has to be used, participants should be told the true nature of the research as soon as possible, during the debriefing.

BPS Guidelines for Deception

Deception should be avoided wherever possible and only be used when it's scientifically justified — when the study would be meaningless otherwise.

Deception shouldn't be used if it's likely that the participant will be unhappy when they discover the study's true nature.

Informed Consent Should be Given

Giving consent means **agreeing** to participate in a study. When a participant is told the research aim and procedure and then agrees to it — this is **informed consent**. They are fully informed before their decision to participate.
If deception is used, participants **can't** give informed consent until they've been debriefed.

Asch's participants **did not** give informed consent when they agreed to take part.
They were deceived about aspects of the study and didn't have enough information for an informed decision.

BPS Guidelines for Informed Consent

Participants should be given all the information they need to decide whether to participate in research and shouldn't be coerced or pressured.

Some people may not be able to give real informed consent — for example children. In these cases informed consent should be obtained from parents or guardians.

Psychological Harm Means Any **Negative Emotion** (e.g. Stress, Distress, Embarrassment)

Asch's participants may have experienced **stress** and were possibly **embarrassed** about being 'tricked' into conforming.

BPS Guidelines for Psychological Harm

Researchers have a responsibility to protect participants from physical and psychological harm during the study. Any risk of harm should be no greater than the participant might experience in their normal life.

There are Many **Ethical Issues** in Other Social Influence Research

1) **Zimbardo** (see page 90) got **limited consent** from his prison-study participants — they weren't told they'd be arrested at their home. This experience and conditions in the mock prison may have caused **psychological harm**.
2) **Milgram's participants** were **deceived** about the true purpose of the study and about the learner being shocked. They couldn't give **informed consent** until after they were debriefed. Many showed signs of **stress** and were pressured (by the experimenter) to continue when they wanted to stop. They weren't protected from psychological harm. After the study, many participants said they **weren't sorry** they took part. But this doesn't mean that they weren't psychologically harmed by knowing they were willing to give strong electric shocks to someone.
3) **Hofling et al's participants** didn't know they were in a study until after they had participated. They were **deceived** and didn't give **consent**. The nurses may have been **psychologically harmed**, having realised they were willing to break hospital rules and possibly harm a patient.

Ethical Issues in Psychological Research

Confidentiality *and* ***Animal Rights*** *are Also* ***Ethical Issues***

Confidentiality means keeping information private.

1) Participants should feel safe that any **sensitive information**, **results** or **behaviour** revealed through research won't be discussed with others.
2) Information obtained during a study should remain confidential unless the participant agrees for it to be shared with others.
3) The study's report shouldn't reveal information or data **identifiable** to an individual.
4) You shouldn't be able to tell who took part or what their individual data were — these should remain **anonymous**.

Research with non-human animals has caused much heated debate.

1) In **support**, people argue that animal research has provided **valuable information** for psychological and medical research. Some **research designs** couldn't have be conducted on humans — e.g. Harlow's study on attachment, where young monkeys were separated from their mothers and reared alone.
2) Some **disagree** with the idea of conducting research with non-human animals. They may argue that it's **ethically wrong** to inflict harm and suffering on animals, and obviously animals can't give consent to take part.
3) Some argue that it's cruel to experiment on animals that have a **similar intelligence** to humans, because they might suffer the same problems we would. It'd be OK to experiment on animals that are far less developed than us, but there is no point because they'll be **too different** from us to give results that apply to humans.

Ethical Guidelines ***Don't Solve*** *All the Problems*

1) One obvious limitation with ethical guidelines is that there may be researchers who **don't follow the guidelines** properly.
2) If a psychologist conducts research in an unacceptable way, they **can't be banned** from research (unlike a doctor who might be 'struck off' for misconduct).
3) Even when guidelines are followed, it may be **difficult to assess** things like **psychological harm** or to **fully justify the use of deception**.
4) Deciding whether the ends (benefits from the study) justify the means (how it was done and at what cost) is not straightforward either. This creates another dilemma for psychologists.

Practice Questions

Q1 What are ethics?

Q2 According to the British Psychological Society's ethical guidelines, when can deception be used?

Q3 If you have used deception, what should you do immediately after the study?

Q4 What does 'informed consent' mean?

Q5 For the issue of psychological harm, what level of risk is said to be acceptable in research?

Q6 Give one reason why ethical guidelines don't solve all the problems of ethical issues in psychological research.

Exam Questions

Q1 Describe how psychologists have dealt with ethical issues in social influence research. [12 marks]

Q2 Discuss the extent to which the ethical objections about social influence research are justified. [12 marks]

*People question the ethics of keeping a man in a box above the Thames...**

Psychological experiments create many ethical dilemmas. Take Milgram's study — there's no doubting that the results reveal interesting things about how people interact. But do these results justify the possible psychological damage done to the participants? There's no right or wrong answer to this, but the BPS guidelines are there to address exactly this sort of issue.

*I question the ethics of letting him out.

Contemporary Issues in Social Psychology

Just Edexcel. *Psychologists are heavily involved in contemporary issues such as hypnosis, crowd behaviour and racism. These parts of psychology are the practical areas where psychologists' studies can be used to solve current problems...*

*Social Psychology Can Be Used to Explain **Hypnosis***

Hypnosis is often thought to be an **altered state of consciousness**, where the person appears to be in a trance but can respond to requests and suggestions by the hypnotist. Physiological psychology explains hypnosis from a biological point of view, but this is the social psychology section so here's what the social psychologists think is going on:

1) **Baker (1990)** suggests that hypnosis is **actually a social phenomenon** that is a **form of learned behaviour**. The hypnotist and the subject both **play the role that is expected** of them in this particular social context and so reinforce each other's behaviour.
2) **Techniques** such as the hypnotist using a **soft**, **relaxing voice** and **repeating words** and **gestures** all contribute to **expectations about how to behave**. Using this approach, hypnosis can be seen as a form of social conformity, rather than a physiological experience. This is supported by evidence that shows that people who use **fantasy and imaginative thought** are very **responsive** to hypnosis.
3) Some people may therefore have **personal characteristics** that make it **difficult for them to resist** the social pressure to behave in the way that is expected of them. They may also be **more willing** to put themselves into these types of social situations in the first place.

The physiological changes are not unique to hypnosis — they would happen during activities such as daydreaming or concentrating on a topic.

*Social Psychologists have **Six** Theories for **Crowd Behaviour***

People act differently when they're in a crowd, but their behaviour won't always be the same. It'll also depend on the situation. Well that's what them social psychologists reckon anyway, and they've come up with six different types of behaviour for six different crowd situations. And you've got to learn the lot I'm afraid.

1	**Social facilitation**	The presence of other people can lead to improvement in a person's performance. It will only happen if the task is relatively easy or well practised, e.g. running faster when someone else comes into the gym.
2	**Social inhibition**	The presence of other people can also lead to a decrease in a person's performance. This is more likely if the task is difficult, e.g. stalling the car the first time you give someone a lift after passing your test.
3	**Social loafing**	A person deliberately reduces their individual level of effort when others are performing the same task. Safety in numbers means that they think they can get away with it without being noticed, e.g. mouthing the words when singing in the school choir.
4	**Social conformity**	Giving in to the pressure of social groups and changing behaviour — the pressures might not be explicit and might actually be imagined by the person, e.g. getting an unusual nether-region piercing because everyone else is getting one.
5	**Social compliance**	Agreeing with the majority although internally you don't really agree with them, e.g. talking about how you love Eastenders even though you don't really watch it and you're a closet Family Affairs fan.*
6	**Deindividuation**	Personal identity is lowered and replaced by a group identity, resulting in a person behaving in ways that they wouldn't normally. The anonymity provided by the group will encourage deindividuation, e.g. a small proportion of protesters in recent anti-capitalism demonstrations have damaged property and cars and attacked the police. This behaviour would have been less likely if they had been alone without the support of the group.

*Social compliance can be a bad thing as it can push people to do things they don't really want to do — but if you are a Family Affairs fan I think it is best to keep that to yourself.

Contemporary Issues in Social Psychology

Racism is a Contemporary Issue in Social Psychology

1) Racism is an example of a **prejudiced attitude** — people of other races are seen as inferior in some way. The prejudice will probably have a **corresponding stereotype**, an **over-generalised and negative perception** of people who all share the characteristic of belonging to that race.
2) The problem is that stereotypes can be very **resistant to change** because a **racist will avoid** people they dislike. This prevents them from finding out what people from that race are really like and so their **stereotype isn't challenged**.
3) If a racist person does meet a member of the disliked race they tend to either **focus on their negative aspects** to support their prejudice or acknowledge their positive aspects but dismiss them as unrepresentative of the race in general.
4) There are **regular examples of racism and discrimination** in the news.
In 1999, **David Copeland** blew up three separate bombs in London, killing three and injuring seventy-nine. Two bombs were left in areas he targeted because many black and Asian people lived there.
One bomb was left at the bar of a gay pub, targeting homosexuals. He told police he had intended to continue targeting ethnic minority communities if he hadn't been caught and wanted his bombs to trigger a racial war to encourage white people to vote for the British National Party.

The 'Let's kick racism out of football' campaign

This campaign was started in 1993 by the Commission for Racial Equality and the Professional Footballer's Association to tackle racism at football matches.

Black footballers had been subjected to abuse in the form of insulting noises, racist chants and things thrown at them.

Football supporters had a reputation that was seen as very damaging for the sport and some fans were put off attending matches because they felt uncomfortable exposing children to this level of prejudice.

The campaign uses **positive role models** in the form of popular players and managers like David Beckham and Arsene Wenger, discussing their dislike for racist behaviour. The intention is that fans will try to **model** their favourite stars, and racist behaviour will be seen as unacceptable rather than the norm.

"Surely a foul" thought John, but the reason eluded him.

Practice Questions

Q1 What is hypnosis?

Q2 What is social facilitation?

Q3 What is social loafing?

Q4 What is racism?

Q5 What is the 'Let's kick racism out of football' campaign?

Exam Questions

Q1 How can hypnosis be seen as a social phenomenon rather than a physiological one? [5 marks]

Q2 Explain two psychological concepts relevant to crowd behaviour and apply them to racist behaviour in football. [6 marks]

There's no room for racial hatred in football — save your hatred for Man U...

These are all interesting areas, where psychologists are looking directly at problems in today's society and using their theories to find solutions. Take the example of the anti-capitalist marches — if psychologists can help us understand why they lead to violent clashes and unrest in a minority, then it can help to work towards solutions to this problem.

Group Identity and Prejudice

These pages are just for OCR people. *Whether we like it or not, we're lumped into groups—some we choose, like a rugby club, and some we don't, like gender. Social psychologists have done loads of studies to see how prejudices develop between groups, in the hope that it's possible to start breaking them down.*

There are Examples of **Prejudice** and **Discrimination** all Around Us

Prejudice is a **negative attitude** towards a person because of a **characteristic** that they have or their **membership** of a group, for example disliking someone because of their race or religion.

> Common types of **prejudice** include race, gender, sexuality, religion, appearance, disability and economic status. Prejudice has recently led to **physical attacks** on asylum seekers and the racist **murder** of Stephen Lawrence.

Discrimination is **unfair treatment** that results from prejudice, for example not giving someone a job because of their race. Laws such as the **Race Relations Act** are used to try to prevent and reduce prejudice and discrimination.

Sherif Explained Prejudice With **Realistic Group Conflict Theory**

Sherif's (1966) Realistic Group Conflict Theory suggests that prejudice occurs because of **competition**. If two groups want the same limited resources then they will form negative attitudes towards each other, causing conflict.

This theory can be used to explain **Hitler**'s horrifying manipulation of German people before and during WWII.

1) At the time Germany was experiencing **economic problems** and through propaganda Hitler portrayed a **stereotype** of Jews as rich, greedy and selfish.
2) This encouraged people to resent Jews because they were seen as having what other people wanted financially, but couldn't afford.
3) This prejudice made it much easier for Hitler to deport Jews to concentration camps on a massive scale.

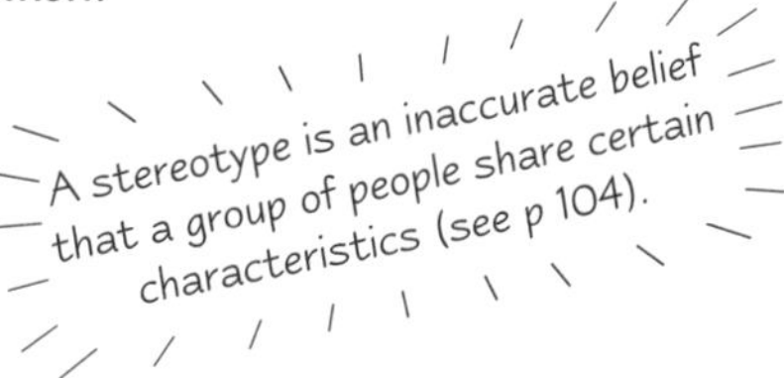

A stereotype is an inaccurate belief
that a group of people share certain
characteristics (see p 104).

> The main strength of Sherif's theory is that it can easily be **applied** to famous examples of prejudice. However, the theory has been criticised because prejudice often occurs in situations where there isn't any apparent **competition** for resources.

Tajfel Explained Prejudice With **Social Identity Theory**

Tajfel's (1978) Social Identity Theory suggests that our **self-concept** (the way we view our self) is partly made up of our membership of social groups (our social identity).

1) If a social group that you belong to is successful and is viewed positively, then this reflects well on you as an individual.
2) Examples of your social groups could include a sports team, college, workplace, a peer group or your family.
3) Nobody wants to be seen as a loser stuck in a losing group, so we are **motivated to belong to groups** that are as good as possible.
4) One way to do this is to **compare our group** (the in group) to **another group** (the out group) and emphasise our group's strengths and the other group's weaknesses. This then makes us look better as individuals.
5) Another way is to **change membership** of groups, but this is **not always practical**. For example, if your family are an embarrassment, you can't easily get a new one.

> A strength of Tajfel's theory is that it appreciates that we still see ourselves as **individuals** when we are in social situations.
>
> A weakness of the theory is that the supporting evidence is mainly experimental which lacks **ecological validity**.

Ecological validity is a measure of how much a conclusion from an experiment is likely to apply to the real world.

Group Identity and Prejudice

Sherif et al (1961) Investigated *Prejudice* Using the *Robber's Cave Experiment*

Cultural context — There was a vast amount of research into social psychology during the 1960s as people became more aware of what had taken place during WWII, and wanted to understand how it could have happened.

Details — Two groups of boys were sent to the Robber's Cave summer camp in the USA. They quickly developed individual group identities with group names, rules and leadership. When competitions were organised, hostility quickly grew and camp staff had to prevent violence and theft between the groups.

To reduce prejudice, the staff created problems such as the water supply failing, which could only be overcome through cooperation between the groups.

As a result, discrimination disappeared and the two groups became friendly.

Evaluation — A practical application of this study is that non-competitive contact between social groups isn't enough to reduce prejudice. They need to work together towards common goals instead. This could be used in situations such as schools to reduce conflict. However, it would be difficult with larger groups.

Tajfel (1971) Investigated *Prejudice* Using a *Minimal Group Experiment*

OCR Core Study

Cultural context — Tajfel acknowledged that competition could cause prejudice, but suggested that the process of **categorisation into groups alone was sufficient to cause prejudice**.

Details — Schoolboys were allocated into two groups with very minimal (trivial) reasons for group membership such as preference for an artist.

They were given pairs of numbers and had to give one number in each pair to their own group and the other number to the other group. The numbers would be converted into money but they wouldn't receive any money themselves. The results showed that the participants would give more points to members of their own group than members of the other group, and would award the points which gave the greatest difference between the two groups.

Participants wanted to favour their own group and emphasise the difference between the groups even without knowing the members of their group.

Evaluation — The experiment was highly controlled, the boys didn't know who the members of their group were and didn't benefit themselves, suggesting that prejudice can happen easily.

It supports social identity theory as the boys tried to improve their self-esteem by increasing the success of their group. However, the study lacks ecological validity as in real life, categorisation into groups often involves some competition. Additionally, the sample consisted only of adolescent boys — these results might therefore be difficult to apply to other groups.

Practice Questions

Q1 Give an example of a type of prejudice.

Q2 What is meant by discrimination?

Q3 What does Sherif suggest is the main cause of prejudice?

Q4 What is a weakness of Tajfel's theory?

Q5 How did the two groups of boys behave towards each other in the Robber's Cave study?

Exam Questions

Q1 Describe and evaluate one theory of the causes of prejudice. [6 marks]

Q2 Describe the minimal group experiment by Tajfel. [4 marks]

Remember prejudice is an attitude — discrimination is acting on it...

It's quite amazing that Tajfel's study suggests that even if we are stuck in arbitrary groups we can still build up a favouritism for the group we are in, and a dislike for other groups. When this is mixed with competition between groups, say for land or money, it's easy to see how prejudices can become strong. But this makes the prejudice understandable — not acceptable.

Reduction in Prejudice

Edexcel only. *Many psychologists have taken on the theories about how and why prejudice develops in order to find possible solutions and ways to reduce prejudice.*

Realistic Group Conflict Theory Can Be Used to Reduce Prejudice

Sherif's theory (1966) on the last page suggested that prejudice is created by **competition for resources**. Therefore getting rid of competition between groups should reduce the opportunity for prejudice to occur.

1) Sherif found that the prejudice between groups only began to be broken down when the groups were involved in **cooperative tasks** (such as fixing the water supply in the Robber's Cave experiment).
2) Therefore **realistic group conflict theory** suggests prejudice can be broken down by putting groups in these kinds of cooperative situations.

Removing competition isn't always a **practical** option — some groups exist because of competition, for example football supporters. However, in social situations like schools it might be possible to arrange activities that involve cooperation rather than competition.

Social Identity Theory Can Be Used to Reduce Prejudice

Tajfel's theory (1978) suggests that prejudice occurs because we **exaggerate the superiority** of our social groups and **exaggerate the inferiority** of other groups in order to make ourselves look good as individuals.

1) **Reducing prejudice** therefore relies on **changing the way we think** about the structure of groups.
2) Rather than thinking about the characteristics that make our group different from others, we should focus on how groups are related to each other and so emphasise the similarities.

E.g. teenagers and elderly people.

- Instead of thinking of them as two completely different groups of people, think about them as just groups at **different ends of a scale**.
- Young people will one day become elderly and the elderly were young at some point.
- This way it is much harder for both groups to be critical of each other as it would mean that the young would be criticising themselves in the future and the elderly would be criticising themselves in the past.

Reducing prejudice in this way involves finding a characteristic that both groups share and bringing this to the attention of people in the groups.
A **practical problem** here is that people with a strongly held prejudice may **refuse to listen** to somebody trying to point out the similarities between the groups, as they prefer to focus on the differences and maintain their views.

Equal Status Contact is One Way to Challenge Stereotypes

Stereotyping means: mentally **grouping** people together on the **basis of a characteristic**, for example their job, **nationality**, **gender** or an **aspect of appearance**. The use of stereotypes will lead to prejudice if we believe that people in the group share characteristics that are negative.

An example is: the labels of '**single mothers**' and '**asylum seekers**'. These are used in some newspapers to identify groups of people who can then be portrayed as lazy and unwilling to work for money. These negative stereotypes can encourage prejudice and lead to discrimination.

What can be done: A method called **equal status contact** can be used.

This involves getting people together of equal status from opposing groups. For example, two violently rival football fans who share the same type of job and social standing.

The fact that both people are similar in almost every way should show up the stereotypes for what they are and hopefully break them down.

Reduction in Prejudice

The *Jigsaw Classroom Method* is Used in Schools to Reduce Racism

The **jigsaw classroom method** is an example of an equal status contact technique. It involves children of **different races** being put into **groups** together and each being given a different part of a task.

1) Each part is of equal difficulty so that everybody is of **equal status**, and the group can only finish the task if each person completes their part and explains it to the rest of the group.
2) They are then **tested** on all the parts of the task, so the children can only pass the test if they have **worked together** as a team and **listened** to what each person has found out.

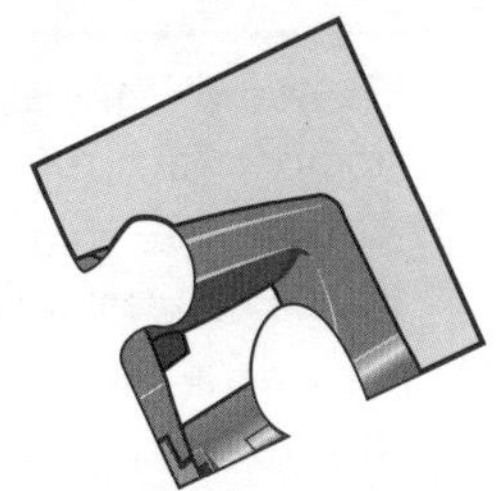

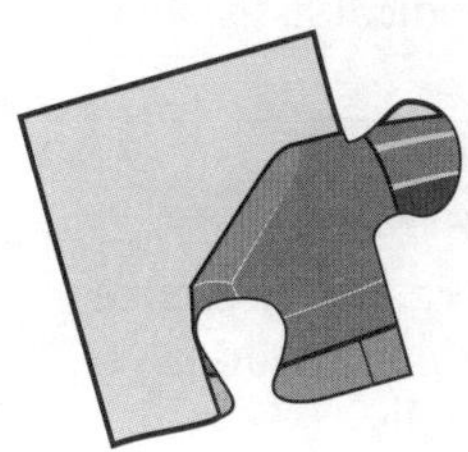

This technique was developed by **Aronson (1971)** in an attempt to reduce the prejudice and discrimination that children were demonstrating in schools in Texas, USA. It was introduced at a time when racial segregation had just ended and children of different races were being taught in the same schools for the first time.

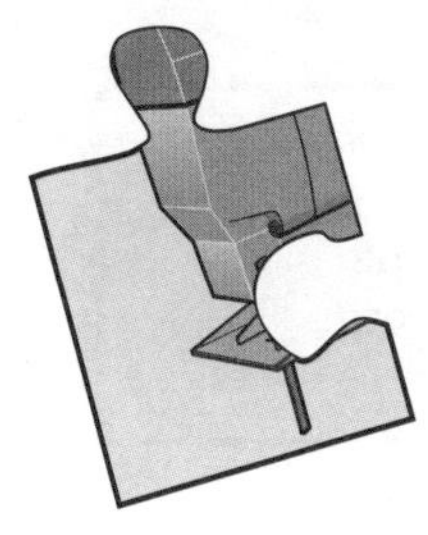

3) The **aim** of the jigsaw method is for children to **learn** that their **stereotypes** of the children of different races are **wrong** and to encourage a more cooperative and supportive atmosphere in the classroom.
4) The jigsaw method has to be carefully planned so that all the children in a group can actually do their part, otherwise there is a **danger** that failure will **reinforce stereotypes** instead of challenging them.

Practice Questions

Q1 What does realistic group conflict theory suggest as a way of reducing prejudice?

Q2 What type of activities did the Robber's Cave experiment use to encourage cooperation?

Q3 What does social identity theory suggest we should focus on to reduce prejudice?

Q4 What is a stereotype?

Q5 Who introduced the jigsaw classroom method?

Q6 What is the aim of the jigsaw classroom method?

Exam Questions

Q1 Compare and contrast how realistic group conflict theory and social identity theory are used to reduce prejudice. [8 marks]

Q2 Describe how the jigsaw classroom technique works. [4 marks]

I guess sat trawling through psychology, jigsaw class sounds quite nice...

The main difficulty with prejudice is that people tend to try to avoid situations in which their stereotypes are challenged. If people can meet on an equal footing and find out that their assumptions about people are wrong, they can begin to break down their prejudices. Remember the methods psychologists have come up with, and how they are supposed to work.

Roles and Situational Variables (Bystander Behaviour)

These pages are for OCR and Edexcel.
*Our behaviour in any situation is affected by a load of different things. These things may be to do with us personally, for example our **social role**. Or they may be to do with the situation itself — these factors are called **situational variables**.*

Social Roles are the Responsibilities that Give Us Identity

1) There are many **social roles** — such as father, mother, husband, wife, son, daughter, politician, doctor. Each role has different **responsibilities** and different levels of **importance**.
2) Some of our social roles **change** over time (e.g. our occupation might change several times), others can last a **lifetime** (such as being a daughter or a sister).
3) Social roles lead to **expectations** from other people — we expect a mother to be sensitive and caring towards her children and a teacher to be responsible and respectable.
4) These expectations can exist even if a person isn't officially in the role at the time. For example, people expect a police officer to always obey the law and a doctor to always be prepared to give medical assistance.

Situational Variables are Environmental Factors that Affect Behaviour

Situational variables are any factors in the **environment** that affect behaviour, such as **noise**, **temperature**, **presence of other people**, **distractions**, **time of day** or **lighting**. A researcher needs to be very aware of possible situational variables when conducting a study as these can influence the findings if they aren't controlled carefully.

1) The **presence of other people** is an important situational variable — it can affect how people behave, especially when they don't know how they should behave.
2) A common time when people don't know how to behave is in an **emergency situation**.
3) This is known as **bystander behaviour**, and is an area of psychology with key terms:

1) Bystander apathy	People prefer not to help when observing an emergency situation.
2) Diffusion of responsibility	People don't help because they know that there are other people around who are equally responsible for helping, so they feel less individual responsibility.
3) Pluralistic ignorance	People don't help because they take their cues about how to behave from other people and so are misled if others seem to be calm and are not getting involved.
4) Evaluation apprehension	People don't help because they are worried about how others will judge their behaviour.
5) Prosocial behaviours	Any action that is of benefit to others.
6) Altruism	Behaviour which helps others, but not yourself, for example giving blood.
7) Cost-benefit analysis	People will decide whether to help or not after comparing the costs (e.g. time, effort and danger) to the benefits (e.g. praise, positive feelings and rewards).

The Murder of Kitty Genovese Resulted in Research into Bystander Behaviour

Kitty Genovese was **murdered** outside her apartment block in 1964.

1) After the attack it was revealed that **38 people** had either seen or heard the attack, which lasted 35 minutes.
2) The killer was **disturbed** twice but both times returned to continue the crime. Individuals reported hearing Kitty shouting that she had been stabbed, that she was dying and pleading for help but it still took **20 minutes** before someone called the police.
3) When people were asked why they hadn't helped the only reason they could give was that they were **afraid**, however a phone call to the police wouldn't have put them at any individual risk.

The case **triggered** several psychological studies into **bystander behaviour**. Two of these studies are on the next page.

Roles and Situational Variables (Bystander Behaviour)

*Two Interesting **Studies** Followed the Kitty Genovese Case*

Darley and Latane (1968) — diffusion of responsibility

Method: Participants were told they were taking part in a discussion using intercoms with at least one other person. They were all in separate rooms so that they couldn't see anybody. The other person then made sounds like he was having a seizure and started begging for help.

Results: When the participant believed they were the only person available, **85%** reported the problem.
When they thought they were in a three-person group, **62%** reported it.
When they thought they were in a six-person group, only **31%** did.

Conclusion: Although all participants considered the situation to be an emergency, they were less likely to help if there were more people involved who also didn't help. This demonstrated **diffusion of responsibility**.

Comments: The laboratory setting means the study has low ecological validity — the results might not show how behaviour takes place in real life. There are also ethical problems as many participants were distressed by what happened.

Piliavin et al (1969) — bystander behaviour on the subway

OCR Core Study

Method: A victim collapsed on a subway train and the researchers observed to see if others would help him and if so, how long they took. The victim was either white, black, drunk or carrying a cane in each trial of the study.

Results: The victim with a **cane** was **helped immediately** in almost all of the trials, the **drunken victim** was helped **50%** of the time. There was no difference in results between black and white victims, although if the victim was also drunk there was a slight tendency towards same race helping. 90% of the helpers were male and the race of helpers reflected the race of the people in the carriage.

Conclusion: People were generally much more helpful than previous laboratory based studies suggested. There was **no support** for diffusion of responsibility.

Comments: The study has **good ecological validity** as it took place in a real-life setting and it was highly standardised — each trial took place in the same way leading to good control of variables.
The **ethics** of the study are concerning as participants did not give consent, may have experienced stress or discomfort and weren't debriefed afterwards.

Practice Questions

Q1 How can we define social roles?

Q2 Give an example of a situational variable.

Q3 How does evaluation apprehension prevent people helping others?

Q4 Who was Kitty Genovese?

Q5 What were the findings of Darley and Latane's study into diffusion of responsibility?

Q6 What positive comments can be made about the study by Piliavin et al?

Exam Questions

Q1 Explain the case of Kitty Genovese using psychological concepts. [10 marks]

Q2 Compare and contrast the research into bystander behaviour by Darley and Latane, and Piliavin et al. [8 marks]

It's no good looking away and assuming someone will learn this for you...

It's always shocking to read about cases like Kitty Genovese's but I'm sure we've all been in situations where we've turned a blind eye because we were afraid to get involved, or we think someone else will deal with it. It's a pretty sobering topic to end the section on. What's that... finished the section? Yep, as far as social goes, it's all done — think a cuppa's in order.

Practical Assessment

The practical assessment is worth a heck of a lot of marks — about a third of the total marks available. So it's worth doing well. And the first step on the way to doing it well is to know what you're trying to do. Read on.

The practical assessment for **OCR** is called **Psychological Investigations**

1) This is assessed by an **hour-long written exam** containing **10 to 12 compulsory questions**, and is worth **33.3%** of the AS level. You get a mark out of **50** for your work in the exam.
2) The questions are based on **four practical work activities**, which you conduct under the guidance of your teacher in class and at home. (If you don't complete the tasks before the exam, you won't have all the information you need to answer the questions.)
3) In theory, you're allowed to work on these practical activities **individually** or in **groups** (although in practice your school or college might want you to work in a particular way for each task).
4) **Notes** about the four activities (including the method and results) are written up in a **practical work folder** that you can then take into the exam with you. These notes are to help you remember what you did for each of the activities. However, to answer the questions you need to understand **research methods generally**. (After the exam, your school or college keeps your practical work folder.)

The four activities are:

Activity A — about **questions, self-reports** and **questionnaires.**
You need to be able to give **examples** of the questions used, and describe the **rating scale** involved.
Notes on these **can** be included in the practical work folder.

Activity B — an **observation.**
You need to be able to describe the **categories of behaviour** and to consider **alternative** ways of sampling the behaviour — notes on these **cannot** be included in the practical work folder.
You also need to be able to describe the **rating** or **coding system** you used — notes on this **can** be included in the practical work folder.

Activity C — a **collection of data** to test the **difference between two conditions.**
You must conduct an appropriate **statistical test** (probably a Mann-Whitney U or a Wilcoxon signed ranks test).
A copy of the calculation or computer print out **should** be included in the practical work folder.

Activity D — a **collection of data** (two independent variables), plus a **test of correlation** (probably Spearman's Rho).
A copy of the calculation or computer print out **should** be included in the practical work folder.

You also need to **know about**, but **not record** in the practical work folder:
1) **Ethical** considerations
2) The **reliability** and **validity** of the measurements used
3) **Different ways** the variables could have been **measured**
4) Ways to reduce any **weaknesses** in the methodology
5) **Advantages** and **disadvantages** of each method or design type

Practical Assessment

The practical assessment for **EDEXCEL** is **Unit 3 — Coursework**

1) The coursework is worth **33%** of the AS level and is given a mark out of **72**. It should be about **1500 words** long.
2) Your investigation must be submitted by a **deadline** set by your school or college. It is then **externally marked** by an Edexcel examiner.
3) You need to demonstrate that the work submitted is **your own** — but you **can** use pooled data, provided you've collected at least **some** of the data sets **yourself**. In theory you're allowed to work as an individual, in small groups or as a class — however, your teacher may have a preference for the way you should work.
4) Your report should be presented in the **order shown**. To get all the marks available for each section, you need to include certain things — ask your psychology teacher for a complete list.

> 1) Introduction — worth 18 marks
> 2) Method — worth 14 marks
> 3) Results — worth 11 marks
> 4) Discussion — worth 24 marks
> 5) References and Appendices — worth 5 marks (and includes marks for overall presentation)

There is **No Practical Assessment** for **AQA A — hurrah**

But on the down-side, there are **3 exams** — boo.

There are things you can do to **Make Life Easier**

> **Tip 1** — If you have access to a **word processor**, use it to write up your **coursework** (even if your college or school doesn't ask you to). It'll be easier to **make changes** later to anything you've written.

> **Tip 2** — You don't have to produce an **original** piece of research for your coursework — it's okay to **replicate** an **existing study** to see if you get **similar results**.

> **Tip 3** — **Plan ahead** so that you don't get caught out by **deadlines**. And don't leave everything until the last minute — it might take you **longer** than you **expect** to collect your data or write up your work. **Expect the unexpected** — your computer might crash, the ink cartridge might run out, all the computers at school or college might be occupied by other panicking psychology students.

Practice Questions

Q1 Is there a practical assessment for your syllabus?

Q2 If so, what percentage of the AS level is it worth?

Q3 Does it consist of an exam, a piece of coursework or a practical investigation?

Q4 Briefly describe your practical assessment.

Q5 Why should you use a word processor?

Q6 Should you plan ahead or leave it to the last minute?

In AQA A, you practically do nothing...

I'll be the first to admit it — these two pages won't get your heart racing with excitement. But then again, that's not the point. The practical assessment is worth loads of marks (unless you're doing AQA A), and these are marks you can earn before the stress of sitting exams really sets in (maybe). So read the stuff, work out what you've got to do, and then do it well.

Research Methods

Useful for everyone. *There are various ways of studying behaviour and gathering data — all have their pros and cons...*

Laboratory Experiments are Controlled and Scientific

1) An **experiment** is a way of conducting research in a **controlled** way.
2) The aim is to **control** all relevant variables except for **one key variable**, which is altered to see what the effect is. The variable that you alter is called the **independent variable** (see page 113).
3) Laboratory experiments are conducted in an **artificial setting**, e.g. Milgram's and Asch's studies (see pages 90-94).

Advantages

Control — effects of confounding variables (those that have an effect in addition to the variable of interest) are minimised.

Replication — can run the study again to check the findings.

Causal relationships — it's possible to establish whether one variable actually causes change in another.

Disadvantages

Artificial — experiments might not measure real-life behaviour (i.e. they may lack ecological validity).

Demand characteristics — participants may respond according to what they think is being investigated, which can bias the results.

*Field Experiments are Conducted **Outside** the Laboratory*

In **field experiments** behaviour is measured in a **natural environment** like a school, the street or on a train.
A **key variable** is still altered so that its effect can be measured.

Advantages

Causal relationships — you can still establish causal relationships by manipulating the key variable and measuring its effect.

Ecological validity — field experiments are less artificial than those done in a laboratory.

Demand characteristics — avoided if participants don't know they're in a study.

Disadvantages

Less control — confounding variables may be more likely in a natural environment.

Ethics — participants didn't agree to take part, might experience distress and often can't be debriefed.

*Natural Experiments Measure but **Don't Control** Variables*

A **natural experiment** is a study that measures variables that **aren't** directly manipulated by the experimenter.
For example, comparing behaviour in a single-sex school and a mixed school.

Advantages

Ethical — it's possible to study variables that it would be unethical to manipulate, e.g. are people less aggressive in a community without TV?

Disadvantages

Participant allocation — you can't randomly allocate participants to each condition, and so confounding variables (e.g. what area the participants live in) may affect results.

Rare events — some groups of interest are hard to find, e.g. a community that doesn't have TV.

*Correlational Research Looks for **Relationships** Between Variables*

Correlation means that two variables rise and fall together, or that one rises as the other falls — but **not** necessarily that one variable **causes** a change in the other, e.g. as age increases so might intelligence, but age doesn't cause intelligence.

Advantages

Causal relationships — these can be ruled out if no correlation exists.

Ethical — can study variables that would be unethical to manipulate, e.g. is there a relationship between number of cigarettes smoked and incidence of ill-health?

Disadvantages

Causal relationships — cannot be assumed from a correlation, which may be caused by a third, unknown variable.

Misinterpretation — sometimes the media (and researchers) infer causality from a correlation.

*Naturalistic Observation — **Observing** but NOT Interfering*

Advantages

Ecological validity — natural behaviour and no demand characteristics, as participant unaware of being observed.

Theory development — can be a useful way of developing ideas about behaviour that could be tested in more controlled conditions later.

Disadvantages

Extraneous variables — can't control variables that may affect behaviour.

Observer bias — observer's expectations may affect what they focus on and record. This means the reliability of the results may be a problem — another observer may have come up with very different results.

Ethics — you should only conduct observations where people might expect to be observed by strangers. This limits the situations where you can do a naturalistic observation.

Research Methods

Questionnaires — Written, Face-to-Face, on the Phone, or via the Internet

Advantages

Practical — can collect a large amount of information quickly and relatively cheaply.

Disadvantages

Bad questions — leading questions (questions that suggest a desired answer) or unclear questions can be a problem. Or you might miss out an important question, so the participant doesn't have the opportunity to give certain information.

Biased samples — some people are more likely to respond to a questionnaire, which might make a sample unrepresentative.

Self report — people sometimes want to present themselves in a good light (social desirability bias). What they say and what they actually think could be different, making any results unreliable.

Interviews — More Like a **Conversation** than a Face-to-Face Questionnaire

Structured interviews follow a fixed set of questions that are the same for all participants.
Unstructured interviews may have a set of discussion topics, but are less constrained about how the conversation goes.

Advantages

Rich data — detailed information, as there are fewer constraints than with a questionnaire. Unstructured interviews provide richer information than structured interviews.

Pilot study — a good way to gather detailed information before further investigation.

Disadvantages

Self report — can be unreliable and affected by social desirability bias (see questionnaires).

Impractical — conducting interviews can be time-consuming and requires skilled researchers.

Ethical Guidelines Advise and Protect

1) Different research methods present different **ethical issues** — dilemmas about how acceptable such research is.
2) **Ethical guidelines** have been developed by organisations like the British Psychological Society to **advise** researchers and **protect** participants, e.g. observational research should only be carried out where people can expect to be observed by strangers.

Other ethical guidelines are discussed on pages 98-99.

3) The ethical issues depend on the actual research method used:

Method	Possible Ethical Issues
Laboratory Experiment	Deception often used, making informed consent difficult.
Field Experiment	Deception often used, making informed consent difficult. May be difficult to offer debriefing if people leave the location. Observation must respect privacy.
Natural Experiment	Deception often used, making informed consent difficult. Confidentiality may be compromised if community identifiable.
Correlational Studies	Misinterpretation of results.
Naturalistic Observation	Informed consent a problem. Observation must respect privacy. Debriefing may be difficult if people leave the location.
Questionnaire Surveys	Confidentiality — especially around sensitive issues.
Interviews	Confidentiality — especially around sensitive issues.

Practice Questions

Q1 What advantage is gained by running an experiment 'in the field' rather than in the laboratory?

Q2 Describe a disadvantage of studies where correlational analysis is used.

Q3 What ethical considerations are important when conducting observational research?

Q4 Why might you get an unrepresentative sample when carrying out questionnaire-based research?

Q5 What is the difference between a structured and unstructured interview?

Field experiments — fine, if you're really that interested in grass...

No research method is perfect — the one you choose to use is bound to be some kind of compromise. A quick warning about correlation — correlation means that two variables rise and fall together, or that one rises as the other falls — but that doesn't necessarily mean that a change in one variable ***causes*** *a change in the other. No, no, no, no, no.*

Aims and Hypotheses

These pages are for everyone. *When research is conducted, the idea is to produce an* ***objective test*** *of something — i.e. a scientifically proven measurement of how people behave, not just someone's opinion. Well that's what I reckon...*

***Research Aims** are Important*

1) An **aim** is a statement of a study's purpose — for example Asch's aim might have been: 'To study majority influence in an unambiguous task'. (See page 90 for the detail of Asch's study.)
2) Research should state its aim **beforehand** so that it's **clear** what the study intends to investigate.

***Hypotheses** are Theories Tested by Research*

Although the **aim** states the **purpose** of a study, it isn't usually **precise** enough to **test**.
What is needed are clear statements of what is actually being tested — the **hypotheses**.

1) RESEARCH HYPOTHESIS

The **research hypothesis** is proposed at the beginning of a piece of research and is often generated from a theory. For example — Bowlby's research hypothesis was that maternal deprivation causes delinquency. (See page 27 for the detail of Bowlby's study.)

2) NULL HYPOTHESIS

The **null hypothesis** is what you are going to **assume is true** during the study. Any data you collect will either back this assumption up, or it won't. If the data **doesn't support** your null hypothesis, you **reject** it and go with your **alternative hypothesis** instead.

Very often, the null hypothesis is a prediction that there will be **no relationship** between key variables in a study — and any correlation is due to **chance**. (An example might be that there is no difference in exam grades between students who use a revision guide and students who don't.)

(Note: It's quite usual to have something you **don't actually believe** as your null hypothesis. You assume it **is** true for the duration of the study, then if your results lead you to reject this null hypothesis, you've **proved** it **wasn't true** after all. See page 124 for more details.)

3) EXPERIMENTAL HYPOTHESIS (or ALTERNATIVE HYPOTHESIS)

If the data forces you to **reject** your null hypothesis, then you accept your **experimental (alternative) hypothesis** instead.

So if your null hypothesis was that two variables **aren't** linked, then your alternative hypothesis would be that they **are** linked. Or you can be more specific, and be a bit more precise about **how** they are linked, using **directional** hypotheses (see below).

4) DIRECTIONAL HYPOTHESIS (also called ONE-TAILED)

A hypothesis might predict a difference between the exam results obtained by two groups of students — a group that uses a revision guide and another group that doesn't.

If the hypothesis states which group will do better, it is making a **directional prediction**.

For example, you might say that students who use a revision guide will get **higher** exam grades than students who don't — this is a directional hypothesis.

Directional hypotheses are often used when **previous research findings** suggest which way the results will go.

5) NON-DIRECTIONAL HYPOTHESIS (also called TWO-TAILED)

A **non-directional hypothesis** would predict a difference, but wouldn't say which group would do better.

For example, you might just say that there will be a **difference** in exam grades between students who use a revision guide and students who don't — this is a **non-directional** hypothesis, since you're not saying which group will do better.

Non-directional hypotheses can be used when there is **little previous research** in the area under investigation, or when previous research findings are **mixed** and **inconclusive**.

Aims and Hypotheses

*Some **Variables** are **Manipulated** by the Researcher — Others aren't*

A **variable** is a quantity whose **value changes** — for example time taken to do a task, anxiety levels, or exam results. There are various different kinds of variable.

*The **Independent Variable** is **Directly** Manipulated*

1) An **independent variable** (**IV**) is a variable **directly manipulated** by the researcher.
2) In the example about students, exams and revision guides, there are two variables.
One is 'whether or not a revision guide is used' (so this variable has only two possible values: yes or no).
The other is the 'exam grade' (and this could have lots of possible values: A, B, C, D, E, N, U).
3) In this case, the **independent variable** is 'whether or not the students used a revision guide' — since this is **directly** under the control of the researcher.

*The **Dependent Variable** is Only Affected **Indirectly***

1) The **dependent variable** (**DV**) is the variable that you think is **affected** by changes in the independent variable. (So the DV is **dependent on** the IV.)
2) In the exam grades example, the dependent variable is the 'exam grade'. The exam grade is dependent upon whether the revision guide was used (or at least, that's what's being **investigated**).

Extraneous Variables** are **Extra** Things that **Might** Affect What You're Trying to **Measure

1) Ideally in a study you'd keep all the variables **constant** and change just one (the **IV**) to see **what effect** it has on the **DV**. Unfortunately, sometimes this isn't done (or isn't possible).
2) An **extraneous variable** is any variable (other than the IV) that **could** affect what you're trying to measure.
3) For example, some students could sit exams at different times, use different revision guides, be different ages or genders. Any one of these could affect the exam results, so they would be **extraneous** variables.

***Confounding Variables** are Extraneous Variables that Have **Actually Had** an Effect*

1) Ideally the **only** difference between groups in a study will be down to the IV under investigation — then any **difference** in the **DV** is caused by a **difference** in the **IV**.
2) However, one or more extraneous variables may also have affected the DV.
If this is the case, it's called a **confounding variable**.
3) For example, if all the students in the group using revision guides were studying Physics and all the students not using them were doing Chemistry, there's possibly a **confounding** variable. If the group using the revision guide do better, it might be because it's easier to get a higher mark in Physics.

Practice Questions

Q1 What is a hypothesis?

Q2 What is the difference between a directional and non-directional hypothesis?

Q3 When would we reject the null hypothesis?

Q4 What is an independent variable?

Q5 What is a dependent variable?

Q6 Why does a confounding variable make it difficult to interpret differences found in results?

Aim to learn this page, I hypothesise you'll need it...

Remember, you assume the null hypothesis is true unless your data suggests otherwise — then you quickly switch allegiance to the alternative hypothesis instead. And remember, the IV is deliberately manipulated by the researcher. This might lead to an effect on the DV, but it's often a kind of indirect, knock-on effect. Yep, I agree — that's enough.

Research Design

Useful for everyone. *Once you've got a theory, this is about how you'd actually go about researching...*

The Research Design Must make the Hypothesis **Testable**

Research example — does the presence of an audience help or hinder people doing the 'wiggly wire' task (moving a loop along a wire without touching it, and setting off the buzzer)?
Based on previous research, we expect people to do this better without anyone watching them.

1) The IV (the variable being manipulated) is the presence or absence of an audience.
2) The DV (the variable being measured) is 'how well' the participants do on the task — but it must be testable. You need a **precisely defined** (or **operationalised**) DV, which should be **quantitative** wherever possible. An operationalised DV for this experiment might be 'the time taken to move the loop from one end of the wire to the other without setting off the buzzer'.

There are Three **Research Designs** that are Used Loads

1) An **independent measures design** means there are **different participants** in each group.
Here, for example, one group does the task *with* an audience and another group does it *alone*.
This avoids the problem that if all the participants did the test in both conditions, any improvement in performance might be due to them having two goes at the task (which would be a confounding variable).

Advantages
No **order effects** — no one gets better through practice (**learning effect**) or gets worse through being bored or tired (**fatigue effect**).

Disadvantages
Participant variables — differences between the **people** in each group might affect the results (e.g. the 'without audience' group may just have people who are better at the task — so we can't safely compare groups).
Number of participants — **twice as many** participants are needed to get the same amount of data, compared to having everyone do both conditions.

2) A **repeated measures design** is where all participants do the task both **with** an audience and then **without**. You can compare the performances in each condition, knowing the differences weren't due to participant variables.

Advantages
Participant variables — now the same people do the test in both conditions, so any differences between individuals shouldn't affect the results.
Number of participants — **fewer** participants are needed to get the same amount of data.

Disadvantages
Order effects — if all participants did the 'with audience' condition first, any improvements in the second condition could be due to **practice**, not the audience's absence. (But see **counterbalancing** on the next page.)

3) A **matched participants design** (also known as 'matched pairs') means there are different participants in each condition, but they're **matched** on important variables (like age, sex and personality).
For example, if a participant in one condition was a 20-year-old male, you'd also want a participant in the other condition to be a male aged around 20 with a similar personality.

Advantages
No order effects — there are **different people** in each condition.
Participant variables — important differences are minimised through **matching**.

Disadvantages
Number of participants — need twice as many people compared to repeated measures.
Practicalities — **time-consuming** and difficult to find participants who **match**.

It's Sometimes Good to Run a Small **Pilot Study** First

1) No piece of research is perfect. To help foresee problems, a small-scale **pilot study** can be run first.
2) This should establish whether the **design** works, whether **participants** understand the wording in **instructions**, or whether something important has been **missed out**.
3) Problems can be tackled before running the **main study**, which could save a lot of wasted **time** and **money**.

Research Design

Variables Can Be *'Controlled'* so Their Unwanted Effects are *Minimised*

Counterbalancing (mixing up the order of the tasks) can solve **order effects** in **repeated measures** designs. Half the participants do the task **with** an audience **first** and **then without**. The others do the conditions **the other way round**. Any order effects would then be equal across conditions.

Random allocation (e.g. by drawing names out of a hat) means everyone has an **equal chance** of doing **either** condition. An **independent measures** study with, for example, more men in one group than the other could have a confounding variable. Any difference in performance may be due to **sex** rather than the real IV. Random allocation should ensure groups are **not biased** on key variables.

Extraneous variables can be controlled by:
(i) keeping them **constant** for all participants (e.g. everyone does the task in the same place so distractions are similar),
(ii) eliminating them altogether (e.g. everyone does the task somewhere with no noise distractions).

Standardised instructions these should ensure the **experimenters** act in a similar way to all participants. Everything should be **as similar as possible** for all the participants, including each participant's **experience** in such studies.

Tests should be *Internally* and *Externally Reliable*

Internal Reliability

1) Is the measure consistent? **Split-half technique** can assess this. Questionnaire items are randomly split into **two groups**. If all participants score similarly on both halves, the questions measure the same thing.
2) Are you measuring what you **think** you're measuring? A way of assessing this is **predictive validity** — do the scores on your test predict actual performance? For example, a test to measure how good someone will be at management will have predictive validity if it picks out those people who go on to become good managers.

External Reliability

1) Is the measure stable over time or between people? This can be assessed by measuring **test-retest reliability** (does the same person always score similarly on the test?) or **inter-rater reliability** (do different assessors agree, i.e. do they both give the same score?)
2) Does the study tell us about **real-life** behaviour? This can be improved by using less artificial surroundings, e.g. field experiments or naturalistic observations.

Research should be designed with *Ethical Issues* in mind

Ethical guidelines assist researchers who have **ethical dilemmas** and should ensure that research is **acceptable** and participants are **protected**.

Practice Questions

Q1 Give one disadvantage of an independent measures design.

Q2 Give one design that overcomes the disadvantage you identified in Q1.

Q3 Give one disadvantage of a matched participants design.

Exam Questions

Choose an example of a famous piece of psychological research to answer these questions:

Q1 Identify the design used in this study. [2 marks]

Q2 Describe one conclusion that could be drawn from the findings in this study. [2 marks]

Q3 Describe one problem that may limit the validity of the conclusion you have identified in Q2. [3 marks]

Inter-test validity, no... split-rater ethics, no... oh sod it.... zzzzzzzzz...

There are a lot of details here, but they're really important. If you're not really careful when you design a piece of research, the results you get might not be worth the paper you end up writing them down on. Spending a little time thinking at this stage will all be worth it in the end — trust me.

Naturalistic Observation

Useful for all. *Naturalistic observation is the collection of data by observing participants in their natural environments. This may seem pretty simple, but there are still lots of important design decisions to be made.*

Making **Naturalistic Observations** Needs a Lot of Thought

Recording data

If you want **qualitative data** (e.g. words, pictures, etc.) you could just make **written notes**. But **video** or **audio recording** means that you have a **permanent** record, and also ensures no behaviours are missed.

Categorising behaviour

You must **define** the behaviours you aim to observe. For example, if you were going to observe children in a school playground to see how many behave aggressively, you'd have to decide **what counts as aggression**.

This involves giving an **operationalised definition** (i.e. some **specific**, **observable** behaviours). For example, you might say that *'aggression is any physical act made with the intention to harm another person – such as punching, kicking etc.'*

But you have to be careful not to **miss out** anything important otherwise your definition may not be valid, e.g. aggression can also be verbal.

Rating behaviour

The behaviours that you're interested in may be things that are a matter of **degree**, e.g. behaviours may be *very aggressive*, *mildly aggressive*, etc. — so you might need to use a rating scale to classify behaviour.

You could put each participant's behaviour into one of several **categories**, e.g. *not aggressive*, *mildly aggressive* or *very aggressive*.

Or you could use a **coding system** where each participant is given a **number** (e.g. between 1 and 10) to represent how aggressive they are, where a **higher score** indicates **more aggression**. However, you still have to **define** what kinds of behaviour are included for each number on the scale (e.g. 5 = *pushing* and 10 = *kicking or punching more than once*).

Behaviour rated in this way provides **quantitative data** (data in the form of **numbers**).

Sampling behaviour

You have to decide **how often** and for **how long** you're going to observe the participants. Two approaches are **event sampling** and **time-interval sampling**.

Event sampling — this is when you only record particular events that you're interested in (e.g. aggression shown by the children) and ignore other behaviours.

Time-interval sampling — if the behaviours occur over a long time period you might choose to observe for only set time intervals e.g. the first 10 minutes of every hour, or 10 minutes of each playtime the children have in a week. The time intervals could be chosen randomly.

Inter-observer reliability

Even after you've **defined** the behaviours you're interested in, you have to make sure that the observers are actually putting each participant in the **right category** or giving the **right rating**. This might involve **comparing** the data from two or more observers to make sure they're giving the **same** scores (i.e. that they are 'reliable').

Naturalistic Observation

And there's more...

Questionnaires *Need to be Designed* ***Carefully***

There are various things you need to consider when designing a questionnaire for a survey.

1) **Type of data** — whether you want **qualitative data** and/or **quantitative data** will affect whether you ask **open** and/or **closed questions**.

   a) **Open questions** are questions such as *What kinds of music do you like?*
   The participant can reply in **any way**, and in as much detail as they want. This gives detailed, qualitative information, although it may be **hard to analyse**, as the participants could have given very different answers.

   b) **Closed questions** limit the answers that can be given, e.g. *Which do you like: Pop, Rock or neither?*
   They give **quantitative** data that is relatively **easy to analyse** — e.g. you can say exactly **how many** people liked each type of music. However, less detail is obtained about each participant.

2) **Ambiguity** — you have to avoid questions and answer options which are **not** clearly **defined**, e.g. *Do you listen to music frequently?* What is meant here by 'frequently'? — Once a day, once a week?

3) **Double-barrelled questions** — best not to use these, since a person may wish to answer **differently** to each part. For example, *Do you agree that modern music is not as good as the music of the 1960s and that there should be more guitar-based music in the charts?*

4) **Leading questions** — these are questions that **lead** the participant towards a particular answer. E.g. *How old was the boy in the distance?* They might have seen an older person, but by saying '*boy*' you're leading them to describe the person as young. You're also leading them to think that the person was male, but they might not have been sure. (Leading questions are really important in eyewitness testimony — see pages 16-17.)

5) **Complexity** — whenever possible **clear English** should be used, avoiding **jargon**.
   However, if specialist terms are included, they should be clearly defined.
   (So the question *Do you prefer music written in unusual time signatures?* probably isn't ideal for most people.)

All of the Above Goes For ***Interviews*** *As Well*

But you also have to consider the following:

1) **How structured** the interview will be:
   Interviews can be very **informal** with **few set questions**, and new questions being asked **depending on** the participant's **previous answers**. This gives detailed qualitative data, which may be difficult to analyse.
   Alternatively, they may be more **structured**, with set questions and **closed answers**, giving **less detail** but being **easier to analyse**.
2) Using a **question checklist** — if the interview is structured, a checklist ensures that no questions are left out and questions aren't asked twice.
3) The behaviour or appearance of the **interviewer** — this could **influence** how the participants react.

Practice Questions

Q1 Explain the difference between quantitative and qualitative data.

Q2 How can behaviour be sampled in observational studies?

Q3 What is 'inter-observer reliability'?

Q4 Distinguish between open and closed questions.

Q5 Explain three of the issues involved in designing questionnaires and/or interviews.

Big Brother — naturalistic observation at its finest...?

This is all about observing behaviour that's as natural as possible. What you don't want is for people to put on an act just because they're aware that they're being watched — that defeats the object of doing the study in the first place. Makes you wonder about Big Brother — can they keep an act up for ten whole weeks, or do we actually get to see some natural stuff?

Selecting and Using Participants

Useful for everyone. *In a study, you could ask everyone in the world some questions, but that's not really practical. This is why in most cases it's best to survey just a sample of participants. But you have to be careful how you choose them.*

Selecting a **Sample** of Participants Can Be Done in **Three Main Ways**

The part of a **population** that you're interested in studying (e.g. all the people in a particular city, or all people of a certain age or background) is called the **target group**. Usually you can't include everyone in the target group in a study, so you choose a certain **sample** of **participants** (or **Pp** for short).

This sample should be **representative**, i.e. it should reflect the variety of characteristics that are found in the target group. A sample that is unrepresentative is **biased**. There are various methods of selecting a sample:

RANDOM SAMPLING

This is when **every** member of the target group has an **equal chance** of being selected for the sample. This could be done by giving everyone in the target group a number and then getting a computer to randomly pick numbers in order to select the Pp.

Advantages: Random sampling is 'fair'. Everyone has an equal chance of being selected and the sample is **likely** to be representative.

Disadvantages: This method doesn't **guarantee** a representative sample — there's still a chance that some sub-groups in the target group may not be selected (e.g. people from a minority cultural group). Also, if the target group is large it may not be practical (or possible) to give everyone a number that might be picked. So in practice, completely random samples are rarely used.

OPPORTUNITY SAMPLING

This is when the researcher samples whoever is **available and willing** to be studied. Since many researchers work in universities, they often use opportunity samples made up of students.

Advantages: This is a **quick** and **practical** way of getting a sample.

Disadvantages: The sample is **unlikely** to be **representative** of a target group or population as a whole. This means that we can't confidently **generalise** the findings of the research. However, because it is **quick** and **easy**, opportunity sampling is **often used**.

VOLUNTEER SAMPLING

This is when people actively **volunteer** to be in a study by responding to a request for Pp advertised by the researcher, e.g. in a newspaper, or on a notice board.
The researcher may then select only those who are **suitable** for the study.
(This method was used by Milgram — see page 94.)

Advantages: If an advert is placed prominently (e.g. in a national newspaper) a **large number** of people may respond, giving more Pp to study. This may allow more **in-depth analysis** and **more accurate** statistical results.

Disadvantages: Even though a large number of people may respond, these will only include people who actually saw the advertisement — no one else would have a chance of being selected.
Also, people who volunteer may be more **co-operative** than others. For these reasons the sample is **unlikely** to be **representative** of the target population.

No method can guarantee a representative sample, but you should have confidence that your sample is (quite) representative if you want to generalise your results to the entire target group.

Selecting and Using Participants

Participants Sometimes *Act Differently* When They're Being *Observed*

Human Pp will usually be aware that they are being **studied**. This may mean they don't show their **true response**, and so their data may not be **valid** or **reliable**. Some of these effects are explained below...

1) **THE HAWTHORNE EFFECT**: If people are **interested** in something and in the attention they are getting (e.g. from researchers), then they show a more **positive** response, try **harder** at tasks, and so on.
   This means their results for tests are often **artificially high** (because they're trying harder than normal), which could make a researcher's conclusions **inaccurate**.
   The opposite effect may occur if the Pp are **uninterested** in the task.

2) **DEMAND CHARACTERISTICS**: This is when Pp look for **clues** to the aims of a study.
   If they think they realise what kinds of response the researcher is **expecting** from them, they may show that response to '**please**' the researcher (or they may **deliberately** do the **opposite**).
   Either way, the conclusions drawn from the study would be **inaccurate**.

3) **SOCIAL DESIRABILITY BIAS**: People usually try to show themselves in the **best possible light**.
   So in a survey, they may **not** be completely **truthful**, but give answers that are more **socially acceptable** instead (e.g. people may say they give more money to charity than they really do).
   This would make the results **less accurate**.

The *Researchers* Can *Affect* the Outcomes in *Undesirable ways*

The **reliability** and **validity** of results may also be influenced by the researcher, since he or she has **expectations** about what will happen. This can produce the following effects:

1) **RESEARCHER (or EXPERIMENTER) BIAS**: The researcher's **expectations** can influence how they **design** their study and how they **behave** towards the Pp, which may then produce **demand characteristics**.
   Also, their expectations may influence **how** they take **measurements** and **analyse** their data, resulting in errors that can lead, for example, to accepting a hypothesis that was actually false.

2) **INTERVIEWER EFFECTS**: The interviewer's **expectations** may lead them to ask only questions about what *they* are **interested** in, or to ask **leading questions**.
   Or they may **focus** on the aspects of the Pp's answers which **fit** their **expectations**.
   Also a Pp may react to the **behaviour** or **appearance** of an interviewer and then not answer truthfully.

Practice Questions

Q1 What is a biased sample?
Q2 What is a random sample?
Q3 Give a disadvantage of opportunity sampling.
Q4 Give an advantage of volunteer sampling.
Q5 What is the Hawthorne effect?
Q6 How may demand characteristics affect a study?
Q7 How may a researcher's expectations affect a study?

Volunteers needed for study into pain and embarrassment... (and stupidity)

In a study, you could survey everyone in the world, but it might be expensive and time-consuming. This is why in most cases it's better to survey just a sample of participants. But you have to be careful how you choose them. There's no point in going to your local club and surveying all the crazy dancing people, cos I bet down at the old folk's home they'd disagree.

Data Analysis

For everybody. *Data analysis may sound vaguely maths-like — but don't run for the hills just yet. It isn't too tricky...*

Data From **Observations** Should be Analysed **Carefully**

1) If you've got **quantitative** data (i.e. numbers), you can use **statistics** to show, for example, the most common behaviours. (Quantitative data can be obtained by **categorising** and **rating** behaviour — see page 116.)
2) **Qualitative** data might consist of video or audio **recording**, or written **notes** on what the observers witnessed. Analysis of qualitative data is **less straightforward**, but it can still be done.
3) Whatever kind of data you've got, there are some important issues to bear in mind:

   a) There must be **adequate data sampling** to ensure that a **representative** sample of Pps' behaviour has been seen.
   b) **Language** must be used **accurately** — the words used to describe behaviour should be **accurate** and **appropriate** (and must have valid **operationalised definitions**).
   For example, it might not be appropriate to describe a child's behaviour as 'aggressive' if he or she is play-fighting.
   c) Researcher **bias** must be **avoided** — e.g. it's not okay to make notes *only* on events that **support** the researcher's theories, or to have a **biased interpretation** of what is observed.

The Same Goes For Data Obtained From **Interviews**

1) When **closed** questions are used as part of an interview's structure, **quantitative** data can be produced (e.g. the **number** of Pps who replied 'Yes' to a particular question). **Statistics** can then be used (see pages 122-129) to further analyse the data.
2) When **open** questions are used, more **detailed**, **qualitative** data are obtained.
3) Again, whatever you've got, there are certain things you'll need to remember:

   a) **Context** — the **situation** in which a Pp said something, and the way they were **behaving** at the time, may be important. It may help the researcher understand **why** something was said, and give clues about the **honesty** of a statement.
   b) The researcher should clearly distinguish **what** was said by the Pp from **how** *they* interpreted it.
   c) **Selection** of data — a lot of **qualitative** data may be produced by an interview, which may be difficult for the researcher to **summarise** in a report. The researcher must **avoid bias** in selecting what to include (e.g. only including statements that support their ideas).
   The interviewees may be consulted when deciding **what** to include and **how** to present it.
   d) The interviewer should be aware of how *their* feelings about the interviewee could lead to **biased interpretations** of what they say, or how it is later reported.

And Likewise For Data From **Questionnaire Surveys**

1) Like observations and interviews, **surveys** can give you both **quantitative** and **qualitative** data, and so most of the points above are relevant to surveys as well.
2) Again, it's especially important to distinguish the **interpretations** of the **researcher** from the **statements** of the **participant**, and to be **unbiased** in selecting what to include in any report on the research.
3) However, the analysis of **written** answers may be especially difficult because the participant is not present to **clarify** any **ambiguities**, plus you don't know the **context** for their answers (e.g. what mood they were in, and so on).

Data Analysis

Qualitative *Data Can Be* ***Tricky*** *to* ***Analyse***

Qualitative data are sometimes seen as 'of **limited use**' because they're difficult to **analyse**.
This is why they are often **converted** into **quantitative** data using **content analysis**.

CONTENT ANALYSIS

a) A **representative sample** of qualitative data is first **collected** — e.g. from an interview, printed material (newspapers, etc.) or other media (such as TV programmes).

b) **Coding units** are identified to analyse the data. A coding unit could be, for example, an **act of violence**, or the use of **gender stereotypes** (though both of these must be given valid **operationalised definitions** first — e.g. a definition of an 'act of violence').

c) The qualitative data are then **analysed** to see **how often** each coding unit occurs (or **how much** is said about them, etc.).

d) A **statistical analysis** can then be carried out (see pages 122-129).

ADVANTAGES OF QUANTIFYING DATA

1) It becomes **easier** to see **patterns** in the data, and easier to **summarise** and **present** it (see pages 128-129).

2) **Statistical analysis** allows statements regarding **significance** to be made (see page 124 for more info).

DISADVANTAGES OF QUANTIFYING DATA

1) Care is needed to avoid **bias** in defining **coding units**, or deciding which behaviours fit particular units.

2) Qualitative data has **more detail** (**context**, etc.), which is **lost** when converted into **numbers**.

1) Because of the **detail** (and hence the **insight**) that **qualitative** data can give, some researchers prefer to **avoid** 'reducing' them to **numbers**.

2) Instead they analyse the data into **categories** or '**typologies**' (e.g. sarcastic remarks, statements about feelings, etc.), **quotations**, **summaries**, and so on.

3) **Hypotheses** may be developed during this analysis, rather than being stated previously, so that they are 'grounded in the data'.

Quantitative Data *Allow You to Make Statements Regarding* ***Significance***

1) There's always the chance that results might be due to **chance** rather than the **variables** of interest.

2) One advantage of quantifying data is that it allows you to use **inferential statistics** (see pages 124-125). These allow you to check whether results are likely to be due to chance. If the **probability** of the result being down to **chance** is sufficiently **small**, you say that a finding is **significant**.

Practice Questions

Q1 Distinguish between qualitative and quantitative data.

Q2 Why is data sampling an issue in observation studies?

Q3 Why is context important in analysing interview data?

Q4 How may bias occur in analysing interview or survey data?

Q5 Why may survey data be harder to analyse than interview data?

Q6 How is a content analysis done?

You must keep an open mind — but just don't let all the facts escape...

It's fairly obvious-ish, I guess, that qualitative data need to be analysed with an open mind — it's not OK to fit the facts to your theory... you have to fit your theory to the facts. The same goes for analysing quantitative data — it's not just a case of 'doing some maths' — you have to be sure you're not being biased in your interpretations. Keep an open mind...

Descriptive Statistics

Useful for all. *Run for your lives... panic. This really looks like maths... Well, actually, it's not too bad. So calm down.*

Descriptive Statistics *— Just Say What You See...*

1) **Descriptive statistics** simply describe the **patterns** found in a set of data.
2) Descriptive statistics uses the fancy term '**central tendency**' to describe an **average**. For example, the central tendency (average) for the height of a group of 18-year-old boys might be about 1.70 metres.
3) Measures of **dispersion** describe **how spread out** the data are. For example, the difference in height between the shortest 18-year-old boy and the tallest might be 35 cm.

There are 3 Measures of ***Central Tendency*** *(AKA Average) You Need to Know*

The Mean *— This is the 'Normal Average'*

You calculate the **mean** by **adding** all of the scores in a data set and then **dividing** by the number of scores.

$$\text{Mean} = \bar{X} = \frac{\sum X}{N}, \text{ where } \sum X \text{ is the sum of all the scores (and there are } N \text{ of them).}$$

Σ (pronounced 'sigma') just means you add things up.

Example: If you've got scores of 2, 5, 6, 7 and 10, then $\sum X = 30$ (since all the scores add up to 30), and N = 5 (since there are 5 of them)...

...so the **mean** is $\bar{X} = \frac{30}{5} = 6$.

For example, the scores 10, 40, 25, 20 and 650 have a mean of 149, which is not representative of the central tendency of the data set.

Advantages

a) It uses **all** the scores in a data set.
b) It's used in **further calculations** (e.g. standard deviation, see next page), and so it's handy to work out.

Disadvantages

a) It can be **skewed** (distorted) by extremely **high** or **low** scores. This can make it **unrepresentative** of most of the scores, and so it may be **misleading**. In these cases, it's best to not use the mean.
b) It can sometimes give an **unrealistically precise** value (e.g. the average home has 2.4 children — but what does 0.4 of a child mean...?)

The Median *— The* ***Middle Score*** *When the Data are Put in* ***Order***

Example: The **median** of the scores 4, 5, 10, 12 and 14 is **10**.

In this example there was one score in the middle. If there are two middle scores, add them together and then divide by 2 to get the median.

Advantages

a) It's relatively **quick** and **easy** to calculate.
b) It's **not** affected by extremely high or low scores, so it can be used on 'skewed' sets of data to give a '**representative**' average score.

Disadvantages

a) Not **all** the scores are used to work out the median.
b) It has **little further use** in data analysis.

The Mode *— The Score that Occurs* ***Most Often***

Example: The **mode** (or the **modal score**) of 2, 5, 2, 9, 6, 11 and 2 is 2.

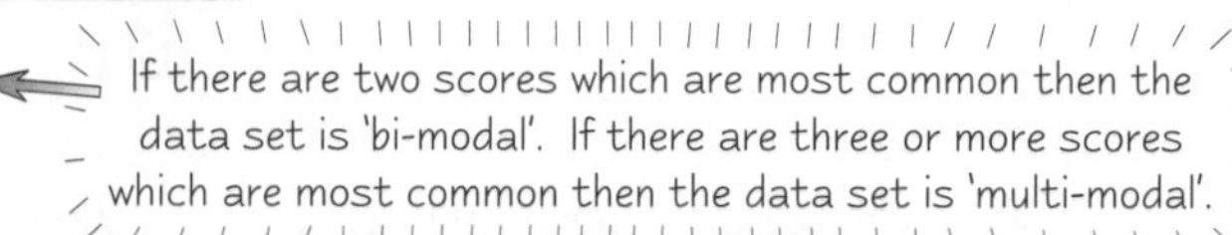

If there are two scores which are most common then the data set is 'bi-modal'. If there are three or more scores which are most common then the data set is 'multi-modal'.

Advantages

a) It shows the **most common** or 'important' score.
b) It's always a result from the actual **data set**, so it can be a more **useful** or **realistic** statistic, e.g. the modal average family has 2 children not 2.4.

Disadvantages

a) It's not very useful if there are **several** modal values, or if the modal value is only **slightly** more common than other scores.
b) It has **little further use** in data analysis.

Descriptive Statistics

Measures of *Dispersion* Tell You How *Spread Out* the Data Are

There are two of these you should learn.

Range — Highest Score Minus the Lowest Score

Example: The range of the scores 6, 10, 35 and 50, is 50 – 6 = 44

Note that (highest-lowest)+1 can also be used, so the range would then be = 45.

Advantage — it's **quick** and **easy** to calculate.

Disadvantage — it completely ignores the **central** values of a data set, so it can be misleading if there are very **high** or **low** scores.

1) The **interquartile range** (**IQR**) can be calculated to help **avoid** this problem.
2) First the **median** is calculated (this is sometimes called **Q2**).
3) Then the value **halfway** between the **median** and the **lowest score** is found (called the **lower quartile**, or **Q1**).
4) Then the value halfway between the **median** and the **highest score** is found (called the **upper quartile**, or **Q3**).
5) The **IQR = Q3 – Q1**.

Example: 3, 3, **4**, 5, 6, **8**, 10, 13, **14**, 16, 19.
There are 11 values, so median (Q2) = 6th value = 8.
Then Q1 = 4, Q3=14, and so IQR = 14 – 4 = 10.

Standard Deviation — Measures How Much Scores Deviate From the Mean

$$s = \sqrt{\frac{\sum (X - \bar{X})^2}{N}}, \quad \text{where } s = \text{standard deviation}$$

Example: Scores = 5, 9, 10, 11 and 15. The mean = 10.
So the standard deviation is:

$$s = \sqrt{\frac{(5-10)^2 + (9-10)^2 + (10-10)^2 + (11-10)^2 + (15-10)^2}{5}} = 3.22$$

A high standard deviation shows more variability in a set of data.

Advantage — **all** scores in the set are taken into account so it is **more accurate** than the range and it can be used in further analysis.

Disadvantage — it's **not** as quick or easy to calculate as the range.

Practice Questions

Q1 Explain how to calculate the mean.
Q2 When is it best not to use the mean?
Q3 What is the difference between the median and the mode?
Q4 Why is the mode sometimes more 'realistic'?
Q5 How is the range calculated?
Q6 What is meant by 'standard deviation'?

Dame Edna Average — making stats fun, possums...

These statistics are used to describe a collection of scores in a data set (how big the scores are, how spread out they are, and so on), so they're called... wait for it... descriptive statistics. Don't be put off by the weirdy maths notation either — a bar on top of a letter (e.g. $\bar{X}$ *) means you work out the mean. And a sigma (Σ) means you add things up. There... not so bad.*

Inferential Statistics

Just OCR here. *Descriptive statistics say nothing about whether a theory is right or wrong. It's inferential statistics that let you make an 'inference' (or educated guess) about what your results show, or whether they're just due to chance.*

Inferential Statistics are about Ruling Out Chance

1) You can never be 100% certain that results aren't all down to chance. So instead of 'proving' a hypothesis, you have to be content with finding out whether it's **likely** to be true. This is called **statistical significance**.
2) If your results are statistically significant, it means that you can '**read something into**' them — they're unlikely to be just down to chance.
3) If your results are **not statistically significant**, it means they could have happened by chance rather than being the effect of your variable, and you can't really read anything into them.

Use Statistical Tests to find out if your Results Mean Anything

OK, it's not easy, this bit — so stop texting people and concentrate...

1) The first thing you do is write out your **null hypothesis** (see page 118) — this is the theory you want to **test**. In a statistical test, you assume your null hypothesis is **true** (for the time being, at least). (So a null hypothesis might be *"rats that eat are poison and rats that eat sugar pellets are equally likely to be ill"*.)
2) Next you choose a **significance level** — this is a '**level of proof**' that you're looking for before you read anything into your results. (The smaller the significance level, the stronger the evidence you're looking for that your results aren't just down to chance.)
3) A significance level is a **probability**, and so is a number between 0 and 1. (Probabilities near 1 mean things are very **likely**, and probabilities near 0 mean things are very **unlikely**.) Significance levels are always **very small** — usually 0.05 (= 5%) or less. (Because a significance level is very **small**, events with probabilities smaller than the significance level are very **unlikely** to happen.)
4) You then turn all your experimental results into a single **test statistic** (fortunately for you, you don't need to know much about this bit for AS Psychology). Then you can find out how likely this test statistic is (and so how likely your results are) **assuming the null hypothesis is true**.
5) If the probability of getting your results (assuming the null hypothesis is true) is **less than the significance level**, then they must be **really unlikely** — and so it's pretty safe to say that your null hypothesis **wasn't true** after all. This is what stats-folk mean when they talk about 'rejecting the null hypothesis'. (If you reject your null hypothesis, you assume your **alternative hypothesis** is true instead — see page 118.)
6) If you reject your null hypothesis, you can proudly say that your results are **statistically significant**. (So rejecting the null hypothesis above would mean that *"rats that eat poison and rats that eat sugar pellets are not equally likely to be ill"*.)
7) If you **don't reject** the null hypothesis, it means that your results could have occurred **by chance**, rather than because your null hypothesis was wrong. If this happens, you've proved **nothing**. (So don't go thinking that not rejecting the null hypothesis means it must be true — cos it doesn't.)
8) Using a significance level of 0.05 (= 5%) is okay for most tests. If the probability of your results is **less** than this, then it's **pretty good evidence** that the null hypothesis **wasn't true** after all. If you use a significance level of 0.01 (= 1%), then you're looking for **really strong evidence** that the null hypothesis is untrue before you're going to reject it.

There are Two Types of Potential Errors — Type 1 and Type 2

1) A **Type 1 error** is when you **reject** the null hypothesis when it was **actually true**.
   The significance level gives you the **probability** of this happening.
   (This is why significance levels are small.)
2) A **Type 2 error** is when you **don't reject** the null hypothesis when it was **actually false**.
   This can happen if your significance level is **too small** (e.g. if you want very strong evidence of the need to reject a null hypothesis and so use a 0.001 significance level).
3) Choosing significance levels is a **compromise** — too big and you risk making a Type 1 error, too small and you could make a Type 2 error.

A very small significance level (e.g. 0.01 or 1%) is used when you need to be very confident in your results, like when testing new theories.

Inferential Statistics

There are Different Kinds of **Statistical Test**

The appropriate significance test to use on your data depends on:

1) The **research design** — some tests need '**unrelated**' data from an independent measures design (e.g. the heights of 10 different people). Others need '**related pairs**' of data from a repeated measures design (e.g. memory scores from people before and after each of them have been trained).
2) The **type of data** you have — e.g. some tests use **ranks** (the position of a score in an ordered list, from smallest to biggest, for example).
3) The **research aim** — maybe you're looking for a significant **correlation** between 2 variables (see pages 126-127), or a significant **difference** in the scores between two groups (like if you're trying a new treatment for an illness).

The **Wilcoxon Signed Ranks** Test — A Test of Difference for **Related** Data

Example: A group does a memory test with two methods of memorising, in a **repeated measures** design:

	Participant no.	1	2	3	4	5	6	7	8
No. words recalled	Method 1	6	5	10	6	8	5	9	8
	Method 2	7	7	8	8	7	6	9	9

1) The **difference** between each participant's two scores is calculated:

Participant no.	1	2	3	4	5	6	7	8
Difference	1	2	2	2	1	1	0	1
Sign (+/-)	-	-	+	-	+	-		-

Always subtract in the same direction, noting if the result is a positive or negative value. Any differences of zero are removed from the results.

2) The differences are placed into **rank order**, lowest gets rank one. Ignore +/- signs.

Difference	1	2	2	2	1	1	0	1
Rank	2.5	6	6	6	2.5	2.5		2.5
Sign (+/-)	-	-	+	-	+	-		-

When there are a few of the same number, calculate their mean rank. e.g. Here, there are four 1s, which should be rank 1, 2, 3 and 4, so they all get the mean rank 2.5.

3) **Total** the ranks for the positive differences and for the negative differences. The smallest is the **observed value of 'T'**.

> Total negative differences = 2.5 + 6 + 6 + 2.5 + 2.5 = **19.5**
> Total positive differences = 6 + 2.5 = **8.5**
> So, the **observed value of T = 8.5**.

4) The observed value must be **less than or equal to** the **critical value** to be significant. Critical values for each number of participants can be found in a special table that you'll be given. The 'number of participants' is the actual number of people taking part in the trial, so 8 in this case.

Practice Questions

Q1 Why can we never be completely certain about a hypothesis?

Q2 What is a significance level?

Q3 When would you reject your null hypothesis?

Q4 Distinguish between Type 1 and Type 2 errors.

Q5 What factors determine which test of inferential statistics should be used?

Don't be put off by the maths — statistic with it (ahem)...

It's 'statistics this and statistics that' at the moment, I'm afraid. But stick with it, as it's actually not that bad. And it's pretty important as well if you want to interpret results of an experiment. But you're right, it's probably not quite as exciting as lion-taming, trapeze artistry, sky diving or even... well... watching paint dry. Sorry, excitement-mongers.

Correlations

Useful for everyone, I reckon. *You know what they say — correlation is as correlation does. Remember that as you read this page... then you won't go far wrong.*

Correlation Measures How Closely Two Variables are Related

1) **Correlation** is a measure of the relationship between **two variables**, e.g. it would tell you whether exam grades are related to the amount of revision that someone's done.
2) **Correlational studies** are done to collect data for some kind of **correlational analysis**.

The Correlation Coefficient is a Number Between –1 and +1

1) To find the correlation between two variables, you first have to collect some **data**.

   For example, you could ask every student in a class how many hours of study they did each week, and note their average test results.

Student	Hours of study	Average test score — %
A	4	58
B	1	23
C	7	67
D	15	89

2) You can then work out a **correlation coefficient** (e.g. Spearman's rho — see next page). This is a number between –1 and +1, and shows:

   (i) **How closely** the variables are linked. This is shown by the **size** of the number — if it's **close** to **+1** or **–1**, then they are **very closely** related, while a smaller number means the relationship is **less strong** (or maybe not there at all if it's close to 0).

   (ii) The **type** of correlation — a **positive** correlation coefficient (i.e. between 0 and +1) means that the variables rise and fall together, while a negative correlation coefficient (i.e. between –1 and 0) means that as one variable rises, the other falls. (See below for more info.)

Correlation is Easy to See on Scatter Graphs

1) **Positive Correlation** — this means that as one variable rises, so does the other (and likewise, if one falls, so does the other).

   Example: hours of study and average test score.

   Correlation coefficient roughly **0.75** (close to +1)

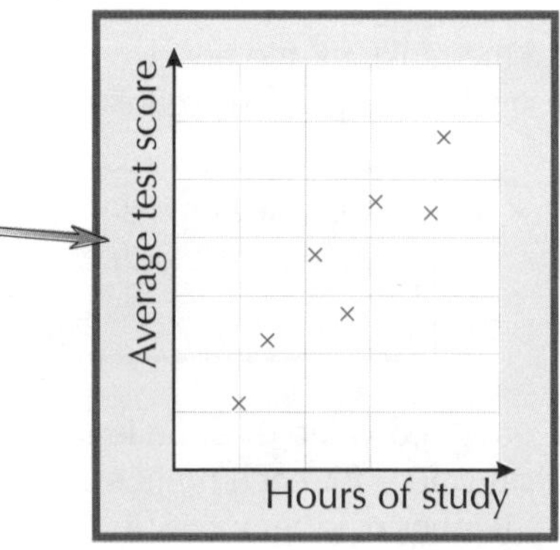

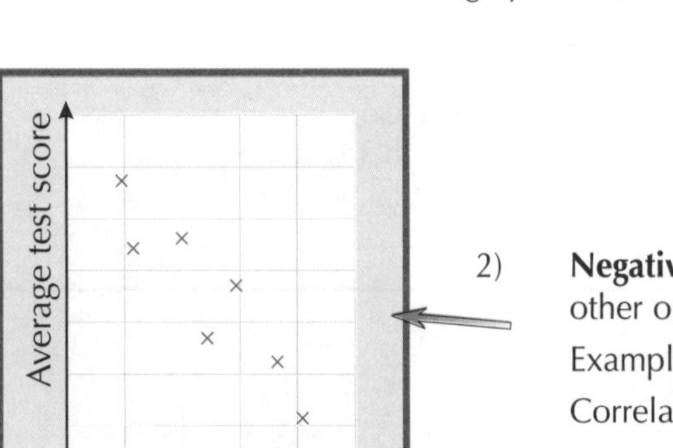

2) **Negative Correlation** — this means that as one variable rises, the other one falls (and vice versa).

   Example: hours of TV watched each week and average test score.

   Correlation coefficient roughly **–0.75** (close to -1).

3) **No correlation** — if the correlation coefficient is 0 (or close to 0), then the two variables aren't linked.

   Example: a student's height and their average test score.

   Correlation coefficient roughly **0.01** (close to 0)

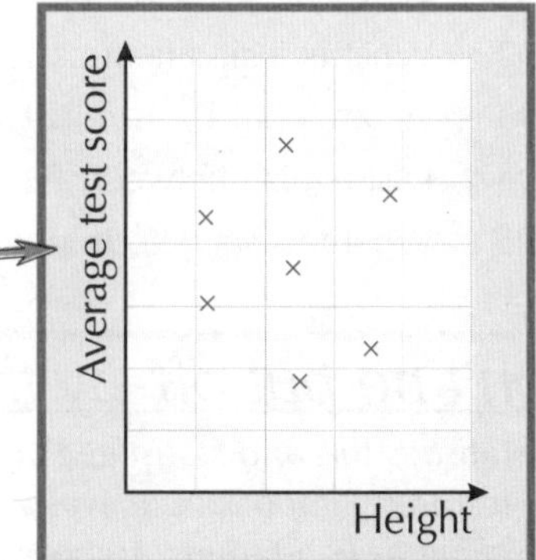

Correlations

Correlational Research Has Some Advantages...

1) Because correlational research doesn't involve **controlling** any variables, you can do it when (for **practical** or **ethical** reasons) you couldn't do a **controlled experiment**.
   For example, an experiment into the effects of smoking on humans probably wouldn't be done for ethical reasons, but a correlation between smoking and cancer could be established from hospital records.
2) Correlational analysis can give ideas for **future** research (e.g. biological research on the effects of smoking).
3) Correlation can even be used to test for **reliability** and **validity** (e.g. by correlating the results of the same test taken twice by the same people — a good **reliable** test will show a **high correlation**).

...but some Limitations

1) Correlational analysis **can't** establish '**cause and effect**' relationships — it can only show that there's a **statistical link** between them.
   Variables can be closely correlated without one causing the other, for example, when a **third variable** is involved. Only a **controlled experiment** can show cause and effect relationships.
2) Care must be taken when **interpreting** correlation coefficients — high correlation coefficients could be down to **chance**. To decide whether a coefficient is **significant**, you have to use a proper **significance test**.

For example, the number of births in a town was found to be positively correlated to the number of storks that nested in that town — but that didn't mean that more storks caused the increase. (It was because more people in the town led to more births, and also to more houses with chimneys to nest in.)

Spearman's Rho is a Correlation Coefficient

To work out (and then test the significance of) **Spearman's rho** correlation coefficient, you need values for two different variables (e.g. hours of revision and average test scores for 10 students).

a) The values for each variable are placed into **rank order** (each variable is ranked separately). The lowest value for each variable gets rank 1 (and in the above example, the biggest value will get rank 10).
b) The **difference** (**d**) in ranks for each student's variables is calculated. (So a particular student may have done the most revision, but got the 3rd best results, in which case the difference in ranks will be d = 3 – 1 = 2.)
c) The value of d for each student is **squared**, then the results are added together (to get $\sum d^2$).
d) Then the special **Spearman's correlation coefficient** calculation is done, which is $r_s = 1 - \frac{6 \times \sum d^2}{N \times (N^2 - 1)}$
   (where N is the number of students, or whatever).
e) To find out whether the result is **significant** (and so whether the variables are linked), you compare the outcome of that nightmarish calculation with a **critical value** that you look up in a **statistics table**.

Practice Questions

Q1 Explain what is meant by correlation.
Q2 What is a correlation coefficient?
Q3 What two things are shown by a correlation coefficient?
Q4 What kind of correlation is shown by a scattergraph whose points start in the upper left and fall to the lower right?
Q5 Explain the difference between a negative correlation and no correlation.
Q6 Describe one use of correlation.

Stats sucks...

Look at the graphs showing the large positive and large negative correlations — all the points lie close-ish to a straight line, which slopes either upwards (positive correlation) or downwards (negative correlation). Just learn the steps involved in working out Spearman's rho — don't try and understand it. Well, that's my advice anyway...

Summarising the Data

This stuff's for all. *It's not very scientific or anything, but the only bit about statistics I don't find mind-numbingly boring is the bit where you get to make all the lovely numbers look pretty... P.S. Ignore me, stats has turned my brain to mush.*

Data *Can Be Presented in* ***Various Ways***

1) **Qualitative** data from observations, interviews, surveys etc (see pages 116-117) can be presented in a **report** as a '**verbal summary**'.
2) The report would contain **summaries** of what was seen or said, possibly using **categories** to group data together. Also **quotations** from participants can be used, and any **research hypotheses** that developed during the study or data analysis may be discussed.
3) When **quantitative** data are **collected** (or **produced** from the data, e.g. by a **content analysis** (see page 121), they can be **summarised** and presented in various ways:

Tables *are a Good Way to Summarise* ***Quantitative Data***

Tables can be used to clearly present the data and show any **patterns** in the scores.

Tables of '**raw data**' show the scores **before** any **analysis** has been done on them.

Other tables may show **descriptive statistics** such as the mean, range and standard deviation (see pages 122-123).

Table To Show the Qualities of Different Types of Ice-cream

	Quality (score out of 10)		
Type of ice-cream	Tastiness	Thickness	Throwability
Chocolate	9	7	6
Toffee	8	6	7
Strawberry	8	5	4
Earwax	2	9	8

Bar Charts *Can be used for* ***Non-continuous Data***

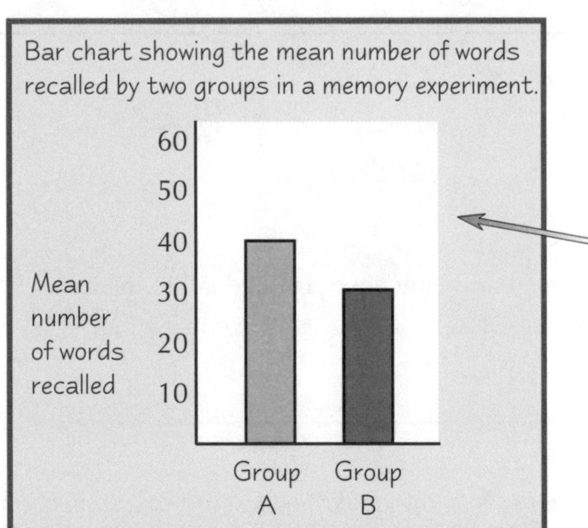

Bar charts (bar graphs) are usually used to present '**non-continuous data**' (like when a variable falls into **categories** rather than being measured on a numbered scale).

This bar chart shows the number of words recalled by different groups in a memory experiment.

Note that the columns in bar charts **don't touch** each other. Also, it's preferable to always show the **full vertical scale**, or **clearly indicate** when it isn't all shown (otherwise it can be **misleading**).

Summarising the Data

Nearly done — just a little bit more...

Histograms** are For When You Have **Continuous Data

Histograms show data measured on a '**continuous**' scale of measurement.

This histogram shows the time different participants took to complete a task.

Each column shows a **class interval** (here, each class interval is 10 seconds), and the columns **touch** each other.

It's the **height** of the column that shows the number of values in that interval. (**All** intervals are shown, even if there are **no scores** within it.)

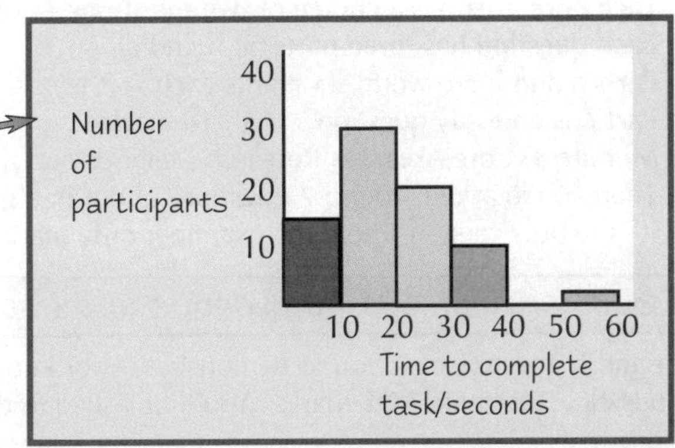

***Frequency Polygons** are Good For Showing **More Than One** Set of Data*

Frequency polygons are similar to histograms, but use **lines** to show where the top of each column would reach.

It can be useful to combine **two or more** frequency polygons on the same set of axes — then it's easy to **make comparisons** between groups.

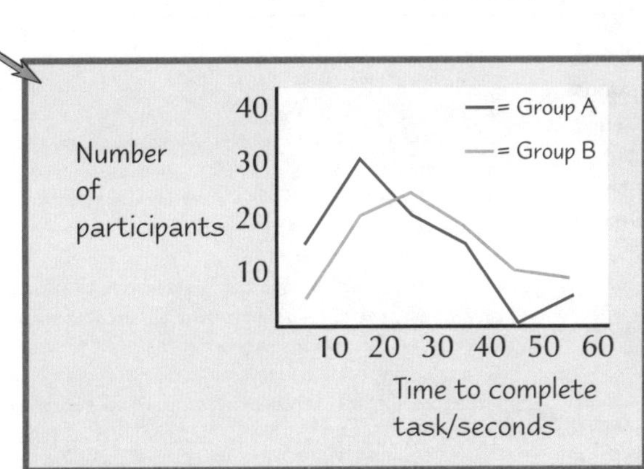

Practice Questions

Q1 How may qualitative data be presented?

Q2 What kind of information is typically shown in tables?

Q3 What kind of data is shown on bar charts?

Q4 Why do the columns on histograms touch?

Q5 What advantage do frequency polygons have over histograms?

*What goes 'Graph graph graph'? A dog with a sore throat...**

That's it. It's done. The book is finished. Well, apart from that pesky bit about essays. I think you deserve a big cake now. Go and tell your mum I said so. Say you want one of those really big gooey chocolate ones from the freezer department in the supermarket. And then you'll need a cup of tea too. And a night of watching soap operas and stupid American sit-coms.

* Or a crowd at a tennis match. Or a maths teacher. Or my dad coughing in the morning. Or... oh think of your own...

Do Well in Your AQA A Exam

This page is all about how to do well in AQA A exams. So don't bother reading it if you're not doing AQA A.

Each Module Has 2 Core Areas, Each Made of 2 Questions, Each Made of 3 Parts

1) **Each** AS module has **two core areas**, e.g. Module 1 has Cognitive Psychology and Developmental Psychology.
2) **Each core area** has a **choice** of **two questions** — pick one of them.
3) **Each question** has **three parts** (a, b and c).
4) **Parts a and b** are worth **six marks each** — they ask you to define terms, describe parts of a study etc.
5) **Part c** is an **essay question**, worth **18 marks**.
6) **Module 3, Core Area 2** is Research Methods and it's a bit **weird**. You get a piece of research described to you. Then you're asked around **7 questions** about it, e.g. identifying variables or interpreting data. IMPORTANT — it's the only section where the examiner **only marks your first answer**, so cross out what you don't want marked.

You Get Marks for AO1 (knowledge and understanding) and AO2 (evaluate and analyse)

Part a and b questions ask you to demonstrate your **knowledge and understanding** of psychological theories, studies, methods etc. These are **AO1** marks. You'll be asked to do something like describe a study or explain a term.

Part c questions award 18 marks in total, 6 of which are for **AO1 skills**, the other 12 for **AO2 skills** (so you've got to **evaluate and analyse** psychological theories, studies etc.)

This means doing things like:
1) presenting **strengths and weaknesses** of a theory/study
2) presenting **alternative** explanations/interpretations of findings
3) using the material to provide a **commentary**, a well-argued essay.

An *Example Essay* to Show You What to Aim at:

"The medical model is the leading approach to dealing with psychological problems."
Describe the biological (medical) model of abnormality and evaluate it in terms of its strengths and weaknesses. (18 marks)

Quotes before essay questions are there to give you ideas – but you can ignore them and just answer the question.

The biological model of abnormality assumes that there is an underlying physiological cause of psychological disorders. Such disorders are considered as illnesses in the same way as the body can be affected by illnesses.

Don't open with a general or meaningless sentence – get straight into gaining marks.

The model includes the idea that genetic factors may be important in psychological disorders. As MZ (identical) twins are 100% genetically identical and DZ (fraternal) twins only share 50% of their genes, MZ twins might be more similar if a condition is inherited. Allen (1976) reported that concordance rates in MZ twins for bipolar disorder are higher than for DZ twins. This suggests that there may be an inherited factor causing bipolar disorder or predisposing someone to the condition.

Interpret findings using sentences beginning with 'This suggests that...' etc.

Another explanation of psychological abnormality is that it is caused by biochemical imbalance. For example, the dopamine hypothesis suggests that excess dopamine may cause schizophrenia. Evidence for this includes the effects of drugs such as amphetamines, which increase dopamine levels and can result in behaviour similar to paranoid schizophrenia. However, an alternative explanation might be that people with schizophrenia are more sensitive to dopamine, rather than they have more of the chemical.

A02 marks for discussing alternative explanations of findings.

Most A02 marks will be awarded for your evaluation of strengths and weaknesses – so don't spend too long describing the model.

Because the medical model assumes there is a physical cause of abnormality, it uses physical treatments. These include drug therapy (e.g. anti-depressants), electro-convulsive therapy (ECT), which is sometimes used in very severe depression and psychosurgery such as prefrontal lobotomies (used to treat aggressive behaviour).

One strength of this model is that there is evidence supporting the view that there are physical causes underlying some psychological disorders. Krafft-Ebbing (1931) discovered that the psychological condition General Paresis (involving mental deterioration) was caused by the syphilis bacterium. This is an example of an infection, which affects the physical body, being the cause of a psychological disorder.

Provide relevant evidence to support the statement.

Physical therapies, such as drugs, have proved effective in treating psychological conditions. Neuroleptic drugs prescribed for schizophrenia are often effective in reducing positive symptoms such as hallucinations and delusions. In some cases, these treatments have enabled people to lead more independent lives. The effectiveness of drugs supports the idea that there are physical causes of psychological conditions.

Write a balanced essay by discussing both strengths and weaknesses.

However, there are problems associated with physical treatments used by this approach. For example, drugs tend to treat symptoms rather than the cause and so do not cure psychological disorders. They may also have serious side effects. Another weakness of the medical model is that there are ethical issues raised by the use of some treatments like ECT. It may be difficult to gain informed consent for treatment from someone with a psychological problem, especially if they don't have insight into the condition. Also, ignoring psychological factors may have negative effects. People may feel more dependent on doctors and take less responsibility for their own psychological well-being.

The medical model has provided evidence that there may be underlying physical causes of psychological disorders. The treatments derived from the approach are often effective, but can have unpleasant side-effects and don't provide a cure. The approach also ignores possible psychological factors that may be involved in psychological disorders. In conclusion, despite its weaknesses, the strengths of the model have maintained its popularity.

Don't repeat stuff in the essay, but do put in a conclusion for full marks.

Do Well in Your OCR Exam

This page is all about how to do well in OCR exams. So don't bother reading it if you're not doing OCR.

There are **3 Exams** for OCR

1) There are **three exams** for OCR — Core Studies 1, Core Studies 2 and Psychological Investigations. Each exam lasts **one hour** and contributes **33.3%** towards the final overall grade.
2) **Core Studies 1** contains one section of 16-20 **compulsory short answer questions** worth 2 or 4 marks each. In total, **60 marks** are available on this exam paper.
3) **Core Studies 2** contains two sections — section A and section B. Section A has a **choice** of one from two **structured essays**. The question asks you to apply methods, themes and perspectives to **one** core study. It's worth **26 marks**. Section B also has a **choice** of one from two **structured essays**, but asks you to apply methods, themes and perspectives to **several** core studies. It's worth **24 marks**.
4) **Psychological Investigations** contains **10 to 12 compulsory questions** about four practical work activities that you will have already conducted. It's worth **50 marks**.

The short questions in **Core Studies 1** are designed to test your **knowledge** of the core studies. The questions are very **specific** and will ask you to define terms and concepts, describe methods, results or conclusions, identify evaluation issues and **understand** the context of the studies. This tests your **AO1** (**knowledge and understanding**) skills.

In **Core Studies 2**, you will need to show your knowledge by **explaining** concepts and findings, and identifying **strengths and weaknesses** of aspects of the study. If the question asks you to include examples, make sure you link them to the points you are making. This tests your **AO2** (**evaluation and analysis**) skills.

An **Example** Core Studies 2 (Section B) Essay:

'Why do people behave in the way that they do? Do they have the freedom to choose their behaviour or is it determined by other factors, such as their culture, their family or their environment, which are beyond their control?'
Using the Core Studies listed below, answer the questions that follow.

Freud (little Hans), Sperry (split brain), Hodges and Tizard (social relationships), Bandura, Ross and Ross (aggression)

(a) Describe what each study tells us about the factors that affect our behaviour. (12 marks)

(b) Using examples, give four problems psychologists may have to consider when they study the factors that influence behaviour. (12 marks)

(a) Freud investigated the phobia of a five-year-old boy called Hans and suggested that unconscious processes were taking place which caused changes in his behaviour. Freud used the Oedipus Complex to explain that at this stage of psychosexual development the boy had sexual feelings for his mother and feared his father, who was his stronger rival. As it was inappropriate for him to fear his father, this fear was transferred to horses, resulting in a phobia. The psychoanalytic explanation for behaviour uses the analysis of unconscious processes to explain behaviour that would otherwise appear unrelated.

Sperry used a biological approach to investigate perception of visual information. He used a sample of 'split brain' people who had undergone surgery for hemisphere disconnection, so communication between their two hemispheres was no longer possible. Through a number of tests involving presenting stimuli only to one side of the body, Sperry was able to show that localisation of brain function takes place in each hemisphere. This study shows that brain structure and function can influence behaviour.

Hodges and Tizard investigated the effect of institutional upbringing on children and their later attachments. Using a longitudinal technique, the development of children who had experienced maternal deprivation was followed. It was found that the attachments they formed depended on the behaviour of the adults in the families the children were placed in — adopted children did better than those returned to their biological families. This study suggests that adults can influence the attachment process in children with implications for their relationships in later life.

Bandura et al investigated how social learning theory could be used to explain aggressive behaviour. They found that children would generally behave aggressively after exposure to an aggressive role model. This study shows that observation and imitation of role models can be an influencing factor on behaviour. Overall these studies show that a number of varying factors such as unconscious processes, brain structure and function, family type, childhood experience and role models can all affect our behaviour.

(b) One problem that psychologists may need to consider is the presence of demand characteristics. This is when participants behave in a way that is expected of them because of a feature of the study. They may try to please the researcher or act differently because they are unsure in the situation. In Freud's study, data came from letters written by Hans' father, who was an admirer of Freud's work. This may have influenced the information he included in his letters. Often, in psychological research, people are put in situations that are out of the ordinary so they will look at the circumstances for clues about how to behave.

Another problem is that ethically, certain variables cannot be deliberately created in a controlled and closely supervised study. Therefore psychologists have to find people already experiencing the variables. Sperry used participants who had already had surgery because of epilepsy. It would be inappropriate and unrealistic to ask people to undergo surgery for a psychological study. For a study to be completely ethical, participants need to leave the study in the same condition that they arrived, but the type of variables that we want to investigate can make this difficult at times.

The representativeness of the sample used is another common problem. This can be because of the sample size (e.g. Freud's study was of one person), or the limited range of people used (e.g. Sperry's study was of people who had epilepsy surgery — not representative of the general population). This is a problem when target population sizes increase or sample sizes decrease.

A fourth problem is controlling for confounding variables, which involves eliminating any variables that could influence the results of the study, other than the independent and dependent variables. In the Hodges and Tizard study, a comparison group of non-institutionalised children was also used . As a control feature they were matched on several variables including gender and family structure. This problem can be a difficult one for psychologists as it can be impractical to match variables and some confounding variables are difficult to predict at the start of a study.

Cover all the core studies requested in the question.

Demonstrate that you understand the studies and can relate them to the question accurately.

Problems can be general problems of all studies, not only specific ones.

Relate an example to each problem by naming a core study.

Don't waffle — make all information relevant to the question.

Make sure sections A and B are balanced with the same amount of depth and detail.

Do Well in Your Edexcel Exam

This page is all about how to do well in Edexcel exams. So don't bother reading it if you're not doing Edexcel.

There are 2 Exams for Edexcel

1) There are **two exams** for Edexcel — both last **an hour and a half** and make up **33.3%** of your final overall grade.
2) The **Unit 1** exam is on cognitive, social and development processes.
3) The **Unit 2** exam is on individual differences, physiology and behaviour.
4) Each exam consists of **6 questions**, broken down into a number of short-answer and some longer-answer questions. The whole exam is worth **72 marks**.
5) The last question is an **essay question**, normally worth **12 marks**.

You Get Marks for AO1 (knowledge and understanding) and AO2 (evaluate and analyse)

57.5% of your marks are for demonstrating your **knowledge and understanding** of psychological theories, studies, methods etc. These are **AO1** marks. You'll be asked to do something like describe a study or explain a term.

42.5% of your marks are for **AO2 skills**. This means you've got to **evaluate and analyse** psychological theories, studies etc. You'll have to do things like:

1) present **strengths and weaknesses** of a theory/study
2) present **alternative** explanations/interpretations of findings
3) use the material to provide a **commentary**, a well-argued essay.

An *Example* of a 12 Mark Essay Question:

Describe and evaluate one study into obedience. (12 marks)

Milgram was interested in how normal German people followed the orders of the Nazis, leading to their treatment of the Jews. He was interested in whether normal Americans would also blindly follow instructions from authority, even if it led to them hurting other people. Milgram set up a study where participants believed they were taking part in a learning experiment. Each participant was a 'teacher', who read out word pairs to a 'learner' (who was actually a confederate). Every time the learner gave an incorrect response, the participant had to give them an electric shock. With each shock, the voltage was increased up to a final level of 450 V, labelled 'XXX'. At 300 V, the learner pleaded to be let out, saying he couldn't stand the pain. Above 300 V, he was silent. If the participant asked to stop, they were told that the experiment had to continue.

Milgram found that no participants stopped the experiment before 300 V, and 65% actually continued as far as 450 V. Milgram concluded that ordinary Americans obey orders even if it leads to them acting against their conscience and hurting others.

Milgram's experiment was repeated in different situations, leading to different results. When run in seedy offices, only 48% of participants gave the maximum shock. This suggests that the original university location made participants more likely to see the researcher as a justified authority figure. Proximity is also an important factor, as when the learner was in the same room as the participant, obedience dropped to 40%. It seemed that participants had lost a buffer protecting them from seeing the consequences of their actions. Likewise, when a confederate gave the shocks instead of the participant, 92.5% of the participants continued to the end of the study — a buffer had been created.

This was a very influential study, which provided great insights into human behaviour. It disproved the 'Germans are different' hypothesis, and led to increased awareness of how easily we can just blindly obey orders, without questioning whether we morally should. However, there are a number of criticisms, including ethical issues and issues of validity.

The participants in Milgram's study suffered a lot of psychological distress. They were also deceived as to the nature of the experiment, which meant they couldn't provide informed consent. Additionally, they were not informed of their right to withdraw, which is now common practice in psychology experiments. Instead, they were urged to continue with the experiment when they asked to stop. This experiment was therefore very ethically questionable, and would never be allowed today. However, Milgram extensively debriefed his participants, including reuniting them with the learner. The participants therefore left understanding that they hadn't hurt anyone. They did, however, leave in the knowledge that they were capable of hurting people, which may have caused them distress.

Milgram's study can also be criticised in terms of external and internal validity. Some people claim that it lacks internal validity — that it wasn't actually measuring obedience rates at all. Perhaps instead, participants were just acting along with the experimenter, not actually believing they were hurting the learner (showing demand characteristics). The experiment has also been criticised in terms of external validity — that it doesn't represent traits that would happen in the real world, with different people, and different situations. However, similar obedience rates have since been shown in other studies (e.g. Hofling et al), which do have high external validity.

Don't get carried away describing all the details — you just need the aim, method and conclusion.

Make sure the study you choose is the one you can describe and evaluate best — not just your favourite.

Don't worry if you can't remember exact figures — just make sure you know the general findings and what they mean.

Interpret findings using sentences beginning with 'This suggests that...' etc.

Evaluations need to include positive points too — not only problems.

Make sure you know the different types of validity — you'll probably need to mention them in any evaluation.

Explain what you mean when you use terms like 'external validity' etc.

Index

Index

Index

Index

Index